Santia

the Dept. of Economic

UB.

Global Finance at Risk

Also by Sunanda Sen

Colonies and Empire: India 1870–1914 (1992)

Finance and Development: RC Dutt Lectures on Political Economy (1998)

Financial Fragility, Debt and Economic Reforms (ed.) (1996)

Trade and Dependence: Essays on the Indian Experiences (2000)

Global Finance at Risk

On Real Stagnation and Instability

Sunanda Sen

First published 2003 by
PALGRAVE MACMILLAN
Houndmills, Basingstoke, Hampshire RG21 6XS and
175 Fifth Avenue, New York, N.Y. 10010
Companies and representatives throughout the world

PALGRAVE MACMILLAN is the global academic imprint of the Palgrave
Macmillan division of St. Martin's Press, LLC and of Palgrave Macmillan Ltd.
Macmillan® is a registered trademark in the United States, United Kingdom
and other countries. Palgrave is a registered trademark in the European
Union and other countries.

ISBN 0–333–80040–0

This book is printed on paper suitable for recycling and made from fully
managed and sustained forest sources.

A catalogue record for this book is available from the British Library.

Library of Congress Cataloging in Publication Data
Sen, Sunanda.
    Global finance at risk : on real stagnation and instability / Sunanda Sen.
        p.   cm.
    Includes bibliographical references and index.
    ISBN 0–333–80040–0
    1. International finance.   2. Capital movements.   I. Title.

HG3881.S426 2003
332′.042—dc21

                                                                    2003040521

10   9   8   7   6   5   4   3   2
12   11   10   09   08   07   06   05   04

Printed and bound in Great Britain by
Antony Rowe Ltd, Chippenham and Eastbourne

Remembering
Krishna

Contents

List of Tables

List of Figures

Preface

This volume includes my work on international finance, the changing face of which had interested me since the floating of the major currencies and the Eurobank lendings to developing countries in the early 1970s. I have documented and analysed the events which have happened since then, in terms of a theoretical framework which deviates from the mainstream orthodoxy. In my analysis, I have been influenced by the post-Keynesian arguments on related issues which are often made use of in the book. The present study looks into the movements in international financial capital which often have failed to work as a catalyst of real growth. Instead these flows have had a disruptive impact on the real economy, both with unpredictable fluctuations and the related speculation on a short-term basis which is generated. Policies advocated by the powerful national governments as well as by their affiliate international bodies have imbibed a culture to protect the interest of finance which is dominant today. This also fits in the liberalisation doctrine and its applications, pushing to backstage the agenda of the state on real growth and employment. It leaves us with great concern, not only for the continuing job losses and contraction of output in the advanced economies, but also for the doctrinaire applications of the liberalisation agenda in the developing countries with even more severe consequences. The book addresses some of these issues, with analyses of past policies and the current events.

The present study incorporates my research over a long period during which I have been helped by a large number of individuals and institutions. I may mention here the generous invitations from Faculty of Economics and Politics at Cambridge University, Maison des Sciences de l'Homme at Paris, Institute of Developing Studies at Sussex University, Departments of Economics at Grenoble University and at Barcelona University, Nehru Memorial Museum and Library in Delhi, Academy of Third World Studies in Delhi and last but not least, Jawaharlal Nehru University in New Delhi where I have taught for nearly three decades. I also mention some of the economists who took an active interest in my work, offering constructive criticisms at crucial stages. These include Amiya Bagchi, Amit Bhaduri, Geoff Harcourt, Prabhat Patnaik, Krishna Bharadwaj, Michel Aglietta, Ricardo Parboni, Hans Singer, Stephany Griffith Jones, Valpy Fitzgerald, Gemma Cairo, Gerard De Bernis, Dietmar Rothermund, Otto Kreye, Bob Rowthorn, John Wells, Joseph Halevi, Jean-Marc Fontaine, Pierre Salama, to name a few. Former students of mine who now are young colleagues have helped. Arun Kumar, Krishnendu Ghosh Dastidar and Subrata Guha have lent support with the mathematical appendices and Biswajit Dhar and R.U. Das with the logistics of preparing the final manuscript. An unknown referee offered useful hints on improving the quality of the draft submitted to Palgrave Macmillan. I offer my sincerest thanks to all the people mentioned above. Finally, I thank Mishtu and Ishan for being patient in my preoccupation during a rather long period.

The book, hopefully, will help to change the mindset of policy-makers and restrain them a bit from bringing more disasters to the real economy.

Sunanda Sen
New Delhi

Introduction

It has become urgent, with the continuing stagnation as well as recurrent instability in the world economy, to offer a convincing analysis of the current situation. Claims put forth by neoclassical economists that such problems would disappear if the free functioning of the market can be ensured are found erroneous and faulty. Problems with these neo-liberal approaches lie both at the level of their logical structure and their policy prescriptions, especially in terms of the historical experiences of countries which implemented the liberalisation strategy. Despite these limitations, the free market doctrines have continued to reign supreme, with industrialised countries pushing the agenda of economic reforms and liberalisation, especially in their trade and financial negotiations with the developing countries. International organisations dealing with related issues have contributed by pushing the liberal agenda further, particularly in the weaker nations which have little power to withstand these dictates. This is hardly surprising since the industrialised countries more or less dominate the major international organisations like the IMF, the World Bank and the WTO.

Failure of neo-liberal policies to revive the real economy has been a rather generalised phenomenon in the world economy. Despite the ongoing recession in the industrialised countries, liberal economic doctrines and policies are championed from official circles. The package includes cuts in fiscal spending and the lifting of controls over financial and material transactions in the markets. The goal of monetary targeting hinged on fiscal balance, and even a surplus in terms of the EU stability pact in some European countries. The drop in inflation rate has also currently lowered the nominal interest rate in most of OECD. However, in absence of credit demand, the expected revival of the real sector has not come about.

Implementation of the monetarist neo-liberal policies have led to two marked anomalies in the world economy. First, there has been a spectacular growth in finance-related activities, combined with cyclic fluctuations. Second, the financial boom has most often failed to infuse expansions in the real share of economies. However, a lull in financial activities, as during a crash, inevitably had an adverse effect on the real sector, with the financial sector functioning in an asymmetric manner as far as its effects on the real sector were concerned.

The fact that the advanced economies of today are ready to champion the case for the market economy despite its limited success in rejuvenating growth in their own economies can be explained by identifying the interests of industry as distinct from those of finance. As pointed out in the early writings on capitalism, the two may not move in the same direction, especially in mature capitalist economies where the class interest of rentiers living on past dominates over those having income which arises from the current flows of output. The fact that finance has gained ground relative to industry in the industrialised countries since the onset of recession in the mid-1970s explains the uneven balance of power relations betweeen finance and industry in the world economy. The liberal doctrines with their advocacy of financial opening have sought to protect the basic interests of finance with anti-inflationary policies geared to protect the real value of financial assets, exchange rates targeted to achieve similar goals and financial institutions restructured to achieve maximum profits in the new environment of financial activities. In the process, interest of industry in terms of output and employment has been treated as subsidiary. To further the interest of trade and industry, use of 'beggar thy neighbour' policies has continued to prevail, even with the professed adherence to free trade doctrines, as is evident in the WTO-related negotiations between the advanced and the developing countries. However, in the absence of a sustained growth of real output and employment in either the advanced or in the developing parts of the world, demand has been hard to generate for the unutilised resources and workforce. The social costs resulting from the output losses, job losses and destitution have been justified by policymakers as necessary for achieving the free-market equilibrium and efficient growth.

We have deviated, in our analysis, from the framework underlying the mainstream policy prescriptions. The alternative position on related issues as originates from the heterodox circles, and especially from the post-Keynesians, has been our starting point in the present analysis. In terms of the alternative approach that we have relied on, we arrive at the following generalisations on both the genesis and the corrective measures of the current scenerio: First that the advanced countries, in their efforts to appease the dominant financial or rentier interests in their own economies, have been following policies which are against global demand and material activity. This is related to their own economies as well as to developing countries which are persuaded to follow demand dampening stabilisation macro-policies. In dealing with the theories which support the mainstream policy prescriptions, we point out their limitations, especially in the manner in which the theory behind has chosen to ignore or trivialise the relevance of uncertainty despite its crucial significance, in particular for the financial markets. Second, the international financial and trading institutions have followed suit, largely in the interest of finance in the global economy. The consequence has been a concerted move to suppress global demand, which dampens the prospect of economic revival in both the advanced and the developing countries. Third, the manner in which the financial market has performed has negated the possibilities of development. This is due to both the wide-ranging financial liberalisation in these areas and the growing liabilities on their past borrowings. Even the flows of direct foreign investments have generated disproportionately large leakages from their income stream, both as royalties and so on and as imports of goods and services. Gross flows of capital in the direction of the developing countries have thus been used in large measure to meet the external payment liabilities. This, as pointed out in the volume, reflects a 'ponzi game'. With channels of financial speculation made simpler to operate and play on, a large part of these inflows are drawn to speculation in secondary capital markets, the gains and losses in which do not contribute to GDP in these countries. This, however, is not to discount the role of the internal elite in the developing region, who imbibed a mindset from the Bretton Woods institutions in terms of their allegiance to packages of conventional economic policies. At times, those also proved beneficial in their class interest, providing opportunities to make money by moving capital to safer havens. The overall impact of following the doctrinaire policies, once again, was bound to be contractionary in terms of global demand with little prospects of new investments and hence of demand as could be generated in these countries.

The Book

The present work aims to throw further light on the implications of financial liberalisation and the globalisation of financial markets. It covers the period from 1973, which marks the end of the fixed exchange rate system under Bretton Woods and also the phenomenal spurt in oil prices with developing countries joining the international credit market; both with deposits of petro-dollar revenue and large-scale borrowings by the oil-importing middle-income developing countries. Simultaneously, bank credit flows to the developing countries soared up, for the first time in post-war history, and surpassed other forms of capital flows like official loans or FDIs. There was, as a consequence, a spectacular increment in the stock of outstanding long-term debt held by these countries. Thus, privately held debt rose from one-third of the public and privately held debt stock at the beginning of the 1970s to three-fourth in 1982, the year when the debt crisis erupted. The meteoric rise seems to be far more if one considers the sum of undisbursed credit as well. The scene of easy and unlimited credit flows was drastically changed in 1982 with a drastic fall in the offer of new credit by banks. This reflected the altered perceptions of the creditor institutions which no longer were confident with the value of assets held as third-world debt. There resulted, as a consequence, an overhauling of balance sheets and a restructuring of the creditor banks along with a swift pace of structural adjustments in the debtor nations, both of which were in line with the economic philosophy of the liberalised regime. The marginalisation of the developing countries in financial markets reflected their reduced share in the global flows of bank credit, at less than 7 per cent of syndicated international bank credit in 1988, as contrasted to their near 50 per cent share in 1981.

Tendencies towards an actual default by the major borrowing countries in Latin America surfaced first in Mexico in August 1982. Heavy exposures to Latin America, and in particular to Mexico, alerted the international community of lenders in the OECD. This led the TNBs to shift from their earlier aggressive 'loan-push' strategy to a defensive stance since the second half of the 1980s. There was a switch from loans to securitised assets as the banks were permitted to invest more profitably in securities, with the newly initiated universal banking principles in most of the OECD. While the new direction of the financial flows averted an impending crisis for the international banks, it simultaneously diverted bank credit flows away from the developing country borrowers. For the risk-averse lender institutions, these opportunities (to maintain a portfolio in securities issued in the advanced regions) improved the quality of their balance sheet while reducing the prospects of reviving new investments. In this process, surplus countries like Japan and West Germany could recycle their investible surpluses by means of the security-led financial intermediation and heavy borrowings by the US in the international capital market.

It is interesting to notice that Japan was drawn in the process with pressures from the financial community, especially in the US, to liberalise the financial market. Simultaneously, the US and the UK emerged, for the first time in recent history, as advanced country borrowers in the international capital market. The consequence of this reveals a story of financial instability and volatility in the financial market and an impact on the real sector, which has been narrated and analysed in the present volume.

Emergence of securities and the related circuits with derivative instruments as the major vehicle of capital flows have changed the institutional structure of the international credit market. Fluctuations in prices of stocks, interest rates as well as exchange rates have been common in this period, generating uncertainties which encourage the use of the hedging instruments. Much of these have very little to do with real sector activities. Flows of credit also include FDIs, which have continued to increase, but at a pace dwarfed by the specular growth in speculatory portfolio capital. A large part of these FDI flows also are directed towards mergers and acquisitions which are of little worth in terms of new investments. An emerging pattern such as this explains the dichotomy between the pace of rapid movements in financial flows and the stagnant real sector activities in the advanced economies.

Looking back, the impressive growth in the flow of private international credit as has taken place since the 1970s marks a departure from the development decade of the 1960s when credit flows to the developing area primarily consisted of the official sources of concessional credit. Flows of finance to the developing areas are market-driven today, and as such are subject to the same vicissitudes of the market forces and underlying uncertainties as are prevalent in the advanced economies. One observes, in the recent flows of private international credit to the developing areas, a typical boom-bust cycle, with bank debt explosion of the 1970s followed by the related crisis in the 1980s and more recently, a boom in the Asian markets followed by several other financial crises which broke out in Russia, parts of Latin America and are still continuing.

While dwelling on the accepted paradigms of mainstream economics relating to the beneficial aspects as are expected from free flow of international capital in terms of a liberalised regime, we offer, in the chapters which follow, an alternative point of view. We would indicate the pitfalls of uncontrolled financial globalisation, from the point of view of both capital-rich and the capital-scarce countries. It is pointed out that policies guided by conventional doctrines can be held responsible for much of the malaise in the world economy, which not only include the recurrent instabilities but also tendencies for real stagnation. In particular, the current trends in the flow of unregulated global finance manifest a pattern which lends proximity to speculation and remains distant from real activities. A reversal of such tendencies may demand monitoring as well as regulations, at national as well as international levels, of the trajectory of these capital flows. This demands a role of the state vis-à-vis the market which is dismissed by the currently popular and dominant liberal philosophy determining economic policy.

We have provided, in Chapter 1, the conceptual background, with an outline and a critique of the neo-liberal doctrines relating to international capital movements. We have questioned the limiting assumptions behind the micro-theoretic formulations in these theories to interpret the debt build-up. These include, among others, the microeconomic rational choice and utility maximisation assumptions of the optimal borrowing models. In the alternate approach we rely on, international capital exports are related to the macro-economic savings-investment discrepancies in the advanced economies. We analyse the problems faced by advanced capitalist countries in sustaining net outflows of surplus capital overseas. These generate propensities for under-consumption with related tendencies for stagnation in these areas. However, the outcome is consistent and rather beneficial to interests of global finance and the rentier classes in these countries. As for the capital-importing nations in the developing region, we highlight the implications of the declining net capital inflows, especially with the erosion of creditor confidence when debt is rolled over and accumulated.

The conceptual aspects dealt with in Chapter 1 are followed, in Chapter 2, by an analytical-historical account of the changing pattern of international capital flows. It brings back the long episodes of bank restructuring as well as transformations of the global financial market in the process. Chapter 3 dwells on the implications of global finance for the real economy and its world implications. It provides an insight into the possibilities of reviving global demand by channelising capital flows in the direction of the developing countries and towards real rather than speculatory investments. Chapter 4 brings back the theme to the developmental dimensions of private international capital flows which remain an impending necessity in the interest of real growth in the world economy. It also dwells on the missed opportunities of the so-called development decade and thereafter, with heavily indebted developing countries of Latin America facing the worst possibilities of reverse capital flows from these countries, often with the connivance of the local elite.

Our study has left out aspects which deal with policy responses to international financial crisis. These include the vast area of reforms and regulations, which have been initiated by creditor governments, banks, security houses and other financial institutions like the Bank for International Settlement which provides a surveillance over the credit flows from the OECD. The study also leaves out the regime change in the developing countries, which happened as these countries accepted Fund conditionality as a part of the co-financing package on the aftermath of the debt crisis, and currently, with financial liberalisation which came with globalisation. The study also does not deal with issues of official development finance which still has a lot of relevance, especially in capital-scarce poor developing economies.

1
International Capital Flows: Some Theoretical Insights

1.1 Introduction

Of late, international financial markets have been subject to an increasing degree of instability. The fact that this has been matched by a deepening crisis in the real sector activities makes it important to analyse the underlying connections between the financial and the real turmoil. A starting point for this clearly departs from what in orthodox economics is cited as 'neutrality' of money. Contesting such positions, the present study views money and finance as active agents of change in the real economy, especially in an uncertain world.

Volatility in financial markets today includes not only the fluctuating turnover in the capital market but also fast movements in asset prices, exchange rates and interest rates. These can have a marked impact on real forces in national economies, in addition to what is caused by the uneven flow of finance itself. The following are the significant aspects in the links between international finance and the real economy in recent times:

1   Real activity has failed to respond to the spectacular boom in the financial activities as has often taken place, especially in the Organisation for Economic Co-operation and Development (OECD), over the last few decades. Of late, a similar pattern of financial boom in financial activities has emerged in the emerging economies of Asia and Latin America. Most of these countries had gone

through financial reforms to prepare themselves for these massive capital inflows from international markets. Financial boom in these countries failed to have a continuing expansionary impact on the real sector, especially in terms of generating industrial activity. The opposite, however, has been the case with down-turns in the financial sector which inevitably swamped the real sector as well.

2   Finance in OECD and elsewhere has been increasingly engaged in meeting the uncertainty-related demand for precautionary and/or speculative funds in these economies. Thus, with the build-up of uncertainty, finance tends to cater more to short-term instruments which are designed to provide insurance against risks. Deregulation in the financial sector has prepared the ground for a mushrooming of instruments which today cater to the market for derivative financial instrument market covering futures and options, the inter-est rate or currency swaps as well as the over the counter (OTC) arrangements. Incidentally, the OTCs avoid an entry into the balance sheets of banks since these are intermediated directly between customers. Most of these off-balance transactions also remain outside the net of supervisory bank regulations.

3   By the mid-1980s, securities as the major vehicle of financial intermediation had already taken precedence over banks in the international capital market. Unlike bank credit flows, especially when lent at fixed interest rates, securities traded were subject to market-risks, thus automatically encouraging hedging and other related activities. Transactions in securities also have so far been largely beyond the jurisdiction of the supervisory authorities, both at national and international levels.

4   The emergence of non-bank financial institutions with pension funds and similar other agencies operate in the market as powerful institutional investors. As with the newly innovated instruments, operations by these financial institutions are also outside the domain of supervisory banking regulations.

Changes, as above, in the pattern of international private capital flows over the last two and a half decades thus seem to have been both qualitative and quantitative. While the magnitude of cross-border financial flows, which cover capital as well as currency markets, has reached unprecedented heights, the relative ease of moving funds across national borders and the uncertainty in the markets both have provided incentives for quick movements of funds. The proportion of capital flows which is locked in long-term real investment projects has, as a consequence, been less attractive, with portfolio investments of short maturity taking precedence over long-term bonds and direct foreign investments.

Volatility in the international capital market today encompasses, in addition to the magnitude of these flows, similar fluctuations in exchange rates as well as interest rates. *With a major part of financial flows geared to the hedge funds, returns on finance today can be sustained by the volatility in finance itself.* Thus, calculations of the stock market call/put premiums in the much celebrated formulation of Merton[1] and earlier, of Black and Scholes in the standard models indicate that these premiums move up when stock prices are subject to a wider range of variance. The rising volume, the frequent instabilities, the changing pattern and their dissociation from real activities have increased the importance of analysing private global finance in recent times. In this chapter it is intended to approach the subject from a theoretical angle. A critical survey of the prevailing interpretations, especially the micro-theoretic formulations dealing with developing country debt, is followed by an analysis of the macroeconomic implications of these flows, both for the capital-exporting and -importing nations. The alternative approach, as embodied in our analysis, provides the much needed relevance of theory as an interpretation of reality.

There exists, in the literature, an interpretation of the bank-led debt cycles of the 1970s and the early 1980s in terms of a microeconomic optimality criterion in international lending and borrowing. An explanation is provided, in these formulations, to the boom-bust cycle in bank credit which took place during the period. Attention, in particular, is also drawn to the fact that refinancing and debt conversion programmes – which include debt-equity swaps – are also a part of the optimisation process. Section 1 provides an exposition of the optimal borrowing models of developing country debt which was accepted in mainstream economic theory and policy as an appropriate answer to events connected with the debt crisis. A brief sketch of the central arguments in these models is followed up with a critique of the micro-level profit maximising argument as is implicit in these models. In particular, it can be argued that the assumptions of 'rational' borrowing as well as lending in these models fail to handle the basic properties of uncertainty in loan markets. Models of these genre thus provide a distorted account of the behaviour of loan-giving agencies, even in terms of assumptions regarding the asymmetric information and credit-rationing in the market. Built around the micro-level profit maximisation on the part of lenders and social welfare maximisation on the part of borrowers, these models fail to recognise the fact that actual lending and especially borrowing are hardly transacted by these norms of optimisation. These models also fail to capture the macroeconomic aspects of the global savings-investment balance as an explanation of the credit flows across regions. Our critique of optimal borrowing models is followed up in Section 1.3 with a macroeconomic perspective of global capital flows. In our judgement, the latter provides a better understanding of the pattern and the implications of international capital flows.

In Section 1.4, an analysis is offered of the observed failure of the financial boom to infiltrate the real sector in terms of higher growth. This section also brings up the issue of uncertainty in the capital market and seeks to provide an appropriate framework for analysing financial fragility. This includes an attempt to unravel the weakening of the links between financial and real flows, especially in the advanced economies where finance has scaled new heights with deregulation.

1.2   Debt under optimality

We provide, in this section, a sketch of optimal international borrowing models while pointing out the limitations in terms of their failure to interpret what happened in reality. Modelling of international debt became popular during the years 1982–92 which also mark the aftermath of the debt crisis. By this time, international credit was dominated by private banks which, as can be expected, were primarily concerned with the maximisation as well as the continuity of profits through lending. Optimisation models of foreign borrowing which were developed in this period were based on both the profit maximisation behaviour of the lenders and an assumed (social) welfare maximisation norm which was to be set by the borrowers themselves, the two interacting to determine the flow of credit at its optimum level.[2] In terms of these models of optimal borrowing (under certainty), the long-term solvency criterion for the borrower is met when the latter can liquidate the discounted stream of debt and the related liabilities accumulated over a time period by means of trade surpluses earned over the same period.[3] It is thus necessary to meet the solvency criterion which ensures that the country is finally left with no more than the discounted value of the initial debt. Since the trade balance measures the gap between real output and real expenditure within the economy during the same period, solvency criterion also implies fiscal self-sufficiency for the country.[4]

Institutional limits to credit are assumed to be set by individual banks in terms of credit ceilings which thus set a liquidity constraint for the borrowing country. This, as has been argued in this literature, would never fall below the limit which is consistent with the solvency criterion as long as the market operates under certainty. Even when individual banks are credit constrained, loan syndication on the part of banks would thus succeed to restore the credit flows up to the limit set by the individual borrowing country's solvency. Figure 1.1 depicts the credit ceiling set by the solvency criterion with a reverse L-shaped loan supply function which puts credit at solvency limit as L_t^{max}.

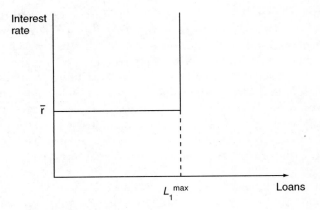

Figure 1.1   Credit limit and solvency

Incidentally, a similar argument was advanced in the debt-cum-growth models of the 1960s, which suggested that with domestic growth it is possible on part of the debtor countries to liquidate their debt by means of additional savings and trade surpluses.[5] It may be pointed out here that, in effect, both these models were based on the assumption that there is neither a ceiling on the global supply of credit nor any uncertainty in the credit market, especially concerning the default potentials of individual borrowers.

In more recent models of optimal borrowing, default risks for lenders have also been incorporated, subject, however, to the assumption that transactions in the credit markets are subject to perfect foresight. Thus both lenders and borrowers are assumed to operate as risk-neutral rational agents.[6] In terms of this framework, defaults can prove beneficial to the borrowers once their debt liabilities exceed the net flow of new credit. Default is thus treated as an *option* for the borrower (country) which will only be exercised if the latter is able to attain a higher level of consumption (and hence social welfare) via default.[7] The lender, however, can impose on the borrower a penalty on default which covers seizure of its assets, loss of trade channels and denial of new loans. Thus the borrower is assumed to exercise a 'rational choice' vis-à-vis default as well as the size of borrowing which is viewed as optimal.[8]

Since defaults may imply gains as well as losses to the borrowers with the perceived penal action on default by lenders, it has been argued that lenders may persuade borrowers to avoid default through co-operative or coercive strategies. In such situations borrowers may be induced to borrow beyond the limit at which default options prevailed earlier. While a pre-commitment on the part of borrowers to set aside a part of the borrowed funds as investment provides an insurance to the lenders against risk of default, the same achieved through policing by lenders permits a larger flow of credit which is similarly considered as safe. Paradoxically, from the point of view of the borrower, policing by the lender is considered in these models as superior to co-operative solutions in terms of the volume of credit![9]

With uncertainty and the related default risks, it is difficult to assess the future flow of tradable output (or the debt servicing capacity), the time rate of discount on loans, or even the real rate of interest.[10] These aspects are encapsulated in the optimal borrowing literature in terms of a backward bending loan supply curve, with higher real interest rates compensating for the risks which are likely to increase with the sanctioning of loans in larger quantities. With lenders continuing to fetch the 'normal' (or competitive) profits on loans extended, there exists a critical limit for loan supply beyond which loans offered would actually contract at higher interest rates and the loan supply function would turn backwards. This is because of the lender's perception regarding the declining creditworthiness on the part of the debtor, as in the case of lending up to a maximum limit under certainty.

Default, in these cases, is explained by the mismatch between the willingness of the lender to lend (along LL in Figure 1.2 with profits π under competition at zero) and of the borrower not to default (as long as the borrower utility function is above the acceptable minimum welfare indicated by U_{min} in Figure 1.2). As pointed out above, if the penal losses are less than the cost of loan servicing, the borrower has an incentive to default. The borrower also has an additional reason to default when loans offered are less than what is considered as the minimum by the borrower country in terms of subsistence at a national level as shown by the U_{min} schedule. Thus, with an initial level of outstanding debt, it may be profitable to default even in the initial period if the new loans offered turn out to be less than the debt charges and/or are inadequate to ensure a U_{min}. In such

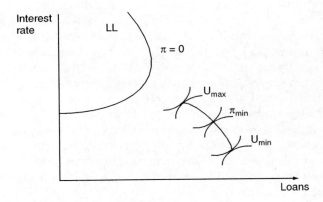

Figure 1.2   Loan supply under credit risk

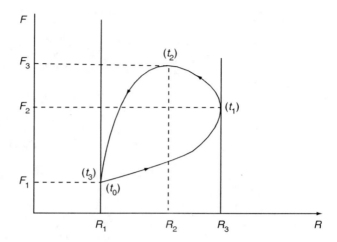

Figure 1.3   Real and financial growth rates

cases a stiffening of loan terms (with higher interest rates) would be incapable of averting a default. Default on individual loans may be responsible for a generalised crisis and in such cases the loan supply curve would shift backward as lenders refuse to offer loans at the prevailing rate. Such a situation may prompt the lenders to initiate collective actions to continue with lendings by refinancing which effectively augments loan supply at each rate of interest. In terms of Figure 1.2, this strategy would be indicated by a rightward shift of the loan supply curve. While refinancing enables lenders to restore the loan supply, borrowers in turn would voluntarily rule out the default option as long as they are able to achieve the necessary minimum flow of loans to provide subsistence. Additional doses of refinancing may even allow the borrower to achieve higher levels of consumption and social welfare. However, negotiations for such refinancing can be effective only when profits enjoyed by lenders are at least at the critical minimum at which the potential default losses can be compensated by gains via additional loan servicing. Simultaneously, it is necessary that the minimum level of refinancing enables the individual borrowing nation to attain the level of subsistence.[11] Refinancing, in such situations has been termed a public good.[12]

Models of optimal borrowings with loan recontracting (refinancing) recognise the problem of free-riding amongst banks which may render it difficult to initiate refinancing. Official interventions are sometimes recommended as a way out, especially when penalties imposed by lenders, say, by boycotting exports from the borrowing country, turn out as sources of losses in the lending country as well; in particular, for its exporters who suffer income losses as a consequence. Official interventions can, in such situations, be used to initiate 'side-payments' which are paid to both private lending agencies (banks and so on) and the borrowing nations, the latter to provide incentives against default.[13] Situations are thus created of a non-default cum non-penalty situation which would improve welfare for the borrower or the lender or both. Side-payments can also be arranged by taxpayers (exporters) in the lending nation who lose with default. In such cases these payments are offered to both lenders (banks and so on) as well as to borrowers.[14] One thus arrives at the paradoxical situation where the borrower's bargaining position *improves* as the size of debt is larger and penalty conditions are more stringent.

The functional value of the optimal borrowing models has been marred by the limiting assumptions on which these are based. In this context the following comments seem to be relevant:

- First, the description of countries as industrial agents which harmoniously maximizes some sort of welfare function over the Nash games where 'all decision paths are mapped at the game's outset ... when ... the game just widens' rests on a set of assumptions which do not relate to reality.[15]
- Second, since in the models of optimum borrowings uncertainty is assumed away, the validity of the arguments relating to default as well as penalties remains limited. Thus while the solvency criterion depends on the borrower's expected value of trade balance, the latter is bound to reflect the changing opportunities of trade which are essentially uncertain. Similarly, the costs of default to the borrower which consist of the stiffening of penal actions are, in absence of uncertainty, assumed to be known in advance. A debt default or its absence is thus of endogenous origin in these models as long as the risk-neutral rational agents transact business both as lenders and borrowers.

- Third, while the simpler version of these models (under perfect foresight) assumes that the loan market operates under perfect competition, with normal (zero) rate of profits to lenders, the more sophisticated versions introduce collusion, side-payments and so on, without, however, exploring the implications of the uneven bargaining strength between the lenders and the borrowers. The omission misses out a decisive factor for exercising options relating to default as well as penalty. Possibilities, in particular, of wielding the power of a discriminatory monopolist on the part of lenders remain, which is thus not considered in these models.
- Fourth, the notion of the utility maximising social welfare function for the borrower relies on the notion of diminishing marginal utility of consumption. The notion may not be tenable in developing countries with poverty as well as uneven distribution of income and wealth distorting the generality of a diminishing marginal utility scenario, even at an aggregate level. This, in particular, would have a lot of relevance when distribution of income and wealth turns regressive under debt-distress.
- Fifth, the treatment of uncertainty, both in the simplified versions with perfect foresight and in models incorporating uncertainty and default risk, remain incomplete. This renders the conclusions derived from these models rather inappropriate to handle the reality. This aspect is handled in Section 1.4 which deals in greater detail with uncertainty.
- Finally, supply of international credit may also be affected by global aspects of savings and investments, especially relating to the rich industrialised countries which are the major source of these flows. Macroeconomic aspects as above are completely neglected in the optimal borrowing models, where supply of credit is constrained by micro-considerations including the opportunity cost of credit which is given by the rate of return on safe lendings. We turn to these aspects of global finance in the next section of this chapter.

1.3   The macroeconomic implications of global capital flows[16]

1.3.1   The underlying paradoxes

The macroeconomic picture of the prevailing pattern of international capital flows unfolds a story with a few underlying paradoxes. These concern the sustainability as well as the implications of these flows in the global economy. The problems can be identified at three levels:

- *First*, in terms of the problems which arise at a microeconomic level and are transmitted to the entire economy as an over-saving or under-consumption problem. The problem is typically faced by lender agencies in their efforts at maximising *both* net advances as well as the returns therefrom. The process can lead to a conflicting situation when the inward flow of returns on past investments tends to swamp the gross outflows, not only at the level of individual lenders but also at an aggregate level, for the nation as a whole. While such situations hamper the ability of the individual lender to sustain the flow of net advances, it also dampens, at a macroeconomic level, the capacity of the capital-exporting nation to make use of its excess savings for generating commodity trade surpluses in overseas markets. The contradiction between higher returns and net exports of capital (and commodities) reflects the classical problems of realisation or under-consumption as are encountered by advanced economies which experience demand constraints on domestic output.
- The *second* aspect of the macroeconomic problem is a mirror image of the first. It is experienced by the borrowing agents (and at an aggregate level, by the capital-importing nations as a whole) neither of which can any longer avail of net inflows of finance. This happens when an increasing share of the gross borrowings is used to meet the rising debt charges when it starts growing faster than the former. If the net inflows of foreign exchange set the binding constraint for supply of output in these borrowing countries, growth in these economies will be thwarted as a consequence. This indicates a situation which, from a borrower's point of view, amounts to ponzi finance, where returns from borrowed money are not commensurate with the cost of servicing. A faltering growth in the borrowing country also shrinks the size of the market in these areas, for exports of goods as well as surplus capital which otherwise remain unutilised in the demand constrained capital-exporting countries.
- The *third* aspect of the macroeconomic problem relating to international capital flows concerns the market-driven path of finance in recent years. With financial innovations geared to provide

hedges against volatility in uncertain markets, little if any, can be the contribution of these instruments in the sphere of real activities. This is because of the fact that the gains and losses of these hedge instruments are in the nature of short-term capital gains/ losses which are treated as transfer payments in national accounts. As financial markets are driven by uncertainty, derivative trade (which caters to the increased riskiness of assets) tends to increase *pari passu*, thus further de-linking spheres of finance and real growth. Instances of these transactions include those secondary market transactions which aim to hedge against fluctuations in currency rates, stocks or money markets. Such issues raise problems, in terms of the macroeconomic impact of global capital inflows, on stability as well as growth in the world economy.

These aspects of the macroeconomic paradox of the international capital market, as described above, are dealt with in the following three parts of the present section.

1.3.2   The lender paradox[17]

For individual lenders, maximising inflows of investment income on past investments often stands in the way of continuing with new loans on a *net* basis. A micro-level conflict, as above, can also prevent the lending nation from maintaining, at a macro-level, *net* outflows of capital and exports of commodities from the country as a whole.

For private agencies which handle credit, it is of paramount importance that *profits on lending*, net of default risk and other transaction costs, are maximised. The goal of profit maximisation is of cardinal importance in influencing the magnitude as well as the direction of private credit flows. Even developmental assistance at concessional loan terms has often been conditional on the return flow of debt charges. For each such financial agent, it thus remains crucial to secure the maximum rate of return as can be achieved after discounting for the costs of probable default. However, as the return flow of investment income and amortisation start swelling, *net* outflows tend to diminish, both in absolute terms and as the percentage growth rate over time. The tendency turns out to be detrimental to the interests of the lender in the long run since the base itself of new investments (which ensures future returns) also tends to contract in the process.

Thus the profit-maximising behaviour of individual financial agents in the capital market seems to stand in the way of sustained net outflows of capital by the respective agents. While lenders would be willing to extend new loans as long as there is no default, growth rate of gross loans would tend to falter as loans outstanding are larger. Conflicts, as described above, between the micro-level profit maximising norms in the international credit market and the macro-economic balances in the economy often result, for demand constrained capital-exporting economies, in an underutilisation of capacity.

The servicing of past loans might generate situations where inflows of capital outstrip the outflows on account of new loans extended. With inflows on account of loan services and amortisation having their origin in past investments, lending nations may thus experience a return flow of capital, a situation which considerably reduces the opportunities of exporting surplus capital and unsold goods to overseas markets. As in closed economies, the problem of sustaining growth and accumulation is equally paramount in open economies, especially in countries which are demand constrained. Net overseas lending and a matching flow of net merchandise exports thus prove difficult to sustain unless gross flows of credit also increase simultaneously at a rate which is higher than that for investment income on past loans. Lender agencies as well as nations thus face the paradoxes of over-lending in their effort to sustain both net lending and high rates of returns abroad. The problem can be identified as an essential aspect of the anarchy of the market mechanism under capitalism. Significantly enough, such problems are *not* related to the limits of debtor capacity. Instead, these are one of an endogenous variant, which are inherent in the process of accumulation, excess capacity and compounding of loans in the advanced economies.

Tendencies on the part of the mature capitalist nations to rely on external markets in order to absorb their domestic surpluses of savings and output reflect propensities, chronic and inherent, towards overproduction. The outcome amounts to a realisation crisis in a Marxist frame of analysis[18] or an excess savings syndrome in terms of the Keynesian[19] Effective Demand principles.

In a model developed by Domar[20] along Keynesian lines, conditions of full-capacity growth for an open economy were spelt out to indicate the two-fold advantages of capital exports in mature capital-exporting economies. The dual benefits include the provisions for (1) the investment outlets for domestic savings which otherwise remain idle; and (2) the overseas export outlets for surplus stocks of output in the domestic economy. Evidently, both processes help to revamp profitability in the capital-exporting countries, in the respective spheres of finance and real activities.

The duality of the lending process corresponds to the distinction, in Marxist writings, between industry and finance under monopoly capitalism.[21] With innovations of financial instruments at advanced stages of overseas lending, rates of return on finance have a tendency to improve along with additional exports of capital abroad. Improved returns, however, do not necessarily prevail for industrial activities in their domestic economy unless the process *also* expands, through export opportunities, overseas markets for those goods and services. In terms of international accounts, it is only when the country exports capital on a *net* basis that it can match export surpluses of merchandise and non-factor services from the economy in its current account. Thus, exports of financial capital net of amortisation and investment income payments can only maintain the macroeconomic balance in the real sector of the capital surplus economies by exporting, in real terms, the excess of domestic output over expenditure.[22]

The above analytic distinction between the two dimensions of overseas investment can be exploited further by drawing a distinction between what characterise as the *rentier effect* and the *trade effect* of capital movements. Relating respectively to the spheres of finance and the real economy in the lending countries, *rentier effects* of overseas investments become strong at advanced stages of capital exports when investment income from externally held assets assumes a greater significance with loan compounding. A similar outcome, however, does not necessarily hold for the *trade effects* unless the gross value of capital exports increases along with inflows of investment income and amortisation payments, so as to permit simultaneous increases in *net* lending itself. If gross capital outflows taper off relative to the inflows on account of the debt servicing and repayments of past loans, the lender nation would eventually turn into a capital importer. This is most likely with creditor-confidence on further lending waning off with accumulation of outstanding loans. Simultaneously, the chances of avoiding stagnation in the real sector of the creditor country's economy through outlets in overseas markets would be weakened as such moves are no longer helpful to absorb the surplus savings/output from the lender country. Loans extended or securities bought in the past, however, would continue to be serviced as long as debtors do not default. Rentiers in the capital-exporting country who live on the past are thus able to sustain the flow of their income. *Under such circumstances, it is possible to expect divergent fortunes for the financier-rentier on the one hand and the industrial-entrepreneur on the other, in capital-exporting countries at advanced stages of capitalism.*

From above, it is logical to expect a structural change in the balance of payments of the capital-exporting countries. Their current account, which in the beginning also records a trade surplus, may now be subject to a change in its composition, with investment income inflows gaining ground in terms of a higher weightage. A declining trade competitiveness may eventually end up with a trade deficit for these capital-exporting countries, as inflows of investment income continue to finance the excess of merchandise imports over exports in their current account. At a later stage, the capital account balance may even turn negative with capital imports financing the current account deficit.

Attention has been drawn in a study by Rowthorn and Wells,[22] to the 'paradoxical results' as lender nations 'start living on past', like a 'rentier nation'. They indicate the stages which eventually transform a lending nation into one which imports capital from abroad. Trade, at this point, ceases to generate income to producers in the domestic economy while financial assets (acquired through past exports of capital) may continue to procure rentals (or investment income from abroad). We have indicated, in Appendix 1A, the implications of this in terms of formal logic.

Global aspects of this exercise may be highlighted further by distinguishing between two groups of borrower nations, designated respectively as borrowing Groups 1 and 2. Group 1 includes the borrowing countries of North and Group 2 those from South. We have tried in Appendix 1A to indicate the effect of the international allocation of gross credit on trade and income flows in each borrowing and lending area, and also on the global pattern of lendings.

As has been pointed out in Appendix 1A, loans to Group 1 nations would generate an outcome which favours the rentiers in the capital-

exporting country who also enjoy the benefits of increased investment income. This penalises the traders in North who now lose
the export markets for merchandise in Group 2 countries who no
longer receive a real transfer of resources from abroad. Thus, the
distribution of aggregate credit flows between different groups of
nations may adversely affect the size of the real transfers which actually flows between the lending and the borrowing nations. Problems
in securing a steady servicing of loans advanced in the past may
generate tendencies, on part of lenders, to set aside funds for loan
rescue operations. The consequent drop in the growth rate of net
lendings, would further dampen the trade-creating effect and initiate
sharper declines in financial and real transfers to the South.

Developments in the recent past, especially since mid-1980s indicate a tendency for increased borrowings by Group 1 countries (the
USA in particular) which caused increases in nominal and real interest
rates till a reversal in the recent past. Thus, US sales of treasury bonds in
the security market increased the share of international borrowings
by the Group 1 countries. Simultaneously, it raised the rate of interest
in the loan market (primarily the bank credit market), creating debt
difficulties and causing lender actions to divert funds towards loan-rescue operations. The situation implied a drop in the 'trade-creating'
effect of foreign credit flows. The above results from the rise in interest
rate and (for a given growth rate of gross loans) declines in trade effect
as are caused by the rise in the share for Group 1 countries. (See Equation (1A.24) for the relation between the three variables, r, i and a.)

The choice open to lenders in terms of the recent pattern in the
distribution of capital flows between borrowers in the international
capital market brings us back to the issue of potential paradoxes in
terms of lender strategies, discussed earlier. Rentiers living on investment income flows and other service income (say from the financial
derivatives) in the lending nations would prefer an allocation which
steps up the share for the borrowing countries in the industrialised
North (Group 1), which has an obvious edge over the Southern
borrowers in terms of creditworthiness. The consequent declines in
the trade effect, as described above are evidently opposed to the
interest of the exporters of material products who face a dwindling
overseas market for their net exports. *With the present tendencies in the*
international capital market towards a reallocation of lendable finance in
favour of the North, the outcome of lender strategies thus seems to boil

down to one on the share as well as the magnitude of North–South finance, increases which are capable of redressing the balance in favour of real activity (as opposed to finance), not only for the foreign exchange constrained capital importers in the South but also in the demand constrained capital-exporting countries of the North.

Analysis of the capital-exporting country problems as presented above highlights, for the lender economies, the macroeconomic conditions for achieving the dual benefits of capital exports which can favour the domestic rentiers as well as traders. The twin goals, as it has been observed earlier, can be simultaneously met by the lending country if it can continue with net exports of capital. As can be seen from Appendix 1A, the above can happen if the savings rate of the capital-exporting country exceeds the ratio between its investment to GDP (which, by assumption, is true) and if its GDP growth rate exceeds a floor which goes up with increases in savings rate as well as the interest rate. This also requires a normal value of the trade effect (of capital exports). Implications of these conditions are spelt out in detail in the model provided in the Appendix 1A.

With global tendencies, which included steep increases in the real rate of interest during the 1980s, it was unlikely that the ceiling on interest rate, if any, ever shifted in the downward direction. With rising interest rates, conditions as above for continuing net exports of capital could only be ensured by a rise in the growth rate of gross lending, and/or with a drop in the savings rates in the lending areas. None of these, as can be witnessed from recent history, prevailed in the past, thus making it difficult to sustain net outflows of capital from the capital-rich North. The other scenario of net capital exports includes the possibility of the trade effect exceeding unity. This implies an excessive trade dependence on the part of the borrowing country. A unit of capital inflow generates, in such situations, a size of import demand which is larger than the capital import itself. (The process is akin to de-industrialisation which actually took place in colonial India during the British rule.) With capital exports from the industrialised North, a major part of which is today retained within the industrialised borrowing nations, it becomes unlikely to encounter such situations. For flows directed to the developing countries (which of late have opened up) it will also be reasonable to assume that the trade effect of capital exports is positive but less than unity.

Recapitulating, the lending nations are thus able to sustain net exports of capital when

(a)   the growth rate of gross capital exports from the lending country is higher;
(b)   the rate of interest is within the limit set by the conditions as above;
(c)   savings rate in the lending country is lower.

As for the ceilings set for interest rate in terms of the conditions spelt out in Appendix 1A, the interest rate on loans to the developing countries often exceeds the prevailing rate (say the libor) in the capital market. This is because of the risk premium (or the spread) which is attached to such loans as an insurance against potential default. This makes it even more difficult to fulfil the three conditions spelt out above. Problems in sustaining net exports of capital and commodities from capital surplus economies lead us to analyse the problems faced by the borrowing economies which are presented in the following section.

1.3.3   The borrowers' dilemma – a case for resource transfers to the South

As an alternative to the conventional approaches to problems faced by the capital importing countries, we have provided, at end of Appendix 1A, a framework which tallies, as a mirror image, with the paradoxes faced by the capital-exporting economies. The issues dealt with dwell on the developmental aspects of these capital flows.

In a world of credit shortages and credit rationing, a heavy debt-servicing schedule may compel a debtor nation in the developing area to enter into loan contracts at high conditionalities, even to continue with its debt servicing. In such cases a higher growth rate for gross credit goes with a stiffening of loan terms. The process makes it harder for the debtor nations to maintain positive inflows of net financial and real transfers, unless the growth rate of gross capital exports continues to grow in excess of the sum of annual amortisation (a) and the rate of interest (i), as pointed out in the Appendix 1A.

Let us now look at the possible flows of net transfers of financial and real resources (RT). In terms of the model specified in Appendix 1A, it is observed that a rise in debt services, relative to net flows of finance which meet the current account deficit (CAD), would generate downward pressures on RT. For a developing debtor we can visualise *three* successive phases in the resulting debt process which can be characterised as follows: (We will use the symbols specified in Appendix 1A to specify the three phases.)

- Phase I: $RT = CAD - iD > 0$ and $CAD > 0$
  where CAD as well as RT are measured in terms of absolute values, as defined earlier. As the initial margin of the growth rate of gross credit over the sum of annual amortisation and interest rates narrows down, RT tapers off relative to CAD (see Equation (1A.15)). This marks the transition to Phase II where RT actually turns negative. The transition also marks the beginning of a debt crisis as well as a debt trap for the borrowing country, the former with the compulsions on the part of the country to follow a path of import-led GDP compression and the latter with the urgency to secure finance from abroad as can meet the debt charges (rather than real transfers). In other words, while the debtor country, short of default, is compelled to borrow, external finance thus secured is used up to meet the debt charges and not the real transfers. This starts the dilemma faced by a typical developing country borrower which does not want to default in order to stay in the capital market and also to grow with foreign capital.
- Phase II: $RT = CAD - iD < 0$ and $CAD > 0$
  During this phase RT turns negative, because gross capital inflows are inadequate in relation to amortisaion and interest charges on foreign loans (as in fact can be seen from Equation (1A.17)). During this phase, expenditure cuts and output compressions (which form the fiscal-monetary component of the conditional loan packages) may reduce import demand, an aspect which is consistent with the reverse flow of transfers from the debtor economy. The output compression will be greater if inflows of capital are packaged with import-liberalisation which adds to import-intensity.
- Phase III: $RT = CAD - iD < 0$ and $CAD < 0$
  In this phase both RT and the CAD turn negative. As for the latter, a negative CAD (a current account surplus) is necessarily matched by a trade surplus as the investment liabilities

continue to be large. The consequences in terms of inflows of real transfers and the related impact on GDP, as in Phase II, are both unfavourable.

It can be gathered from above that domestic growth rate in a typical developing country which imports capital may be adversely affected in the long run with the RT declining and eventually turning negative in Phases II and III of the debt process. The eventuality may be expedited if inflows of capital simultaneously raise the extent of its import-dependence. Experiences of some major debtor countries in Latin America during the 1980s confirm these tendencies, with low negative growth rates of their GDP which were matched by similar low/negative flows of RT and a higher order of import-dependence. In absence of compensating forces which include the mobilisation of domestic savings or the capacity on the part of the country to 'manage' the current account by means of offsetting credit entries like transfers and so on, these countries often found it impossible to avoid a path of GDP compression. With domestic inflation remaining uncontrolled, these borrowing economies also found it difficult to avoid declines in per capita GDP.

In the process of implementing the economic reforms which are considered vital in the interest of stabilisation, the developing countries undergo a process of 'economic retrenchment'.[23] The latter initiates a tightening of the fiscal-monetary policies, which include a cut in government expenditure and fiscal deficits, freeing of the deposit rates and restraining expansions in M2 by means of open market operations in the money market. At times a need arises to monitor consumer prices and real exchange rate variations, especially with rising exchange reserves which can potentially increase domestic money supply. (The latter sequence is described in the literature as a 'Dutch disease syndrome'.) These fiscal-monetary restraints, which target financial stability, can have a detrimental effect on domestic growth. The above deserves attention, especially when implemented as a part of the stabilisation package to mend an external economic crisis.

On the whole, capital flows may not always work as a panacea in terms of their support to the growth process in the developing countries. Combined with the problems faced by the capital-exporting countries in terms of their limited ability to generate demand in their home economy, the capital-importing country's dilemma of non-attainable development goals makes out a case for policy inter-ventions. The latter can be at the level of the lender countries as well as their financial institutions, and targeted to fulfil net capital export targets as well as destinations. At the level of the borrowers, it includes the need to reduce their dependence on imported inputs for domestic growth. We will come back to these issues in Chapters 3 and 4 of this volume.

1.4 Uncertainty and its ramifications

With uncertainty and speculation each having a major role in deci-sions concerning asset preference, a theory dealing with capital flows needs to incorporate these dimensions. We start, in the next few pages, with the approach to uncertainty in mainstream economics and its critique offered from different quarters.

In the mainstream literature dealing with capital market decisions, uncertainty is assumed away, by postulating full information to which all rational operators in the market have free access. In terms of the new classical economics (NCE) models, the maximising rational agents arrive at equilibrium with full utilisation of all resources including labour.[24] Second best solutions at the level of natural rate of unemployment (NRU) qualify the above results while keeping unchanged the basic postulates regarding full information and thus negating uncertainty.

Formulations as above in NCE literature on financial markets include the portfolio (asset market) approach postulating an 'efficient market' equilibrium in terms of allocating capital. All agents operating in the capital market are assumed to have full information regarding the expected changes in variables, thus ruling out uncertain pros-pects.[25] Variants of the optimal portfolio models have recognised the role of trading and information costs at equilibrium. However, it is held that prices have a tendency to quickly adjust to information which is *never* in private domain. On the whole the system tends to set 'conventions' consistent with 'fundamentals', with the process similar to what has been described as a 'random walk along Wall Street'![26]

With uncertainty having no role to play in the market for capital, speculation is reduced to arbitrage even in inter-temporal space, and financial liberalisation follows as a logical policy conclusion.

A variant of these models advocates an end to what is described as 'financial repression' to generate savings, investment as well as growth in the economy. The forces behind include freeing the rate of interest which reaches a level at which the market is cleared which simultaneously makes for a high-risk high-return type of invest-ments in the economy.[27,28]

In an alternative approach which identifies itself as New Keynesian Economics (NKE), short period under-employment equilibrium in the labour market is explained by incomplete (or asymmetric) information. The latter is also supposed to prevail in the credit market which, as is assumed in these models, similarly works under asymmetric information. The credit market models of the NKE variant dwell on the interaction between a principal and an agent having incompatible incentives in the market. With asymmetric information limiting the capacity of the lenders (the principal) to separate out the 'good' ones amongst the borrowers (agents) from those which are the defaulting types (or the 'bad' ones), the lenders resort to credit rationing which keeps out a section of borrowers from the market. The borrowers in turn are assumed to have better knowledge in terms of their own inclinations for default. They are also assumed to have the capacity to choose among projects (and often to prefer the high-risk high-return ones) and also to have an ability to exit by default.[29] Circumstances as above are supposed to initiate strategic games of bargaining and negotiations between lenders and borrowers, with the former co-opting (or pressing) the borrowers with the threat of penalties.[30] The latter include embargoes on trade, credit or even on withdrawal of assets.[31] Actions of both partners are supposed to be guided by principles of 'rationality'. An outcome as above, however, deviates from the conventional arguments in favour of financial liberalisa-tion.[32] An explanation is offered for tendencies towards credit ration-ing on the part of lenders in the credit market. However, on scrutiny these models seem to rely on rational agents, both as borrowers and lenders in the credit market. In the absence of asymmetric information, the equilibrium reached would correspond to the Pareto optima. Even regulations in the form of a Tobin tax on currency speculation to curb noise traders in the market are expected to be Pareto optimal.[33]

Arguments put forth in NKE models in terms of market imperfec-tions and asymmetry, however, are different from the conventional arguments in favour of financial liberalisation. These doctrines advocate a greater degree of financial intermediation to generate real activities, both by raising savings and by ensuring its deployment along more efficient channels.[34] Such arguments do not stand scrutiny once we question their underlying assumptions that all savings are automatically invested and that savings respond favourably to higher interest rates offered in the market. Also the assumption regarding the association of high risks with high returns is found to be empirically unsound.

Critics of the 'efficient market hypothesis' models point at its limitations, much of which is based on a concern for its failure to explain the reality. It can be observed that the limitations are mostly due to an inadequate handling of uncertainty in these formulations.

Aspects which need attention include: (a) a failure to distinguish between new and old stocks which are transacted in the market. The two can have very different impact on the economy. While new stocks sold in the primary market generate demand for real investments in the economy, the stocks when resold in the secondary market, do not necessarily contribute to new investment even when these transactions generate buoyancy in the financial markets by pushing up prices of stocks. Thus rising profits on old stocks of a firm, as has been empirically observed, do not necessarily signify similar movements in the prices of the new stocks launched by the same firm. (b) Contrary to what is postulated in the rational expectations approach, capital markets have failed to serve as an informational/ signalling agent in the real economy. As a consequence the capital market does not always contribute to efficiency and productivity growth in the economy. (c) Finally, capital markets are by no means the sole source of finance for investing firms which can also access credit from banks by using their own source of investible surpluses. Accordingly financial liberalisation does not necessarily generate savings for new investments.

Logic implicit in mainstream economics on related issues thus ignores the fact that there can be financial investments which do not contribute to real investments. This happens typically under uncertainty which provides the impetus to acquire the high-risk financial assets. Hedging in financial transactions is rather common under uncertainty. It includes ranges of derivatives (forwards, futures, options, swaps), the OTC transactions of financial institutions and windfall gains/losses in the volatile markets for currency as well as capital flows. While reliance on these instruments adds to the trans-action cost of each financial deal, the capital gains/losses on these transactions, in terms of standard convention in national accounts, are treated as transfers which do not enter the national output calculations. Thus the multiplicity of financial investments, while originating from the *same* base in terms of specific real activities, do not expand the base itself. Instead, these amount to a piling up of claims which rely on the same set of real assets. Finance thus becomes increasingly remote from the real economy and financial innovations proliferate in the economy, to hedge and insulate finan-cial investments in the presence of uncertainty. Despite the fact that these NKE models are closer to the real world of uncertainty and even involuntary unemployment, the application of the rational choice doctrine in the NKE models,[35] as pointed out in its critique, is subject to severe limitations. It has been argued that rational behaviour is difficult to specify in an uncertain world and such problems can never be minimised by extrapolating behaviour with an actuarial framework of utility maximisation.[36] To treat risk and uncertainty as 'natural (exogenous), time-invariant, parametric and hence probabilistic' thus amounts to an asocial construction which deviates from social reality. The fact that Principal/Agent (P/A) models depend on the property of 'replicability' implies a temporal neutrality of P/A relations. The fact that construction of risk in these models is 'primitive' or exogenously determined is thus a disputed one.[37]

Questioning the legitimacy of the portfolio (or asset market) equi-librium approach, the critics point out the difficulties of calculating the probability of these risks with actuarial precision, especially under uncertainty. It is sometimes argued that uncertainty is 'gradable' and that it is a subjective notion which is based partly on 'epistemic' theories of probability and partly on properties of real world.[38] These interpretations are consistent with Keynes's final position on prob-ability in the General Theory (1936) and in *the Economic Journal* (1937) article. The notion of 'animal spirits' runs through the Gen-eral Theory and is further clarified in 1937 as follows: '... By "uncer-tain" knowledge, let me explain I do not mean merely to distinguish what is known from what is probable. ... About these matters, there is no scientific basis on which to form any calculable probability whatever. We simply do not know'.[39,40]

Let us point out here that the issue of gradeability has been a controversial one in the literature. There lies at one extreme the Keynesian position in his earlier work titled *Tract on Probability* which stated that probability is relative to evidence. Thus it is supposed to take a value between impossibility (zero) and certainty (one), which amounts to a logical approach to probability. However, as mentioned above, Keynes seems to have deviated from the above position in his 1937 article. Positions as those have later been interpreted as one of 'ergodicity' where probability is solely a property of the real world.[41]

As an alternative it can be suggested that knowledge (and uncertainty) is subjective and hence 'non-ergodic'. Thus it is not a natural phenomenon which is time invariant. Accordingly it is ontological and is embedded in social reality which, as Shackle described it, is 'kaleidoscopic' and also relates to what Joan Robinson called 'historic time'.[42] Other interpretations of uncertainty in the literature emphasise the fact that investors in the credit market are tuned to what are treated as 'conventions' and as such are subject to 'bounded rationality'.[43] This is due to an innate tendency on the part of the risk-averse investors to distaste uncertainty and hence to converge to 'conventions'. The argument is similar to what Keynes had described as a 'beauty contest' approach in the market where everybody is keen to arrive at what others think. However, 'conventions' as described in these approaches are also subject to day-to-day changes in the market and hence are equally prone to violent fluctuations, especially with contagion and herd behaviour.[44]

Dwelling on the policy implications, one agrees with the diagnosis that it is the combination of uncertainty and availability of liquidity which is responsible for crises under financial deregulation. By making possible the short-run entry and exit of players in the financial market, financial liberalisation makes for short-termism, which fails to generate real assets in the long run. Instead the demand for financial assets are guided by prospects of 'quasi-rents' as determined by profits and losses in the short run.[45] With availability of credit and the information technology to make for fast communications, perceptions are not only subject but also prone to quick revisions. This explains the bandwagon effects as are frequently observed in the financial markets. Connected with the above sequences is the social construction of credit, which speaks for the social exclusion of borrowers relatively weak in terms of their ability to enter the credit market. These borrowers however, have a great deal of potential in a recession-prone economy due to their higher consumption propensities.[46]

Criticisms launched by the post-Keynesians on related issues dispel the 'myth' of the borrower in the rational expectation models as an independent agent. '...who has no history'. The post-Keynesians have rightly argued that borrowers can never systematically cheat by choosing projects which are risky, nor can they exit at will, facts which are borne out by the unequal power structure in the credit market. The extent of power imbalance between creditors and debtors, as pointed out, is thus strengthened or weakened by degrees of income inequality and monopoly power.[47]

Continuing with the criticisms of mainstream approaches to issues relating to the role of uncertainty in financial markets, one comes across a set of arguments along parallel lines which have been offered by George Soros, an active practitioner in stock markets.[48] Soros interprets the presence of volatility in credit markets by relying on the notion of 'reflexivity', which is defined as a two-way binary relation. Both lenders and borrowers are treated as 'participants' in the credit market which in turn is defined as the 'situation'. Actions on the part of these participants are supposed to be linked to such 'situations' in a two-way 'reflexive' manner. Thus actions by creditors (participants) influence the value of the collateral (situation) held by them against loans advanced in the past, (say with the withdrawal of loans). This, in turn influences actions on the part of the creditors themselves. Expectations regarding further declines in the prices of these financial assets are reinforced by tendencies to sell (spot or forward) by those who hold the assets. The circuit is thus governed by the properties of a 'reflexive' function as defined above.[49] It is worth quoting in full Soros' argument which runs as follows:

'...Loans are based on the lender's estimation of the borrower's ability to service his debt. The valuation of the collateral is supposed to be independent of the act of lending; but in actual fact the act of lending can affect the value of the collateral. This is true of the individual case and of the economy as a whole....The connection between credit expansion and economic activity is anything but constant – for instance, credit for building a new factory has quite a different effect from credit for a leveraged buy-out.

This makes it difficult to quantify the connection between credit and economic activity.... The monetarist school has done so, with disastrous consequences'.[50]

Arguments provided by Soros on the reflexive properties of the credit market are useful to interpret the typical credit cycles in capitalist economies.[51] The boom-bust cycle of credit, as it has been observed, is asymmetrical. While it takes time to build up a credit boom,

'...the period of gradual, slowly accelerating credit expansion is followed by a short period of credit contraction,... Bust is compressed in time because the attempt to liquidate loans causes a sudden implosion of collateral values... In the early stages of a reflexive process of credit expansion the amount of credit involved is relatively small so that its impact on collateral values is negligible... As the amount of debt accumulates, total lending increases in importance and begins to have an appreciable effect on collateral values. The process continues until a point is reached when total credit can not increase fast enough to continue stimulating the economy. By that time collateral values have become greatly dependent on new lending... The erosion of collateral values has a depressing effect on economic activity, which in turn reinforces the erosion of collateral values.... a decline may precipitate the liquidation of loans, which in turn may make the decline more precipitous'.[52]

The points raised earlier in this section on uncertainty as a major factor behind the asset price fluctuations can also be used to infer that *during an upswing* the risk-adjusted returns on speculatory finance are pushed up *more than proportionately as compared* to those on real sector investments. This makes real investments even less attractive in terms of relative profitability. Thus returns on speculative ventures rises *faster* in order to attract investments in an uncertain world, especially with increasing risks.

Signs of an impending bust which comes with the usual social and economic costs regenerate governance which aims to avoid financial collapse, both with regulatory measures from Central Banks and a reorganising of portfolio on the part of corporate entities. The moves generate a regulatory cum restructuring process which starts at the peak of a credit cycle and continues along with it in a wave-like pattern. However, it can be assumed that unlike the credit cycle, these regulatory processes are not subject to asymmetric swings.[53] For Soros, however, like other participants, the regulatory authorities are *also* subject to the same reflexive process. The assumption seeks to contest, rather unsuccessfully, the claim that the state can intervene successfully to stall and prevent an impending collapse of the market.

Reflecting further on the above position, it can be held that knowledge (and its opposite, uncertainty) can improve if institutions like contracts and conventions along with the market makers, remain 'stable'; a situation which warrants policies of effective intervention and stabilisation on the part of the regulatory authorities.[54] This view is based on the notion that uncertainty and knowledge are both 'gradable'. Thus '. . . if uncertainty is gradable, government action may reduce it and thereby increase confidence'.[55]

In a paper dealing with investment decisions in Keynesian theory,[56] the authors have stressed the role of expectations along with the weight attached to the latter. These, as argued, are consistent with what Keynes visualised as 'expectations of future profitability' and the 'confidence with which we forecast the future'. The authors provide an empirical test of the hypothesis to explain investment in a market economy.[57] Investment is driven by the expectations of future profits on the part of the decision-making business manager and the confidence as are assigned by them on these forecasts. The findings, as claimed by the authors, 'can be viewed more broadly as a test of those theories that suggest that expectations matter in the determination of investment'.[58] The model is specified as

$$I = f(BEF, weight)$$

where I, investment; BEF, business executive forecast and weight, or confidence associated with that forecast.

It can also be expressed as

$$I = f(BEF, MISS)$$

where MISS stands for forecast inaccuracy and is the inverse of weight (for example, MISS = 1/weight).[59] Testing the model on the basis of sample data, the authors arrive at the conclusion that '...whether ill-informed or not, whether rational or not, whether stable or not, they (managers' perceptions) are of fundamental importance in the determination of investment, and hence, macroeconomic stability.'[60] One can interpret the low weight as 'paucity of evidence' in terms of probability. Thus uncertainty implies situations where knowledge is incomplete and not totally reliable. This is consistent with the theoretical position that '...uncertainty is not total ignorance'.[61]

Observations as above indicate the crucial role of expectations in an uncertain world, where forecasts can never be accurate. With pyramiding of financial assets, a multiple number of these can now pile up and be backed by the same real/financial asset, especially in deregulated financial markets. The new range of financial instruments provides options to those held against investments in the real sector. While these new financial instruments cater to the need to hedge against uncertainty, the latter in the respective realm of financial or the real sphere continues to spillover to the other, thus reinforcing the speculative tendencies in the economy as a whole. As for the role of financial innovations in launching the new derivative instruments, it becomes doubtful whether these can improve the efficiency of the market by cutting down transaction costs alone. Thus the financial markets under uncertainty are subject to a set of in-built structural changes which tend to turn it more unpredictable. As a consequence the non-ergodic (non-repetitive) character of the social world adds to rising uncertainty.[62] The adverse effects of the financial innovations on the real economy work via (a) the rising uncertainty in the organised financial market and (b) the financial exclusion of the lower income sections (both households and countries) which reduce consumption, investment and as such, often lead to a shrinkage of the money multiplier in the economy.[63]

The range of assets, in a situation described above, can be spaced between liquid (cash and short-term demand deposits) and physical assets (which include real estate). The portfolio choice by the investor in such cases is heavily influenced by the expected changes in prices as well as in the return on each such asset. With uncertainty extorting a heavy discount on future, the investor may prefer to move away from long-term to short-run assets which are liquid. Similar to Keynes's liquidity trap, this characterises the tendencies in a money/credit economy. Assets here, however, are not subject to a binary classification (of money/bonds) as in Keynes, but have a range with varying degrees of liquidity along a whole spectrum.[64] The composition of assets and investments in these economies is influenced both by material conditions of production and by changing perceptions of future. The latter is necessarily subjective, both at the level of individual decisions and as a collective swing (one which is akin to what Keynes had described as 'animal spirit'). Changes in holdings of assets and liabilities thus relate to the speculatory activities; returns on these and as such their net demand are not possible to anticipate at a point of time. Possibilities as characterised earlier in the literature, identify the related investments as 'fictitious', as opposed to 'productive' capital.[65]

1.4.1   The 'finance motive' of liquidity demand

Liquidity needed to finance the purchase of equities is separate from that needed to purchase the fixed rate-fixed price long-term bonds.[66] With an uncertain future the market will have a tendency to hold shorter term assets, which may accommodate liquidity demand to meet pure financial transactions. Long-term equities can also contribute to the flow of these short-term financial assets by having a quick turnover in the secondary market. Financial innovations in a deregulated financial market add to the ranges of derivative financial instruments, expand the liquidity base and provide sources of finance which do not directly contribute to real growth.[67] This happens with divergent and disproportionate gaps between the rates of return on assets, and in particular, between those backed by direct creation of long-term real assets and others based on the pyramiding of financial assets which are backed by the *same* real/financial asset.

In deregulated financial markets, the average risk-adjusted rate of return on speculative activities tends to exceed the returns on real activities, especially under uncertainty. This happens as financial markets are prone to increasing risks, which goes with the fact that the margin in the rate of returns on financial assets over those achievable on real assets is often higher. Financial deregulation encourages innovations to hedge and speculate, which in turn generates demand for credit at higher risks. The latter can be identified as the 'finance' motive of liquidity demand, as pointed out by Keynes in 1937. While the real rate of return on productive investments corresponding to each long-term *expected* rate of return on bonds was central to Keynes's seminal contribution in his General Theory, the position was modified by Keynes himself in his 1937 articles.[68] Thus, the 'finance' motive for holding liquidity was shown as separate from the speculative or transaction motives. The above separation of the finance motive from the rest of liquidity demand has led post-Keynesians[69] to stress the role of financial innovations. This was to accommodate (endogenise) liquidity demand as arise with the finance motive. A failure on the part of the financial institutions to match credit demands by financial innovations, as is argued in terms of the argument, diverts finance away from the sphere of real investment and hence real growth in the economy.

1.4.2   On capital flows under uncertainty – a stylised framework

A stylised framework which captures the symbiotic relation between the real and the financial sectors in an economy is offered below. The model provided in Appendix 1B can be used to interpret the significance of cross-border financial flows in terms of growth in open economies.

Let us assume that the economy concerned is in a phase of post-crisis recovery. In terms of the taxonomy which is offered in Table 1.1, the situation relates to *Phase I Part 1*, characterised by real and financial upswing. Firms can continue with expansionary policies in this phase, both by borrowing and by floating equities. Real investments continue to grow over time, with positive investor-expectations. While the firms are in a position to raise money by floating equities which improves their gearing ratio and reduces the ratio of interest payments to profits earned, it also remains true that '... the existing debts are easily validated and units that were heavily in debt prospered: ... it (then) pays to lever'.[70] The easy access to borrowed funds leads to a piling up of debts, especially as long as profit expectations continue to be revised upwards. With financiers and investors both turning optimistic, the snowball effect in the credit market also continues as long as there exists a shared consensus in discounting the future. Asset prices as well as new real investments continue to rise as a result, with simultaneous increases in debt servicing.

As the process continues, the real sector boom may taper off over time, say with external shocks or with a saturation of technological innovations along with full utilisation of existing capacity. This pushes up risks on extending further credit and encourages the financial institutions to further '... innovate financial products and/or entrepreneurial

Table 1.1 Stages of the credit cycle: a taxonomy

Institutions Stages	Investing firms	Banks and other FIs	Regulatory authorities
Phase I			
Part 1: Real and financial upswing	Borrow and float equities easily to invest with high profits; Low D/E ratio	Lend freely	Do not intervene
Part 2: Real deceleration and financial upswing	Growth rate of real investment turns negative with drop in profit rates and rise in D/E ratio and debt servicing	Lend cautiously and only to 'best customers' out of 'purchased funds' from CDs and CPs, bonds, repurchases and so on and to finance the hedging instruments. Some of the banks and FIs collapse	Institutes credit control and bails out banks and FIs
Phase II			
Real deceleration – financial upswing	Growth rate of real investment turns negative with drop in profit rates and rise in D/E ratio and debt servicing; New borrowing to cover ponzi deals	Banks and FIs tend to meet demand for speculatory finance	Institutes credit control and bails out banks and FIs
Phase III			
Real and financial downswing	Liquidation of firms and bankruptcy	Credit tightened by private banks and FIs	Institutes credit control and bails out banks and FIs
Phase IV			
Real and financial upswing	Borrow and float equities easily to invest with high profits; Low D/E ratio	Lend freely	Do not intervene

subsidies in a fashion which reduces their own liquidity (relative to demand)'.[71] This happens since each unit of new or old investments is now backed, under the impact of greater uncertainty, by instruments of hedging. The process triggers off a rise in interest rate which is initiated by the market (and not by monetary authorities) with a consequent dampening of asset prices. For the investing firms, the liquidity constraint emerges while their gearing ratio moves up. Liquidity problems faced by the investing firms are compounded by factors which include the rising debt services, a drop in internally available finance (due to the drop in profitability) and problems in floating equities due to a reversal of their prices in the stock market. For the investing firms there is thus a genuine cash-flow problem, with the steady rise in debt charges on the one hand and the tapered flow of receipts on the other, from returns on past investments which are combined with sporadic gains/losses from asset prices.

As for banks, the shortfall in liquidity is compounded by tendencies for debt default which goes up with rising interest rates and falling prices of stocks. The banks/other financial institutions respond by financing the hedge instruments, while lending cautiously to the 'best' customers in the market. In a bid to avoid inflation, the monetary authorities may initiate credit-control, which imparts a 'shock' to the financial market. However inflation may work temporarily as a palliative by sustaining asset prices, the resale proceeds of which could be a major source of income to the investing firms in this period.[72] With expectations turning averse, prices of assets soon start tumbling down, thus affecting the financial balance sheet of firms, especially for those laden with a higher debt/equity ratio.[73] This may initiate defaults by firms facing a financial crunch while most of the borrowings in the economy are now channelised to hedging and later to speculation. In the meantime, some financial institutions may collapse and the regulatory authorities may act by both tightening credit and bailing out banks and other financial institutions. The situation described above has been identified as *Part 2 of Stage I* in terms of our taxonomy.

A scenario as above creates the atmosphere for what Minsky once described as a 'euphoric economy',[74] one where capital appreciation rather than returns on such assets provide the firms the means to meet the rising liabilities due to the rising debt charges. The scene characterises a state of 'ponzi finance', namely, one where the returns from investments do not cover the costs of borrowings. Credit advanced by financial institutions to firms in the meantime is utilised not as much for new investments in real activities as to meet debt charges and/or speculation in the capital market. The process of credit creation which starts off with hedging is transformed over time into speculation and then to ponzi finance.[75] As pointed out earlier, returns on these risky investments turn out to be high as compared to those in the real sector transactions. It is also natural that these speculatory investments are easier to be financed as long these are lucrative in terms of profitability.

During the phase of credit expansion, banks follow practices as are found profitable in terms of the newly opened up opportunities in the deregulated financial markets. This leads to a re-structuring of credit, not just by moving away from the equitable as well as socially desirable channels of productive investments but also by generating a reduced level of effective demand in the economy. In this process '... banks are circulating the balance and creating credit for smaller proportion of the populace than before, and thus augmenting effective demand less than previously ... (Again) the reach of the banking system has contracted as standardized products have emerged, ... and as the functions of bank branches have been redefined. So the savings/investment nexus (efficient transfers of idle funds for investment) covered by the banking system is less extensive than before. ... Expansion overseas – which involves primarily Northern banks entering Southern markets – only accentuates these trends.'[76] The new orientation of banks and banking in these cases is no longer limited to the 'passive behavioural approach' of depository institutions as '... memorialized in the money multiplier routinely used in the Keynesian models'.[77] Emphasis is often placed in the conventional doctrines on the micro-foundations of bank behaviour. However, the above, even with its emphasis on imperfect (or asymmetric informations)[78] end up on the role of banks in absorption of risks. This neglects the no less important role expected of the banks in the macroeconomic savings–investments balance achievable in the economy.

The economy then enters into a phase which is one of real deceleration along with continued financial upswing. Real investment comes to a standstill and is followed by deceleration. This happens with the continuous drop in profitability of such investments over time, due to an exhaustion of technological innovations and the near full utilisation of capacity. Borrowings by firms now follow a pattern of ponzi finance which is supported with credit from banks and other FIs. The regulatory authorities continue with their credit control and bail-out operations. This characterises Phase II of the boom-bust credit cycle of the economy where financial upswing continues with real deceleration. With returns on real assets continuing to taper off, the growth rate of net real investments in the economy turns negative, while assets in the financial sector continue to grow for some more time. Thus the end of the real growth channelises credit in the direction of 'high-finance'. The latter is typically characterised by speculation, and is led by a 'euphoria' which eventually comes to a close. However, in the meantime there takes place a reversal of asset prices with a concomitant rise in the ratio of interest rates to profits on real investment, measured at constant prices. This is characterised by debt deflation[79] which is matched by the downswing in real activities. The process, however, ends at a point of time where the negative real growth is no longer compatible with expansions in finance. Credit sources now fail to satisfy the liquidity demand to acquire the spurious financial assets whose real backing is too thin. The credit cycle is then complete with financial deceleration leading the economy to a deeper recession, which now waits for signals of recovery. The economy now faces a complete collapse in Phase III with both real and financial downswings. While the continuing deceleration in the real sector is a consequence of the lack of replacements and depreciation during earlier years, the financial boom ends as expectations of speculators remain unfulfilled. Firms face liquidation and bankruptcy while financial agencies try their best to save the situation by tighter controls on credit advanced. Regulatory authorities may step in with their credit control and bailing operations. This may be followed by a regenerative beginning in Phase IV which will follow the pattern as and when the economy gets ready for a revival.

A recovery, as above, however, may even start at a point where the stock of real assets has already depreciated beyond the stage of restoration and capacity has actually fallen below the level when stagnation had started. This will make the economy recover along a path where the composition of investment and of the stock of assets is one which consists of a large proportion of financial investment as compared to the rate of real investment.

We provide, in Table 1.1 a taxonomy of the four phases of credit cycle as described above. The table outlines the role of the borrowing and lending institutions which include the investing firms, banks and the regulatory authorities (which step in as the cycle nears the end of the boom).

The course of the real-financial investment cycle can be mapped more precisely by identifying the functional relations underlying the respective growth rates of financial and real investment in an economy. A simple model which defines the relation is provided in Appendix 1B. Equations (1B.1) and (1B.2) show the three phases of the credit cycle as in Table 1.1 and Figure 1.3, depicting the growth rates of financial investment (F) as a function of time (t) and the corresponding growth rate of real investment (R) (p. 8). Real investment growth, however, is viewed as a function of time alone, thus determined by exogenous factors. It is noticeable that while the growth rates for both financial and real investments are positive in Phase I, finance grows faster than the real sector. However, despite deceleration in terms of real growth which sets in at time period t_1, F continues to rise in Phase II over the time period between t_1 and t_2 with R lying between the full and critical capacity utilisation levels (R_3 and R_2). The rise in F starts tapering off in Phase I itself and the credit boom gets over at time period t_2 as real sector deceleration reaches the critical level at R_2. F now drops *sharply* until it reaches a low at F_1 while R remains stationary at its minimum level R_1. This marks the final phase of the boom and bust cycle in credit with a turnaround as and when inevitable.

Deceleration of real activity may generate a situation where the full capacity level of output starts eroding and as such the maximum level achievable is less than what it could have been. This is due to obsolescence as well as depreciation of the capital stock. We can capture the possibility with R_3 pushed to the left. The eventuality heightens the social cost of having a deceleration, which now includes, over and above unemployment of labour and underutilisation of capital, depletion of the capital stock.

For regulatory authorities facing the speculatory attacks on national currency in the foreign exchange market, especially in Phase II of the cycle, policy options in deregulated financial markets are not too many.[80] These include the direct interventions in the foreign exchange market by *selling* foreign exchange for local currency, and *hikes* in domestic interest rate to attract foreign investments with capital mobility. The two measures may respectively cut back the growth rates of money supply and credit (via cuts in high powered money) and credit demand in the economy. While exchange market interventions by monetary authorities may reduce the stock of high-powered money, a hike in the domestic interest rate would reinforce the monetary contraction initiated by the former. The process may conflict with the domestic target of monetary expansion, especially with an initial credit stringency and unused capacity. Finally, efforts to restore confidence in the international capital market by stepping up the domestic rate of interest may not achieve its goals when the market is uncertain as well as volatile.

1.4.3 The impossible trilemma or failure of policy in open economies

Efforts on the part of national monetary authorities to protect a run on its currency may thus face difficulties, not just with limits on sterilisation of domestic money supply but also with the ineffectiveness of monetary interventions in deregulated financial markets. Currencies weak in the international markets are typically backed by a stock of reserves which often proves inadequate to support an exchange rate peg or a band if there is a speculative run on it. This has been characterised in the literature as an impossible trilemma.[81] As monetary authorities in the domestic economies try out the route via interest rate hikes, capital flows may not be forthcoming to improve the exchange rate. This is due to the built-in expectations in the capital market, which, with anticipations of further depreciation and interest rate hikes, may not improve the exchange rate at all. We work out in Appendix 1C, a model indicating such possibilities.

To summarise the arguments which are spelt out in the Appendix 1C, we observe that monetary policy to generate positive inflows of capital from abroad can only be temporarily successful, and that too in special situations when μ, as defined in Equation (1C.4) is greater than unity and the sum of the respective responses of net capital flows to exchange rate and interest rate variations $[(\alpha + \beta)$ in Equation (1C.10)] is positive. Paradoxically, it is necessary that exchange rates are subject to extrapolative expectations when the net impact of the exchange rate and interest rate variations on capital flows is positive.

The outcome, however, would be different if, like the exchange rate movements, the hikes in interest rates are also subject to uncertainty, and expectations are not necessarily fulfilled. In such situations it is not guaranteed that the hike in interest rate would be once for all. The monetary authorities may keep raising the interest rate over time. As a consequence, stock prices are expected to drop further while foreign purchasers in the market would prefer to sell stocks and/or wait before their next purchase. In such cases, $\beta < 0$ and changes in K_t as a result of a hike in interest rates can never be positive. For such situations the monetary authorities would simply find it impossible to control the slide in exchange rates by influencing capital flows through interest rate variations. Accordingly, a rise in interest rate would never be able to improve the exchange rate by increasing the net capital flows to the country when interest rates are expected to increase further.[82]

Regulatory authorities, as mentioned earlier, usually start operations in the market as signs of over-lending are visible, especially on speculation without any real backing. This can start a regulatory cycle which now overlaps with the boom-bust credit cycle and tones it down to narrower limits. The tempering of the extremes of financial volatility however, as pointed out above, do not reverse or eliminate the path of the credit cycle, as can be seen from Figure 1.3.

Institutional changes which quicken the transmission between the financial and real activities are initiated by the financial deregulation which permits the switches between assets of different dimensions. However, the process of deregulation changes the composition of capital flows which now can be of varying duration and currency denominations. Simultaneously exchange rates as well as interest rates are also subject to market fluctuations, imparting further volatility to capital flows across nations. There is often a qualitative change in the credit structure with short-term credit gaining ground as the real sector transactions start tapering off. Short-termism in the credit market thus becomes common, especially as long-term investments turn out to be risky and hence subject to higher time rate of discounts. Investors in such cases prefer assets with quick turnovers which are incapable of financing real investments. As serial risks become common, long-term investments become even less attractive leading to increased demand for short-term financial assets, including cash, which are held while waiting for better returns.

The transmission of shocks between the financial and the real sector has its institutional correlates. These include the wide range of financial products which are generated by financial innovations in the deregulated markets. Thus one witnesses the growth of financial consultancy services which overshadows the R&D expenses under the brick and mortar technology and a steady erosion of monetary control as a means of controlling liquidity which is generated by ranges of financial derivatives, adding to the flexibility of trans-actions, especially in the financial sector.[83]

Globalisation, which is an essential aspect of deregulated finance, thus encourages the parallel process of volatility and stagnation in the economy, with the real sector failing to come out from stagna-tion even when the financial sector is at its upswing. Contagion in terms of financial crisis now spreads across national boundaries and the collapse of the real economy in one part of the world has similar repercussions on the rest of the world via trade links. Aspects as above bring to the fore the need for regulations and the role of the nation state against international forces.

Appendix 1A

A model on capital exports[84]

Using the Domar model[85] developed in the context of an open econ-omy facing potential problems of full capacity growth, we can relate it to our observations concerning capital exports. The ability of a country to continue with capital exports depends on the relative value of inflows and gross outflows of capital, as measured, say, by the ratio R. For countries at advanced stages of lending, the claims on past investments which consist of interest and amortisation receipts may at some stage exceed the gross outflows. This indicates situations of *net* capital inflows with R at less than unity.

In symbols,

$$R = (A + I_n)/G \tag{1A.1}$$

where A stands for amortisation charges, I_n is interest payments and G relates to gross capital exports over an identical time period. Situ-ations where R is less than unity indicate that the country is exporting capital on a net basis.

Now

$$A = aD \qquad\qquad (1A.2)$$

where the annual amortisation rate a is determined by the *net value method* of repayments, while D measures the stock of outstanding credit, the flow of which is measured by $(G-A)$.
Similarly

$$I_n = iD \qquad\qquad (1A.3)$$

where i is the rate of interest.
Again

$$\dot{D} = dD/dt = G - A \qquad\qquad (1A.4)$$

where

$$G = G_0 e^{rt} \qquad\qquad (1A.5)$$

with r measuring the growth rate of gross capital inflows G_0 in the initial period.

We now draw attention to factors which determine R. From Equations (1A.1) to (1A.5), one can identify a set of four variables which determine R.
Thus

$$R = R(i, a, r, t) \qquad\qquad (1A.6)$$

On substitution one obtains from Equations (1A.3) and (1A.4), a first order difference equation for D, which by solving, yields the time-path for $\dot{D}$

$$\dot{D} = \left[\frac{e^{rt} - e^{-rt}}{(a+r)} \right] \qquad\qquad (1A.7)$$

From (1A.1) to (1A.5),

$$R = \left(\frac{a+i}{a+r} \right) [1 - e^{-(a+r)t}] \qquad\qquad (1A.8)$$

which for $a>0$ and $r>0$ yields the long-term limiting value of R at

$$\underset{t \to \infty}{\text{Lim}} \ R = R_L = \frac{a+i}{a+r} \tag{1A.9}$$

One can sum up the functional relation between R_L and the determining variables as

$$\partial R_L/\partial i > 0$$

and

$$\partial R/\partial r < 0 \quad \text{always}$$

$$\partial R_L/\partial a \gtreqqless 0 \quad \text{for} \quad i \gtreqqless r \tag{1A.10}$$

A rise in *the* annual amortisation rate, a can have different implications for R_L according to whether the rate of interest is less/greater than the growth rate of gross lending. Thus interest receipts are reduced relative to gross outflows of capital only if the outstanding stock of credit is successively reduced with steeper rates of amortisation. It can, however, be checked that during the short-run changes in R as are caused by changes in a is always positive.

The above indicates the manoeuvrability of the limiting value of net capital exports (R) to possible changes in policy. In terms of the inequality, a, capital-exporting nation can, in principle, seek to reduce a, i and/or increase r in a bid to prevent R_L from unity. (The above, of course, excludes situations of $i<r$.) In practice, however, it may be beyond the capability (or even willingness) of the lending nations (institutions) to manipulate all three variables.[86] For a lending nation facing uncertainties in the capital market, the device of stretching a by extending the loan period may not be feasible. Finally, possibilities of raising r (the growth rate of gross lending) might, again, be inappropriate in situations of an impending debt crisis at a global level. Instead, private financial institutions and official loan disbursing agencies may divert part of the lendable resources towards rescue operations. (Examples can be provided with reference to the debt crisis of 1982 and thereafter. These include the loan loss provisioning, debt-equity-swaps and refinancing arrangements of loans.) For a given growth rate in gross lending, difficulties of

sustaining net lending would tend to be more real over time, even before approaching an actual debt distress situation, as can be expected from the incoming flows of debt services under loan compounding. In absence of the unlikely event of compensating increases in gross finance made available by the lenders, debt servicing would tend to diminish and eventually eliminate the net outflows.

In terms of the Domar model, it is possible to discern the areas of discord within the domestic economy of a capital-exporting country. With the net flow of finance $(G - A - I_n)$ tapering off over time, finance and production in the capital-exporting nation would have very different implications in terms of their respective contribution to income generation through the country's external sector. Faced with possible depreciation of externally held assets (through repudiation of debt) and lapses in loan servicing, lenders may divert a part of the gross loans towards loan protection. These would lead to a simultaneous cut in net lending as well, thus jeopardising the prospects of maintaining export surpluses in the current account of the country.

Situations of conflict between financial and real interests in the mature lending countries open up areas of paradox or dilemma to the international lenders, especially when the short-run gains achieved by the financial conglomerates and their clientele are difficult to sustain in the long run. It is evident from conditions provided in inequality (1A.10) above that except for situations where $r > i$, lender strategy to raise profitability of lending through increases in i and/or a actually reduces R_L. Similarly, attempts to protect loan losses through refinancing loans result in a reduction of r which, from inequality (1A.10) above, reduces the value of R_L. The outcome, with a narrower margin of net investment/export outlets, would obviously be unpalatable, even to the financial circles in the demand-constrained lending economy, with possibilities of an eventual realisation crisis. In the lending economies, the outcome is especially injurious to producer interests with profit cut backs, when net exports of capital taper off as a result of lender strategies. Thus the trade-effect of foreign lending ceases to be positive as exports of capital no longer continue on a net basis. The situation entails a 'lender paradox' in the mature capital-exporting countries as attempts to protect the interest of finance proves self-defeating in the long run.

Links between domestic plus external accumulation in the lender country and its savings at domestic origin are worked out in the Rowthorn–Wells model[87] as follows:
From

$$Y = C + I + X \qquad (1A.11)$$

where Y, C, I and X respectively indicate GDP, aggregate consumption, investment and net exports in the lender nation; it is possible to arrive at GNP of the lender nation by adding factor income earned abroad. Savings out of GNP are invested domestically and overseas.
Hence,

$$\dot{K} + \dot{D} = s(Y + iD) \qquad (1A.12)$$

where K is stock of domestic assets, D is stock of overseas assets [or outstanding credits as defined earlier for Equation (1A.2)], s is average propensity to save and i is rate of interest on foreign loans [as in Equation (1A.3)]. Changes in K and D per period are indicated respectively by $\dot{K}$ and $\dot{D}$. The two respectively indicate the *flow* of domestic investment (I) and foreign investment ($\dot{D}$) over a period.
$\dot{K}$ is related to GDP in the following manner:

$$\dot{K} = kgY \qquad (1A.13)$$

where k and g respectively relate to capital-output ratio and the growth rate of GDP in the lender economy.

From Equations (1A.12) and (1A.13), flows of external loans (net of amortisation) can be expressed as follows:

$$\dot{D} = siD + (s - gk)Y \qquad (1A.14)$$

where

$$Y = Y_0 e^{gt} \qquad (1A.15)$$

when Y and Y_0 refer to GDP in current and initial period. Rearranging, we get the first order differential equation in $\dot{D}$ with

$$\dot{D} = siD + (s - gk)Y_0 e^{st} \tag{1A.16}$$

Solving

$$\dot{D} = Ae^{sit} + [(s - gk)/(g - si)]Y_0 e^{st} \tag{1A.17}$$

where A is an arbitrary constant.

Links between foreign capital flows and the balance of payments of the lender economy are given by

$$\dot{D} = X + iD \tag{1A.18}$$

From Equations (1A.11) to (1A.18), it is possible to see the essence of capital exports for the lending economy.

It is now possible to extend the model by relating it to the distinction drawn earlier in the text between the trade and the rentier effects of overseas investment. In Equation (1A.18) the two terms in the right-hand side indicate the respective magnitude of our trade and rentier effects of foreign investment flows or *new* loans on the lender economy. While it is possible to indicate the magnitude of the rentier effect of the flow of overseas investment as iD (which is positive with $D > 0$), the trade effect is captured by net exports. The latter can be negative when, under import substituting regimes, capital exports reduce the import-dependence of the recipient nations.

We choose to spell out the trade-effect of $\dot{D}$ on net exports in terms of the *ex post* trade-creating effect (α) as spelt out below,
Thus

$$X = \beta + \alpha \dot{D} \tag{1A.19}$$

where $\beta > 0$ and $\alpha < 1$.

Using Equations (1A.18) and (1A.19), and assuming $\beta = 0$,

$$\dot{D} = \frac{[X(1 - \alpha) - \beta]}{i\alpha} = X(1 - \alpha)/i\alpha \tag{1A.20}$$

Substituting the value of $\dot{D}$ from Equation (1A.20) in Equation (1A.17) and rearranging,

$$X = [i\alpha/(1 - \alpha)]Ae^{sit} + [(s - gk)i\alpha]/[(g - si)(1 - \alpha)]Y_0 e^{st} \tag{1A.21}$$

Dividing by $Y = Y_0 e^{gt}$

$$X/Y = [i\alpha(1-\alpha)\, Ae^{-t(g-si)}]/Y_0 + [(s-gk)i\alpha]/[(g-si)(1-\alpha)] \tag{1A.22}$$

The expression has a limiting value as t approaches infinity,

$$\lim_{t\to\infty}(X/Y) = [(s-gk)(i\alpha)]/[(g-si)(1-\alpha)] \tag{1A.23}$$

Starting from a positive value of net exports in the initial period (X_0), we obtain from Equation (1A.11)

$$X_0 = S_0 - I_0 = (s-gk)Y_0 > 0$$

By the same logic $s > gk$ always. It is now possible to spell out the trade effect, α from Equations (1A.18) and (1A.19), in terms of interest rate, i and growth rate of capital exports, r. Thus

$$\alpha = 1 - \frac{i}{r} \tag{1A.24}$$

where β as before has been assumed to be at zero.

From equation (1A.24), $r = i/(1-\alpha)$ and it appears that r would remain positive as long as $\alpha < 1$. When α, for reasons spelt out above (as strong import substitution in borrowing country) is negative, the current account $(X + iD)$ may continue to be positive with a strong rentier effect of overseas investment stepping up the inflows of investment income from abroad. The institutional realities of the international capital market indicate the difficulty, on the part of the individual lenders, of influencing the rate of interest. Thus the trade-creating effect, α is determined, in terms of Equation (1A.24), by the growth rate of (gross) lendings, r. In other words, r remains the exogenous variable, which, for a given i influences the endogenously determined variable, α.

It is now possible to generalise on the conditions which ensure a trade surplus $(X > 0)$ for a capital-surplus country. From Equation (1A.18), net export X is positive when $\dot{D}$ *exceeds* iD. In terms of Equation (1A.23) the condition is met in the long run when the limiting value of (X/Y) is positive. The twin goals, as it has been observed earlier, can be simultaneously met by the lending country if it can continue with net exports of capital. In terms of Equation (1A.23) it can happen if[88]

(a) $s > gk$ (which, by assumption, is true)
(b) $g > si$ when $0 < \alpha < 1$

For both situations, $i < g/s$, that is i is subject to a ceiling which is measured by g/s. Alternately, we have $\alpha > 1$ where g can be less than si and also ensure positive net flows of capital from the lending country.

With positive gross flows of lendings, $\dot{D}$ the net flow of lending $(\dot{D} - iD = X)$ would thus stay positive, if conditions above are satisfied. With the more general case when $\alpha < 1$, net lendings can only be positive when i does not exceed g/s. Conversely, for $\alpha > 1$, the trade effect of foreign investment requires, in order that the net lending is positive, that the interest rate can even exceed g/s. In this case, despite the large weight of investment income inflows in the current account, the strong trade effect of foreign investment implies that the interest rate can exceed g/s and still maintain a positive $\dot{D}$. It is obviously necessary to treat the autonomous components of exports, β as positive, in order to arrive at the above argument. It may be pointed out that for a mature lender it may be difficult to fulfil the condition $g > si$ with rising interest rates. (This had actually happened during the 1980s). It is also conceivable that growth in investment income itself would initiate tendencies for additional savings in the mature lender, pushing up the savings propensities, s, relative to the growth rate of GDP. It would be increasingly difficult, under such circumstances, to continue with net exports of capital (and merchandise) by the capital-exporting nation. Recapitulating the eventualities which delimit the capacity of a lending nation to continue with net lending and net exports of merchandise, we distinguish between the (net) capital-exporting and -importing stages experienced by the lending country. Net exports of capital continue as long as the two conditions (a) and (b) above are both fulfilled, ensuring, in Equation (1A.23),

$$\mathop{\mathrm{Lim}}_{t \to \infty} (X/Y) > 0$$

The country starts borrowing on a *net* basis as

$$\lim_{t \to \infty}(X/Y) < 0$$

a situation which, as noted earlier, arises when conditions (a) and (b) above are not fulfilled. The above represents extreme situations with reverse capital flows to the lending country with perverse effects on its trade balance. The trade deficit of the country now exceeds the investment income inflows. In terms of Equation (1A.18) $\dot{D}$ turns negative since the negative X now exceeds iD. The economic reasoning ensures that with capital imports the lending country now incurs a trade deficit (X) the magnitude of which exceeds gross borrowings ($\dot{D}$). A part of the financing of the trade deficit in the current account can be provided by positive flows of investment income as long as outstanding foreign assets (D) continue to be positive. Situations of fully depleted foreign assets (at $D=0$) or freshly incurred foreign liabilities ($\dot{D} < 0$) demand, with $\alpha < 1$, additional sources of external financing. The above can be avoided through, say a separate channel of borrowing which does not add to net import demand, or through depletion of foreign reserves. In order not to complicate issues, we leave out the eventualities when $\alpha > 1$.

Equation (1A.24) captures the conflicts between trader and rentier interests in the lending nation by highlighting, for given values of r, the inverse relation between i and α. For understandable reasons, a rise in i would swamp the trade-creating effect α, when r, the growth of new credit (net of amortisation), remains unchanged. Problems in securing a steady servicing of loans advanced in the past may generate tendencies, on the part of lenders, to set aside funds for loan rescue operations. The consequent drop in the growth rate of lendings, r, would further reduce the trade-creating effect and initiate sharper declines in financial and real transfers to the borrowing country.

Recapitulating, once again, the lending nations are thus able to sustain net exports of capital, as warranted by the limiting value of (X/Y) at t approaching infinity in Equation (1A.23), when (a) the growth rate of gross capital exports r from the lending country is higher; (b) the rate of interest i is within the limit set by g/s; and (c) savings rate s in the lending country is lower.

Let us now introduce two groups of borrowers which are respectively identified as Group 1 from North and Group 2 from South. Aggregate credit from the lender nation is distributed as

$$\dot{D} = \dot{D}_1 + \dot{D}_2 = (\phi_1 + \phi_2)\,\dot{D} \dots \qquad (1A.25)$$

where $(\dot{D}_1 + \dot{D}_2) = 1$ and ϕ refers to the share of each country. For obvious reasons, a rise in ϕ_1 would imply, at given r, a cut back in ϕ_2. In case a rise in ϕ_1 causes a rise in i, we notice, from Equation (1A.24), that the trade-creating effect α would be generally dampened. And countries in Group 2 would then be doubly hurt, first owing to the cut in ϕ_2 and second, because of the rise in interest rate which causes a proportionate drop in the real transfers (or net exports, X) from abroad which are possible to finance through borrowings.

Let us now look at the dilemma faced by the borrowing countries in Group 2 in sustaining inflows of capital as can provide resources for investment and growth. Using the familiar national accounts, we define, for the capital importing country,

$$Y = C + I + X - M \qquad (1A.26)$$

from which

$$Y = C + I_t - RT$$

where

$$RT = CAD - iD = M - X \qquad (1A.27)$$

Equation (1A.27) is based on the simplifying assumption that all invisibles other than interest payments on foreign loans are non-existent (or that these cancel each other). We now look into the net financial transfer which is identified as the real transfer (RT in short) at current prices. With the simplifying assumption that the net non-factor services are nil, RT measures the value of the merchandise deficit.[89]
Thus

$$sY = I - RT$$

rearranging,

$$g = \Delta Y_t / Y = \frac{s}{k} + \frac{RT}{kY} \tag{1A.28}$$

Equation (1A.28) is a clear indicator that output growth in a borrowing country which is supply constrained would be favourably affected by the flow of current real transfers (RT) from abroad, provided the latter neither reduces nor increases the savings propensity (s) and capital-output ratio (k) in the domestic economy. In absence of offsetting changes, real transfers from abroad can thus have a propelling role for domestic accumulation in borrowing economies. Thus for a capital scarce economy, the magnitude of the RT indicates the developmental dimensions of the external account as distinct from its short-term or liquidity aspects. It is important to stress the point that it may not be possible to sustain a positive inflow of RT even when the CAD and the corresponding capital inflows are in the uptrend. This can be observed from Equation (1A.28) which indicates the possibilities that when investment liabilities (iD) exceed the magnitude of the current account deficit, RT may even turn negative. The process, if continued, may eventually imply a current account surplus. The outcome, it may be noticed, is the mirror image of what prevails in the capital-exporting country facing a CAD.

From Equation (1A.27)

$$RT = CAD - iD \tag{1A.29}$$

From the capital account balance,

$$CAD = \dot{D} - aD \tag{1A.30}$$

where 'a' is the linear rate of amortisation and $\dot{D}$ is the gross inflow of capital, as before.

Combining, we get

$$RT = \dot{D} - (a + i)D \tag{1A.31}$$

For RT to continue as inflows,

$$RT = \dot{D} - (a + i)D > 0$$

or

$$RT = r - (a + i) > 0 \tag{1A.32}$$

where 'r' is the growth rate of gross capital inflows and D is the stock of outstanding debt.

This implies

$$r > (a + i) > 0 \tag{1A.33}$$

Appendix 1B

Relation between financial and real growth

Defining the respective growth rates of financial and real flows of resources in terms of the symbols 'F' and 'R', we have, as in Figure 1.3

$$R = R(t) \tag{1B.1}$$

where

$$R' > 0; \, R'' > 0 \quad \text{for} \quad t_0 \leq t < t_1$$

and

$$R' < 0 \quad \text{for} \quad t_1 < t < t_3 \quad \text{and} \quad R'' > 0 \quad \text{for} \quad t_1 < t < t_2$$

while

$$R'' < 0 \quad \text{for} \quad t_2 < t < t_3$$

As for F, we have

$$F = F(R(t), t) \tag{1B.2}$$

With total differentials,

$$dF/dt > 0 \quad \text{for} \quad t_0 \leq t < t_2$$

and

$$dF/dt < 0 \quad \text{for} \quad t_2 < t < t_3$$

Both $R(t)$ and $F(t)$ are assumed continuous in the interval $[t_0, t_3]$. We notice that
$R(t_0) = R(t_3) = R_1$ at the minimum subsistence level,
$R(t_1) = R_3$ at the maximum full capacity utilisation level, and
$R(t_2) = R_2$ at the level where financial boom stops.
Also we note that

$$F(R(t_0), t_0) = F_1 = F(R(t_3), t_3)$$

$$F_1 = F(R_1, t_0) = F(R_1, t_3); \ F_2 = F(R_3, t_1); \ F_3 = F(R_2, t_2)$$

However, strictly speaking either value of F and R is uniquely associated with a unique value of the other variable.

Appendix 1C

Monetary control under currency convertibility

To simplify our argument, we assume that *all* capital inflows to the domestic economy respond to interest rate variations. This amounts to assuming all such flows as portfolio capital, since the latter responds, via changes in stock prices, to movements in the home interest rate relative to the rate which prevails overseas. We further assume that there is capital account convertibility in the domestic economy. As a consequence capital flows remain market-determined. This rules out all quantitative restrictions on capital flows and the monetary authorities are left with the interest rate and direct exchange rate interventions which remain the tools to combat further declines in the exchange rate.

From an accounting balance, the CAD can be expressed as net capital inflows ($\dot{K}$) less the changes in official reserves (ΔR). Ruling out, by assumption, changes in official reserves,

$$\text{CAD} = \dot{K} - \Delta R = \dot{K} \tag{1C.1}$$

where $\Delta R = 0$ by assumption.

For an economy facing a depreciating exchange rate, the monetary authorities may try to narrow down the CAD by raising the domestic interest rate. Efforts as above would be successful only when the portfolio managers abroad respond favourably. The latter would be a function of both the interest rate variations and the expectations regarding exchange rate movements. To put it formally,

$$K_t = \alpha[E^e_{t+1} - E_t]/E_t + \beta[i^d_t - i^f_t] \qquad (1C.2)$$

where K, E and E^e respectively refer to net capital inflows and the actual and expected exchange rates for foreign currency in units of domestic currency. Subscripts to the respective variables refer to the time period. Finally i^d_t and i^f_t refer to the respective interest rates in domestic and foreign countries in the current period t.

We start with the assumption that that there is no uncertainty regarding the prevailing interest rates (which are given once for all) and in exchange rates (which are expected to change over time). As for the sign of the coefficients, an expected depreciation of the domestic currency (which is equivalent to a rise in E^e) normally reduces the incentives to invest on the part of foreigners, and hence $\alpha < 0$. As a contrast, an excess of i^d_t over i^f_t encourages capital inflows and hence $\beta > 0$. We consider later the possibility that the latter can be negative with expectations of further increases in the interest rate.

We now introduce an additional assumption that financial assets across countries are perfect substitutes of each other. This ensures the uncovered interest rate parity in terms of which

$$i^d_t = i^f_t + [E^e_{t+1} - E_t]/E_t \qquad (1C.3)$$

We now specify the movements in the expected exchange rate. Since the currency in the domestic economy is assumed to be under speculative attacks, we consider the latter to be subject to an extrapolative expectation function. Thus, a movement in the exchange rate in any direction is expected to move it further in the same direction. We thus postulate that

$$E^e_{t+1} = E_t + \mu[E_t - E_{t-1}] \qquad (1C.4)$$

where $E_t > E_{t-1}$ and $\mu > 1$.

Substituting from Equation (1C.4) we get, in Equation (1C.3),

$$i_t^d = i_t^f + \mu[E_{t+1}^e - E_t]/E_t \qquad (1C.5)$$

With expectations always fulfilled, $E_{t+1}^e = E_{t+1}$.
From above Equation (1C.5) can be re-written as

$$i_t^d = i_t^f + \mu(E_t - E_{t-1}) \qquad (1C.6)$$

Now Equation (1C.4) reduces itself to a second-order difference equation

$$E_{t+1} = E_t + \mu(E_t - E_{t-1})$$

Solving we get,

$$E_t = C_1 + \mu^t C_2 \qquad (1C.7)$$

where C_1 and C_2 are two arbitrary constants such that $E_0 = C_1 + C_2$ and $E_\infty = \infty$.

Putting back the value of E_t from (1C.7) in Equation (1C.6),

$$i_t^d - i_t^f = \mu^t C_2(\mu - 1) \qquad (1C.8)$$

Substituting, in Equation (1C.2) values from Equations (1C.7) and (1C.8)

$$K_t = \frac{(\alpha + \beta)C_2 \mu^t(\mu - 1)}{C_1 + C_2 \mu^t} \qquad (1C.9)$$

Rearranging we get,

$$K_t = \frac{(\alpha + \beta)C_2(\mu - 1)}{C_1 \mu^{-t} + C_2} \qquad (1C.10)$$

Equation (1C.10) and Figure 1.4 project the time-path of capital inflows K_t to the country. Given that exchange rate movements are subject to an extrapolative expectation function by assumption so that $\mu > 1$ always, we have the following possibilities:

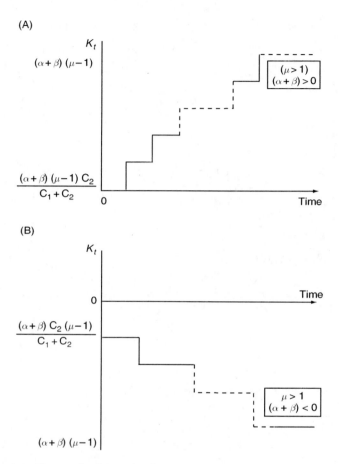

(A)

$(\alpha+\beta)(\mu-1)$

K_t

$(\mu>1)$
$(\alpha+\beta)>0$

$\dfrac{(\alpha+\beta)(\mu-1)\,C_2}{C_1+C_2}$

0   Time

(B)

K_t

0   Time

$\dfrac{(\alpha+\beta)\,C_2\,(\mu-1)}{C_1+C_2}$

$\mu>1$
$(\alpha+\beta)<0$

$(\alpha+\beta)(\mu-1)$

Figure 1.4 Time-path of capital inflow

(a) If $(\alpha+\beta)>0$ there will be an *upward* path of K_t which will lie within the upper and lower bounds as given below:

$$K_t = [(\alpha+\beta)(\mu-1)] \quad \text{at} \quad t\to\infty$$

$$K_t = \frac{[(\alpha+\beta)(\mu-1)]C_2}{C_1+C_2} \quad \text{at} \quad t=0$$

(b) If $(\alpha + \beta) < 0$ there will be a *downward* time-path of K_t which starts at a negative value with

$$K_t = \frac{(\alpha + \beta)C_2(\mu - 1)}{C_1 + C_2} \quad \text{at} \quad t = 0$$

K_t reaches the lower limit of negative value at

$$K_t = (\alpha + \beta)(\mu - 1) \quad \text{at} \quad t \to \infty$$

Interpreting the results, movements in K_t are functions of *changes* in exchange rates and as such always influenced by the value of μ, even at $t=0$. The value of K_t, however, stabilises at the two limits as t approaches zero or infinity since in both situations exchange rate movements also stabilise. Moreover, the sum $(\alpha + \beta)$ as well as the value of μ both have an impact on movements in K_t.

Thus, attempts by monetary authorities to attract capital from abroad by raising the domestic interest rate relative to the foreign rates would be ineffective over time, as can be seen from the flattened part of the K_t schedule in its upper region. Inflows of capital would have its maximum value at a level which will be larger with higher values of μ as well the sum $(\alpha + \beta)$. This reflects the fact that when interest rate hikes counteract the adverse effects of successive exchange rate depreciations on capital inflows (that is, the sum $(\alpha + \beta)$ is positive), the magnitude of the successive rounds of depreciations (μ) as well as that of the net effect of interest rate and exchange rate adjustments $(\alpha + \beta)$ in each time period influence favourably the upper limit of K_t inflows. The minimum level of K_t which is set as the floor, would happen at the beginning when $t=0$ and for similar reasons are influenced by the structural aspects which now also include the constants C_1 and C_2.

We can explore the consequences of a regressive exchange rate function, one where $\mu < 1$. Unlike the previous case, a positive value of $(\alpha + \beta)$ is here self-defeating since exchange rates are expected to move back to the initial level. We now have

$$K_t = -[(\alpha + \beta) C_2 (\mu - 1)]/[C_1 + C_2] \quad \text{for} \quad t = 0$$

$$K_t = 0$$
$$\lim t \to \infty$$

Continuing further, we can have a negative value for $(\alpha+\beta)$ and find out the consequences for K_t when the exchange rate expectations continue to be regressive with $\mu<1$.

The upper and lower limits of K_t are given by

$$K_t = [(\alpha+\beta)\, C_2\, (\mu-1)]/[C_1+C_2] \quad \text{at} \quad t=0$$

$$K_t = 0$$
$$\lim t \to \infty$$

Interestingly, efforts to maintain the interest rate parity by hiking the domestic interest rate would, in this case, eliminate all capital inflows, thus making $K_t=0$.

2
The Evolving Pattern of International Capital Flows

2.1 Introduction

There have been sweeping changes in the global finance relations since the international bank credit boom of the 1970s. The changes have been all-pervasive, influencing the interrelations between state, industry and finance in a large part of the global economy. The significant aspects of this include the wave of deregulation, which has integrated the major financial markets of the world. With finance crossing the boundaries of nation states, the advanced nations experienced a climate of interdependence as was never witnessed before. The steady rise in the magnitude of cross-border financial flows has been combined by systemic risks with boom-bust cycles in private credit, the amplitude of which also widened markedly over time.

Observations as above set the context for our analysis in this chapter, which relates to the significance of the global restructuring of private sources of finance since 1973. We can identify three distinct phases in the sequential mode of world finance over the last three decades: (1) the period of expansion in bank credit to the developing countries during 1973–81; (2) the debt-led restructuring of finance during 1982–88; and (3) the widely practised securitisation.

2.2 Reaching out to the LDCs: spurts in the LDC exposure of transnational banks during 1973–81

With the formation of the OPEC cartel and its success in generating a financial surplus for the oil producing countries in Middle East, transnational banks (TNBs) operating in the Euro-currency market turned out to be the depositories of the dollar-denominated oil revenue of the Middle East. These banks could recycle most of these by on-lending to a few middle-income developing countries.

2.2.1   Banks and credit expansions during the 1970s

Three factors operated to initiate the unprecedented expansions in international bank credit flows to the LDCs during the 1970s. These included, first, the expanded credit base of the Euro-currency market, both with restraints by the US monetary authorities on overseas operations of the US banks and with deposits of the OPEC surpluses with the TNBs. Second, the fast pace of financial deregulation, which permitted the banks to go international. Third, there was the expanding demand for credits from some oil-importing LDCs, which, as mentioned above, also made possible a recycling of these financial surpluses, especially with recession in the North. In the process, the US money-centre banks started having a close nexus with third-world debt, a fact which explains much of the later developments in the area of prudential legislation, especially in the US. Examples of financial deregulation in the 1970s include the exemptions in the US, which permitted, in June 1979, the domestic banks to exceed the prevailing 10 per cent limit on loans to a single party and also to violate other domestic regulations when lending abroad. In the UK, similar restrictions (on reinvestment of profits and on outward portfolio as well as direct investments) were removed around the same time. In Japan, a similar process slowly started with a 7-point plan to relax restrictions on capital inflows by allowing non-residents an access to the Gensaki market and the issue of yen-denominated 3–6 month CDs by Japanese as well as non-Japanese banks.[1] Despite the problems which came up later in the 1980s and the 1990s, the pace of deregulation in the financial sector continued unabated over the next few decades.

2.2.2   Bank failures and reforms: national and international measures during the early years

Internationalisation of credit entrusted newer responsibilities on nation states as TNBs branched out to overseas markets, thus moving away from their national origin. The ability of individual nation states to control the operations of these TNBs turned out to be rather limited. With a large number of these banks having large exposures and some actually facing the risk of a potential default, especially from clients in the developing regions, the G-10 had to come forward with a set of prudential regulatory norms to protect the lending institutions. A collapse of the Herstatt Bank in the US in the summer of 1974 had earlier swung the BIS into action with the forming of a Standing Committee on Bank Regulation and Supervisory Practices (CBRSP). The latter led to the *Basle Concordant of 1975* which was designed to consolidate supervision of solvency and liquidity of most OECD banks. While solvency and liquidity of the branches were to be decided by the parent bodies, those of the subsidiaries were left to be decided by the host country. The collapse of Banco Ambrosiano, a major Italian bank, led to a revision of the CBRSP of 1974, permitting a dual supervision of banks by both host and home countries.[2] It was recognised by the international financial community that strategies for international regulation of banks had already been diluted, thus transgressing the individual capacity of the national monetary authorities. It may be pointed out here that the 10 per cent limit in the US on bank lending to a single borrower was never applied to overseas lending! Similarly in 1978, the US Comptroller of Finance had proposed 'a means and ends test for foreign borrowings, subject, however, to the foreign policy interest of the US government.' Such exemptions clearly bypassed the norms of prudent lending.[3] On the whole there was hardly any effective device in those days, either at the behest of the national monetary authorities or at the command of the private institutions, to restrain the TNBs from activities which already were proving both risky and imprudent.

2.2.3 The US banks and third-world credit flows

Profits earned by TNBs through commissions as well as spreads on loans to the third-world encouraged the US 'money-centre' banks to 'push loans' in these directions during the 1970s. As pointed out in a study, '...the commercial banks turn in comprehensive fashion toward the LDCs when loan demand from sources in the developed world weakens sufficiently for the terms to bring forth additional demand to be unprofitable'.[4] However, there was a considerable degree of concentration in banking business. Thus, one witnesses a handful of 25 TNBs initiating the expansions in credit during the 1970s. Of these, the majority were from the US. Working aggressively behind such credit expansions, these banks often ended up in 'over-lending' during these years. One can identify three distinct groups among those 25 banks.

First, there were the big 5 'leaders', all having a US origin,[5] and responsible for leading the syndication of sovereign loans in risk-prone markets. One notices the rush for loan syndication on the part of the banks during the 1970s, which goes with the changing financial environment as well as institutions. In terms of a neo-classical inter-pretation, such moves could be related to the so-called 'wisdom' of a handful of syndicated banks. Euro-currency loans proved as a potent financial instrument especially for the US banks, which had been debarred from the bond market in terms of the Glass-Stegall Act since 1933. Problems experienced with the Interest Equalisation Tax of 1964–73 as well as with the floating of exchange rates since 1972, further prompted these US banks to syndication of loans via the Euro-currency market.[6] High-priced loan packages were offered in uncharted territories where these banks often operated as 'loan pushers'. Often separate deals were struck with 'riskier clients at higher fees and com-missions', thus achieving a 'relational' arrangement.[7] Evidently, it paid to enter into those arrangements in terms of bank profitability.

In contrast to the 'leaders', the *second* group of banks included ten others which acted as 'challengers'.[8] Those consisted of banks of different national origin including four from the US. These banks operated in competitive loan markets. The resulting cuts in returns often failed to cover the uncertainty premium, and even led to exces-sive lending with potential insolvency. The process amounted to a transactional approach on the part of the 'challenger' banks that were keen to expand their exposures in the low-risk but highly competitive loan markets in the developing area. Transactions as above created a built-in bias for a technical failure with a 'systemic tendency' in terms of eventual losses faced by the banks concerned. As problems compounded, efforts later were made by the same banks to protect the value of these debt-denominated assets, especially as the process turned out to be an over-extended exposure.

The *third* group consisted of ten other 'organising' banks that were the 'followers'. Of these two were from the US and the rest from Canada, the UK, Germany and Japan.[9] For the banking industry as a whole, concentration was thus quite high with top 15 of the OECD banks (which included both the US leaders and challengers in LDC loan markets) dominating the syndicated credit market. During the bank credit boom 50–66 per cent of credit offered by these banks went to the major LDC borrowers with the remainder to the less import-ant ones.[10] In a study of six major borrowing countries (of which five were in Latin America), the challenger banks were found to be active during the 1970s, venturing out to the less risky but competitive loan markets with lucrative loan packages. This was in contrast to the 'leaders', which preferred to operate in the risky credit markets.[11] For reasons provided earlier, both groups were responsible, on different grounds, for over-lending during the 1970s. As could be expected, the US banks cornered between them most of LDC credit.

2.2.4 De-linking of credit flows and the real economy

Credit offered to the third-world countries, however, did not have much of an impact on the real sector of these economies. Most of it was used to meet the escalations in the oil import bill during the 1970s and also to meet the steep increases in the debt-related liabilities of the bor-rowing nations. This can be witnessed from the statistics on net finan-cial flows to developing countries (Table 4.1). With the OECD engulfed in a continuing recession, credit flows in the direction of the developing countries provided alternate outlets to the creditor banks during these years, especially since these countries at the moment were growing faster. As for the recession in the OECD, which began on a full swing since the second half of the 1970s, the outcome was largely due to a demand shortfall. This was evident in the widening Okun Gap, which recorded the shortfall of the actual output in the area as compared to the potential.[12] Not much respite to the demand-led recession in the OECD was forthcoming from additional exports, especially, in the direc-tion of the debt-ridden developing countries. The problem, as expected, was due to the ongoing debt-overhang experienced by these countries.

Banks in the OECD were on a lending spree vis-à-vis in the devel-oping areas, all through the 1970s. However, by the end of the 1970s, these loans were often offered on a compulsive basis, to avert the impending loan defaults. In effect, this was an example of an ongoing ponzi game! In the process, the OECD retained very little of its financial surpluses for investment within the region, because it could hardly be used for productive purposes within the area. At the same time, not much new investment was possible to undertake in the debt-ridden developing countries where gross inflows of credit were used to meet the debt-related liabilities.

Table 2.1 Net private capital flows to emerging market economies

	DFI	Portfolio	Other	Total Asia	DFI	Portfolio	Other	Total L.Am	DFI	Portfolio	Other
1996	150	23	-93	-27	50	-6	-71	54	64	11	-20
1997	143	9	-77	-43	58	-18	-83	70	56	15	-1
1998	139	53	-44	-1	55	4	60	86	53	19	13
1999	113	98	25	104	53	13	38	72	40	41	-8

Source: BIS 70th Annual Report.

Table 2.2A   Net issue of debt securities

	Total	Developed countries	Other countries
1991	204.7	159.0	16.0
1992	149.9	117.4	12.7
1993	189.0	123.0	24.7
1994	251.8	204.1	32.5
1995	260.6	226.9	22.0
1996	534.0	404.2	87.7
1997	563.2	439.0	89.1
1998	680.9	574.8	30.1
1999	1225.2	1149.4	35.5

Source: BIS, 70th Annual Report, p. 112.

One can notice the following *two* distinct aspects of the debt build-up process which started during the beginning of the 1970s: *First*, a continuous transfer of investible surpluses from the OECD to overseas countries, largely due to a lack of complementary demand in the OECD economies. *Second*, the inability of the borrowing countries to make use of these flows for new investments in the domestic economy. Instead the credit flows were mostly used by the borrowers to service their external debt on an *a priori* basis. This clearly ruled out a possible expansion of import demand in the borrowing countries which could be a potential source of external demand in the lending areas.

A de-linking of finance and industry was thus very much in the cards, especially for the OECD countries where the state was fast losing control over the globalised financial agents. Financial expansions thus had already outgrown the limits of surveillance by the nation state in the era of deregulated finance in the OECD. As pointed out above, even efforts by individual banks to protect the value of their assets which were locked up as third-world debt proved inadequate, when the highly indebted nations were at the brink of insolvency and default by the early 1980s.

2.3   Debt crisis and the restructuring of the financial institutions: 1982–88

As the heavily indebted countries including the three most affected in Latin America came up with threats of default, portfolios held by the

Table 2.2B   Net bank lending and security financing of major emerging economies

	Total Asia	China	Crisis economies	Total Latin America	Argentina, Brazil, Mexico	Russia	Total Africa
Bank lending							
av 1990–95	37	7	28	1	NA	1	–2
1996	80	13	58	28	22	6	NA
1997	5	10	–10	31	14	10	3
1998	96	–11	–83	–8	–10	–6	–2
1999	–53	–15	–31	–16	–13	–8	–1
Debt securities							
av 1990–95	15	2	11	13	12	NA	NA
1996	42	2	38	41	46	NA	NA
1997	34	4	25	42	32	7	NA
1998	NA	NA	NA	22	16	12	NA
1999	3	NA	2	32	27	–1	NA

Source: BIS, 70th Annual Report, p. 39.

Table 2.3   Net claims of BIS reporting banks ($ billions)

	Total	Inside area	Outside area
1992	165	80.4	66.0
1993	200	251.4	11.6
1994	190	228.3	36.6
1995	330	506.5	20.8
1996	420	446.2	141.4
1997	500	1115.2	94.8

Source: BIS, 68th Annual Report, p. 144.

highly exposed banks in the OECD were in trouble. By the beginning of the 1980s, the money centre banks in the US faced problems with the worst-affected debtor countries in Latin America, which were facing difficulties in servicing their debt. With assets based on third-world debt about to turn non-performing, banks needed a drive to protect their portfolios, especially with the onset of a generalised debt crisis in 1982.

Efforts at a restructuring of bank assets following the debt crisis included several measures initiated by these banks. These ranged from loan loss provisioning, debt sales at discounts to refinancing of loans. Steps were also initiated, at an international level, by the Bank for International Settlements (which was an organ of the G-10) to regulate bank activities with prescribed capital adequacy and prudential norms. As it happened in the US, the national monetary authorities in the rest of the OECD were also losing control over the expanding international business of their private financial agencies. A co-ordination of international banking practices was thus an impending necessity.

Measures introduced by the BIS started with the Basle Accord in July 1988 which stipulated a minimum capital adequacy norm. One more bank failure, with the BCCI collapsing in 1991 led the BIS replace the dual supervision norm of the CBRSP with an implementation of the minimum capital adequacy standards over the next two years.[13] Simultaneously, the national monetary authorities tried to encourage the loan-loss provisioning by banks, offering tax concessions (see Tables 2.4 and 2.5). Measures as above were expected to bring down the size of outstanding debt held by the developing debtors,

Table 2.4   Financial markets for derivative instruments – notional amounts outstanding ($ trillions)

End year	Exchange traded instruments	OTC instruments
1991	3.51	4.44
1992	4.63	0.34
1993	7.77	8.47
1994	0.86	11.30
1995	9.18	17.70
1996	9.87	25.45
1997	12.20	28.73

Source: BIS, 68th Annual Report, p. 155.

Table 2.5   Financial derivative instruments traded on organised exchange turnover in notional amounts ($ trillions)

	Total	Interest rate futures	Interest rate options	Currency futures	Currency options	Stock future	Stock options
1991	135.2	99.6	17.3	2.7	1.5	7.8	6.9
1992	181.9	141.8	25.5	2.3	1.4	6.0	5.7
1993	227.8	177.3	32.8	2.8	1.4	7.1	6.3
1994	340.5	271.7	46.7	3.3	1.4	9.4	8.0
1995	333.9	266.3	43.3	3.3	1.0	10.6	9.2
1996	321.5	253.5	41.0	3.0	0.9	12.9	10.1
1997	356.8	274.6	8.6	3.5	0.7	16.4	13.0

Source: BIS, 68th Annual Report, p. 156.

while improving the asset quality as well as performance of the creditor banks, much of which was achieved in reality.

2.3.1   Bank profits, loan loss provisions and tax laws in the OECD

With banks from different parts of the OECD controlling the flow of international credit, bank profits rather than credit turnovers were treated by the financial community as a relatively more important index of financial standing. This was especially true with the ranks of individual TNBs changing considerably, both in terms of credit flows and with the depreciating dollar after the Plaza agreement. However, in the meantime there was a general reduction in bank profits as a consequence of the developing country debt crisis. This created an atmosphere of eroded investors' confidence on bank stocks (Table 2.6). Banks were already loaded with provisioning against loan losses which however were not initially disclosed to the public. In Europe, the 'hidden' reserves of banks were tacitly approved, by the respective governments, as indications of provisioning. However, by 1978, banks started disclosing their loan-loss provisioning, largely to win over the disenchanted clients.[14] It took a few years for the creditor governments to come forward with a seal of approval, announcing special accounting and tax privileges for banks which were declaring loan loss reserves. These reserves were treated at par with bank capital, which was up to 100 per cent in the US and France and up to 14 per cent of reserves in Japan. Full tax deduction was allowed in France as well as in Germany against the reserves, while in Japan the concession was partial. In terms of official sources, with most of OECD governments there was an implicit encouragement of loan-loss provisioning. These were done by allowing their inclusion in bank capital, and permitting tax deductions against those items. While the inclusion of provisioning as part of bank capital strengthened the capital/asset ratios of banks, tax deductions augmented the post-tax bank income and profits.[15] However, in the US the prevailing real interest rates proved too high as compared to the real returns earned on bank assets, especially by small banks which often failed to provide for loan losses. Mergers and acquisitions were actively encouraged by the Federal government in the US, especially at an interstate level, thus putting up a front against the dominance of the handful of leader banks.[16]

Table 2.6 Profitability of major banks in OECD (percentage of total average assets)

Pre-tax profits				
2000	1999	1990	1984–86	1980–82
1.79	2.17	0.59	0.83	0.83
0.37	0.42	0.33	0.46	0.40
0.55	0.43	0.83	0.97	0.50
1.53	1.43	0.59	1.05	1.04

Source: BIS, 71st Annual Report, p. 130.

2.3.2 The US money-centre banks, the Fed and the IMF

As pointed out earlier in the previous section, a large number of money-centre banks in the US were involved in third-world debt in a big way. By the end of 1982, 60 per cent of the $200 billion debt owed by the four largest debtors (Argentina, Brazil, Mexico and Venezuela) was held with three major US banks, which included Citicorp, Bank of America and Manufacturer Hanovar. (This amounted to more than a quarter of aggregate developing country debt at around $450 billion in 1982.) By June 1986, share for the same three banks went up further.[17] Clearly, the above reflected a high degree of concentration, both in terms of borrowers and lenders. As a response, the US Fed tried to initiate a set of measures which were more prudential than regulatory in terms of bank supervision.

With Mexico's call for debt default in August 1982 which was echoed in several other indebted countries of Latin America, the Fed initiated the International Lending Supervisory Act (or ILSA in short) in the year 1983.[18] In terms of ILSA, banks could preserve the value of their assets by involuntary loans to the borrowing countries which were approved by the IMF in terms of loan conditionalities. Thus, loans offered through these windows were not market determined. To prevent interbank rivalry in fetching these payments, the ILSA made it obligatory that pre-payments should not be confined to a single creditor bank and rather be shared by others. This in effect amounted to a creditor's cartel, one where the individual debtor country had little scope of negotiating directly with its creditor bank. While the Act aimed to prevent a collapse of the financial system as could occur through a non-payment of interest charges, a steering committee of nine US money-centre banks demanded an implementation of the prevailing 90-days non-accrual interest rule. (In terms of the latter, non-payment of interest beyond 90 days was supposed to render an asset non-performing.) Almost simultaneously, the IMF announced its 'case-by-case' debt strategy which formally codified the borrowing status of countries in terms of the fund-approved loan agreements.

Between the ILSA and the conditional loan package instituted by the IMF, it was expected by the financial community that the flow of bank credit would be uninterrupted to countries having the seal of approval from these supra-statal authorities.[19] While debtors were

Table 2.7 Provisioning expenses as a percentage of total average bank assets in selected OECD countries

	Number of banks	1999	2000
USA	12	3.84	0.63
Japan	16	0.89	0.52
Germany	4	1.65	0.18
UK	4	2.40	0.21

Source: BIS, 71st Annual Report, p. 130.

Table 2.8 Net non-interest income as a share of banks' annual gross income (%)

	1981	1983	1985	1988	1990
United States	24.0	26.5	26.6	30.1	32.8
UK	NA	NA	34.5	37.6	40.1
Japan	17.8	14.7	21.1	25.8	24.1
Germany	29.1	24.8	30.1	30.4	34.7

Source: OECD, *Banks Under Stress*, Paris, 1992, p. 125.

asked to deal with steering committees of the TNBs, in effect it amounted to their dealings with the US lead banks which filled up 50 per cent of the positions in these committees.[20]

2.3.3 The US official debt-initiative to help debtors 'grow out of debt' – the Baker Plan 1985

Debt restructuring during 1982–84 enforced a discipline of 'forced adjustments' with punitive actions against debtor countries if they failed to conform to the loan conditionalities. It, however, was also evident that the debt issue was more than a liquidity problem and that the debtor countries need to 'grow out of debt'. This led to a growth-oriented approach during 1985–86 in terms of the Baker plan. It aimed towards debt redressal, which, however, met with limited success.

Case-by-case negotiations, between the TNBs, the developing country debtors and the IMF, which were tried out during the earlier part of the 1980s proved inadequate to handle the debt problem by

Table 2.9 Exchange rate of US dollar vis-à-vis Chinese yuan and Japanese yen

	1985	1986	1987	1988	1989	1990	1991	1992	1993	1994	1995	1996	1997
Yen/$	239.0	169.0	145.0	126.0	140.0	145.0	135.0	127.0	111.0	102.0	94.0	109.0	130.0
Yuan/$	2.94	3.45	3.72	3.72	3.77	4.78	5.32	5.32	5.32	5.32	5.32	8.31	8.28

Source: IMF, *International Financial Statistics*, various issues.

the middle of the decade. Possibilities of a generalised debt collapse were quite high by 1985 when James Baker, the US Secretary of State floated his plan to resume the WB guaranteed new loans, to the 15 Highly Indebted countries (HICs). Of the latter, ten were from Latin America. In terms of the Baker Plan, the HICs were to be provided $20 billions of new loans by private commercial banks and $10 billion by development banks. In addition, the World Bank was to offer a package of new loans, which included a sum of $9 billion to the ten HICs of Latin America and $2.7 billions to sub-Saharan Africa, the latter as a supplement to the Bank's IDA loan facilities.

However, even the Baker Plan, when implemented, touched only a fringe of the third-world debt stock held by the HICs which was at $420.4 billion at the beginning of 1985. Total third-world debt soared up to $430 billion by October 1995 of which almost a quarter at $91 billion was owed to the US banks.[21] While the aggregate debt owed by Latin America and sub-Saharan Africa was curtailed by $15 billion during 1985–88 following the implementation of the Baker Plan (1985), it fell further by another $30 billion by 1989. However, voluntary credit from banks to these areas, unlike what was postulated, was hardly forthcoming.[22] The Baker Plan was rather limited in terms of the offer of 'new money' and led to discontent among the smaller regional US banks and the European as well as Japanese banks which could not get any benefit from the scheme. It took a much longer period for third-world debt to cave in than what was projected in the Baker Plan, as can be seen from the rather slow decline of the debt stock from $184 billion in 1987 to $113 billion at the end of 1991. In retrospect, the drop in debt stock was the outcome of a fall in gross inflows of loans rather than of the measures initiated by the Baker Plan.[23]

The US involvement in the debt initiative can also be viewed as a sequel to the frustrated attempts of the G-7 countries at the 1985 Plaza meet, to re-shape and co-ordinate their macroeconomic policies. The discords, in particular, were related to their disagreements regarding the appropriate monetary and fiscal policies. While surplus countries like Japan and Germany refused to concede to the demand from the remaining G-7 for an expansionary policy, deficit nations, and in particular the US retaliated with a refusal to restrain the fiscal deficits. Attention, instead, was focused on the exchange rate target of the dollar, which depreciated considerably after the Plaza meet as a consequence of the co-ordinated efforts of the G-5 Central Banks. Simultaneously, the Libor rate also went down considerably. For the US banks, the outcome, with depreciating dollar and probabilities of a lower libor rate, did not turn out to be a favourable one. It thus became rather imperative for the US authorities to respond to the financial sector concerns by bailing out the troubled banks; with the ILSA and the case-by-case approach, and also with the Baker Plan and other programmes of the US State Department which followed. With smaller US banks and regionals opting out from new money scheme and the non-US banks openly disagreeing with the solution, the 'leaders' finally were left to bear a more than proportionate burden of the debt crisis that had emerged in Latin America.[24]

Measures on the part of the national and international regulatory bodies to avert a bank crisis were inadequate to prevent further bank collapses. This was evident in the crash of several banks in succession during the second half of the 1980s.[25] In October 1986, Mexico's announcement of an impending debt default initiated a package of concessions from the major TNBs, both with pressures from the US government and with indirect supports from the IMF. The Agreement with Mexico sought to provide new money which was backed by effective US government guarantee and was secured at concessional loan terms which included interest rate spread at less than 1 per cent, long maturity and co-financing facilities from the World Bank.[26] The deal provided to Mexico encouraged Brazil to seek a similar deal with the IMF, which however, was not acceptable to the creditor TNBs. This led Brazil to announce a moratorium in February 1987 while the creditor banks sought to avert further defaults by entering into agreements with a few other debtor countries in Latin America.

The Brazilian moratorium led the 'leaders' to devise further actions in self-defence.[27] In particular, provisioning for loan loss reserves (LLR) was a major step, which came up as a reaction. Citicorp, a major US lead bank which was heavily exposed, announced a hefty $3 billion LLR which in turn amounted to 25 per cent of its exposure. Other lead banks, all from US, followed suit, but with a considerable stress which ultimately destroyed the last fragments of leader-bank solidarity.[28]

In reality very little was achieved in terms of debt redressal. Finally, the outstanding debt held by the third-world was diluted with large-scale securitisation of debt-backed assets of banks, a move which was convenient to the latter. As the debt-related assets became nearly non-performing, banks started selling them at heavy discounts in the secondary market, thus reinforcing the drop in the prices of those assets. Uncertainty on the debt front also initiated banks and other FIIs to the grey area of hedge finance, with financial derivatives providing new avenues of operation in risky business. Thus, problems with third-world debt led the international banks to shift to securities and financial derivatives as new instruments. This was reflected in the changes that took place in bank portfolios and in off-balance sheet activities which will be discussed later in this chapter. In the process, the banks showed a much less interest in advancing new loans to the developing areas by mid 1980s.

2.3.4 Break-up of creditor cartel, financial deregulation and growing securitisation in the leading money centres of the US and the UK

By 1987–88, there was a complete break-up of creditor cartel and along with it, of unity over the 'new money' facility to Mexico.[29] With smaller banks switching to debt sales, it heralded the beginning of a menu approach endorsed by the Brady proposals in the US. In the meantime, the pace of deregulation in the financial markets had already speeded up, with the 'big bang' in the UK, on 27 October 1986 permitting all foreign financial agents an open entry to the City. In effect, this allowed the foreign banks and security houses much easier entry into the London money market, which was already attractive because of the practice of 'universal banking' in the City. The 'big bang' blew off the 'barricade' between London's gilt-edged and stock markets on the one hand and the Euro-bond as well as equity market on the other.[30] While 'segregated banking' was still the formal practice in Japan, bank assets held securities were in effect hidden. This pushed up the profitability of the Japanese banks which in turn proved to be all the more attractive when the yen-denominated assets and profits rose in terms of dollar after Plaza agreement. In the US, the vestiges of the Glass-Stegall Act and 'segregated banking' were effectively withdrawn, as the Supreme Court gave a formal ruling in favour of under-writings of commercial paper by the US banks in the year 1988.[31] With as many as 182 banks operating in

the security market and $14 billion securities lead managed by the
US money-centre banks by 1986, it was already apparent that the US
banks were very much involved in the international security market.
The scale of bank operations in the security sector was on the increase
during the next few years, with the banks expressing a preference for
assets held as securities as compared to third-world loans.[32]

Involvement of banks in the security market took various forms.
Instead of lending directly to the sovereign borrowers as during the
1970s, banks now lent more to corporates and that too indirectly by
underwriting. These included the note issuing facilities (NIF) as well
as the revolving underwriting facilities (RUF). As it has been aptly
described, '... The traditional commercial bank role of providing
liquidity to the securities markets was reinstated with the birth of
NIFs and RUFs where the provision of direct funds via the issue of
short-term securities is backed by commercial bank medium-term
liquidity backstops'.[33] In effect, the banks were providing contingent
liquidity against these instruments, and thus enabling the corporates
to raise funds from the market without the hassle of direct transactions.

Commercial banks were active, once again, in the syndicated loan
market by mid-1980s. However, their pattern of involvement, dealing
with large corporate borrowers from OECD, was rather different from
the earlier pattern of involvement during the 1970s when sovereign
debt by the LDCs was their prime target.

Revival of syndicated bank credit during the 1980s can be viewed
as a by-product of several factors which included the following:
(a) the preference for multi-option facilities by corporates with flexible
facilities incorporating a wider array of funding options; (b) growth
of highly leveraged transactions (HLTs), largely to borrowers which
were the 'less primed' corporates and had fewer options in the capital
market; (c) the growth of 'wholesale secondary transaction and loan
trading' creating additional demand for liquidity. It is important to
notice that in none of these cases LDC borrowers were in the picture.

The US banks also participated in the leverage-buy-outs (LBOs).
These were often used to back purchases of the officially guaranteed
Euro-bonds having a triple-A rating from a recognised official agency
in the US. By 1988, LBO transactions amounted to $10 billion in Wall
Street. At 1/10 of the purchasing power of equities, the latter covered
an additional $100 billion equities. Banks funded most of these

deals.[34, 35] Often the margins of the spread over libor for these credits were influenced by the speed of business. In particular, the fast pace of leveraged take-over bids between 1988 and 1991 was a factor behind a rise in the margin. Thus '... the high margin business in the form of loans to finance acquisitions amounted for almost half of announced new syndicated lending in 1989 and 1990'. These transactions generally added to the risk profile of bank portfolios in general.[36]

One should also mention here the role of asset based securities (ABS). These were used by banks to acquire mortgaged as well as other real assets and also claims (including loans) against durable consumer goods, credit cards and so on. Banks in turn sold securities, which were backed by these assets in the market. In terms of estimates done by the Salomon Brothers, aggregate ABS in the US amounted to $476 billion by the end of 1988. Using ABS as a method of acquiring assets was also common in the UK, a practice that soon was popular in other financial centres within the OECD. To handle these complicated instruments, the mighty 'financial boutiques' were active, especially in the US. These were usually managed by a 'small, highly powerful and specialised expertise having contacts at top levels.... With a steady trickle of people from top investment banks who were corporate finance specialists or smart investors'.

As for the other major financial centres, West Germany had virtually no restriction on banks operating in securities while in England universal banking was very much in practice, with finance outperforming industry as a consequence of the continuing supremacy of the City as a financial centre. Both managed their national interest reasonably well, with Germany in a position to lead the EU till recently in terms of a strong as well as stable currency, while England avoided major runs in its financial centre which was its major source of international economic supremacy. Japan, which also was in a very different position in terms of financial stability till the mid-1990s, provides a very different story, which we will deal separately later in this chapter.

2.3.5 Further initiatives from the US in terms of the menu approach

As in 1985, the US took the leadership to protect the interest of the US banks when the Brady plan was announced in 1989. By this time, the situation in the financial market, however, was different in terms of the menu approach which had already begun. Moreover, the use of provisioning against loan losses had changed the asset composition of major banks in the US and the UK with a growing preponderance of the non-interest bearing assets. On the whole, the banks had much less of a stake on third-world debt by late 1980s as compared to what they had in 1985. Finally, the ranking of banks had also changed in the meantime, with banks of Japanese origin moving up in the market in terms of asset holding, size of capital stock and profitability. It was only in 1989 that a crisis in the Tokyo stock market gave these banks a temporary jolt.

In 1988, the G-5 met in Toronto to look afresh at the third-world debt strategy. However, by then the private financial institutions had already restructured their strategies. These changes included the end of cohesion and cartel amongst the TNBs which were no longer dominated by the lead banks from the US. Moreover, there was a considerable diversification of bank portfolios which was now heavily weighed by the holding of securities.

As for the use of regulatory and prudential norms to improve bank performances, the case-by-case approach was substituted by this time with what came to be known as a 'menu approach'. It concerned the debt sales, swaps and wide-ranging use of financial derivatives on the part of banks which by now was quite common. These were the new responses of the financial houses to the crisis faced in the new setting of liberalised financial markets. The menu approach initiated in the Brady deal thus suited the changing scene of the deregulated financial markets. These were already exposed to much greater degrees of uncertainty by the late-1980s, with fluctuations both in exchange rates and interest rates, and in prices of financial assets including the wide range of high-risk products.

The US banks, however, still had a lot of their assets locked up in third-world debt by this time and Senator Brady's plan towards debt redressal was a last ditch effort to save these financial institutions. In his testimony to the US Congress where Mr Brady urged for US initiatives, he made an explicit comment that the plan was '. . . a bid to keep US leadership in debt-related issues'.[37] Conforming to the prevailing tendencies the Brady plan offered a solution to the debt problem which was primarily market-based. It sought debt reductions to the tune of a 20 per cent in the debt stock held with the LDCs and another cut of 20 per cent in interest payments thereon.

All these were to be achieved with a $20–25 billion support from the IMF and the World Bank. With the prevailing stock of LDC debt at $340 billion and the $102 billion interest bill on the latter, the reductions were supposed to be of the order of $70 billion and $20 billion respectively. Also, zero-coupon US bonds could be used to support the debt sales at discounts. It was argued from the US official quarters that the measures would help to reinstate growth of output and enhance import capacity in the heavily indebted countries, both with the direct debt reductions and the heavy market discounts on their debt, with the latter ranging between 30 and 60 per cent in the market. In reality, the debtor performances worsened. Thus, negative transfers from Latin America amounted to $179 billions. These flows were to meet the debt-servicing which amounted to 4 per cent of their combined GDP. The picture conformed to what was implicit with the German reparations at the end of the First World War as analysed in the famous Keynes–Ohlin controversy.[38] Incidentally, the sum even exceeded the previous record of war reparations from Germany which amounted to 2.5 per cent of the latter's GDP in 1917.[39]

As it could be expected, the Brady plan had little impact on the debt stock of the 38 heavily indebted countries. Of the latter, only five countries, which included Costa Rica, Philippines, Mexico, Morocco and Venezuela, had already entered the structural reform programme of the IMF. Hence, these were considered eligible to adopt the Brady plan proposals. A failure to reach an accord with the IMF explains the exclusion of two other large debtors, Argentina and Brazil, from the Brady plan.

Senator Brady's approach to third-world debt cancellation, especially under the head of interest payments, was criticised by other creditor countries, especially by the UK, West Germany, Sweden, Netherlands and Canada. It was alleged that the plan '...smacks of interest subsidy'. However, the G-10, in principle, did support both the US initiatives on debt strategy and the Fund responsibilities regarding third-world debt including the actions by the latter against deliberate defaults. But when the Fund and the Bank showed an interest in '...lending into arrears', creditor countries including the UK, Sweden and Netherlands were apprehensive that such actions may generate a 'free-rider problem', not just for banks but also for the lender governments.[40]

Emphasis, once again, was laid on *new money* from private banks at the Interim Committee meeting of the IMF which was held in April 1989. This was a part of the officially supported debt package under the Brady plan. Some creditor governments objected to the practice of transferring the credit risk to tax payers in advanced countries. According to the private credit rating agency, the Moody's Investor Service, the World Bank guarantee to third-world debt was a device to 'legitimise debt forgiveness to debtor governments'.[41] Even Japan, which had a consistently liberal stance so far on debt cancellation and was even willing to put in money in the Exim Bank at a parallel level, was quite apprehensive by 1989. This was because Japan by this time had a substantial LDC exposure, at $80 billion in March 1989. The country rather wanted to wait for green signals from other creditor governments and the World Bank before committing to the Brady proposals.[42] The Brady plan in effect opened a pandora's box by admitting, on an official basis, that the LDC debt was no longer sustainable and that this provided the main reason for the US to take an initiative in terms of cutting back bank debt.

It was no surprise that the Brady plan touched only a fringe of the developing country debt problem. As mentioned above, even the most heavily indebted countries like Argentina and Brazil were left in the lurch, simply because they could not reach an agreement with the IMF. While the Brady plan continued to be under-funded, debt prices dampened further in the secondary market. The consequence was adverse for both banks as well as the debtor countries; the former in terms of the value of bank assets which depreciated as a result of discounts in the market and the latter with the related disincentives on the part of the creditor banks to offer new loans. Thus, a cut in the debt-overhang, which came through the market did *not* contribute additional resource inflows from abroad which could be invested in these capital-scarce economies. And the low magnitude of debt relief was hardly adequate to bring about a change in the scene.

The Brady plan did not meet with much of an appeal even with big debtors in Latin America like Mexico which was one of the beneficiaries. This was reflected in Mexico's finance minister Herzog continuing to reiterate his country's demand since 1984 to link the debt issue to oil prices. In Venezuela, President Perez was keen to sell debts only when bonds were at the market rate of interest while

President Alfonsin in Argentina demanded interest rate cuts on its $56 billion debt from 9 to 2 per cent. It was thus evident that the large debtors covered by the plan were actually not satisfied with the deal.[43]

2.3.6 The prudential measures and bank performance

It will be interesting, at this point, to have an assessment of the various prudential measures in terms of the financial restructuring which came about since the 1980s. These included the loan-loss provisioning, the capital adequacy norms prescribed by the BIS, debt sales and swaps by banks and the Brady proposal discussed above. In the following pages we propose to critically view, in the same sequence, the *three* aspects mentioned above.

Provisioning of reserves against loan losses was tried out by major banks in the US and in other OECD countries which had a stake in terms of their debt exposures. In 1988, the US government's General Accounting Office (GAO) observed that the ILSA of 1983 was rather inadequate to tackle the problems of the creditor banks. Accordingly, the GAO advised the banks to provide for loan loss reserves against debt as revalued at the discounted prices in the secondary market.[44] Until about 1985, banks in the US had been encouraged to treat those reserves as undisclosed assets. However, within a few years large-scale sales of loans at discounts led banks to push up the margin of loan-loss provisioning. Reserves set aside as provisioning by banks amounted, on average, to 25 per cent of developing country debt for the six major US money-centre banks in 1987, a year when debt sales were quite high. For the remaining four money-centre banks, the range was even higher, ranging between 39 and 55 per cent during the same year. For regional banks in the US, loan-loss provisioning as proportions of developing country debt varied between 20 and 75 per cent.[45] In Europe, these hidden bank reserves against probable loan losses were officially encouraged with tax concessions. Loan-loss provisioning was also in practice in the UK, and the share of assets similarly set aside increased over the 1980s.[46]

A major impact of loan provisioning on the performance of the banks was felt on their profit rates. Profitability of banks did temporarily improve since the assets on which profits were calculated now excluded the reserves set aside in terms of the provisioning. Banks with improved profitability also achieved higher prices for bank equities which were selling better in the market.[47] However provisionings continued, not only against the growing stock of LDC debt but also on real estate, agriculture and energy. As a consequence, banks, especially in the US, started facing losses with an erosion of their income earning assets.[48] Thus, the pre-tax profit rates of the US banks fell sharply from 24.76 per cent (1981) to 5.73 per cent (1987), which fell further, to a low of 15.34 per cent (1989) after recovering to 20.80 per cent (1988).[49]

Profitability of banks in Europe were also subject to declines along with the provisioning against losses, as can be seen from statistics provided by the OECD.[50] As a contrast, banks in Japan, which from the beginning had less of exposure to LDC debt, went through an expansionary phase as overseas banking was substantially deregulated by 1988. We have explained above the reasons behind such expansions. Profitability of banks in Japan also went up, with pre-tax profits moving up from 25.15 per cent (1981) to 40.68 per cent (1988) and then to 35.26 per cent (1989).[51]

Prudential Regulations have been subject to criticisms from different quarters. While many banks were happy to abide by the norms, they were also keen to disclose them in order to push upwards the prices of equities they wanted to float in the market. The step, however, as argued by banks, led to an excess holding of the safer government securities on their part, since there was a uniform 100 per cent risk weight for all commercial papers. It has also been argued that the capital adequacy norms, as pointed out below, might have generated a credit squeeze in the OECD and also that loan-loss provisions had been entirely subjective, thus impairing its worth in judging the relative financial strength of banks.[52]

A device which similarly aimed to protect the ailing banking industry during the debt crisis included the *capital adequacy norms* of the BIS, as instituted in July 1988. In terms of the latter, banks in OECD which reported to the BIS were to achieve a minimum ratio of capital to risk-weighted assets at 8 per cent by April 1993. Constituents of bank capital included, as core or Tier I capital, all equities and disclosed capital and general reserves (of banks) from post-tax earnings. Tier II or 'supplementary' capital included undisclosed reserves, revaluation reserves, general loan-loss reserves (upto 1.25 per cent of risky assets) and long-term subordinated debt, upto limits as set down in terms of the regulation. Tier II capital could also be included in the capital adequacy ratio as long as their value was less than that of Tier I capital. Thus, bank assets in principle were weighed according to a pre-supposed risk of counterparty failure. To arrive at the ratio, all on-balance sheet assets were assigned categories, each having a risk weight, the range of which was between 0–100 per cent. These included a zero per cent risk for all advances in general to the OECD and to all Central Banks, 20 per cent on claims relating to residential mortgages in OECD, and 100 per cent on assets relating to advances to non-OECD private sector unless these were funded in national currency. Off-balance sheet loans were also classified, after converting these to putative on-balance sheet amounts by applying appropriate credit conversion factors.[53] Obviously, there was an in-built system of preferences in the BIS capital adequacy norms in favour of bank assets held within the OECD or with monetary authorities, in terms of the provision that these needed a zero or only a 20 per cent risk cover in terms of the BIS capital adequacy norms.

Capital adequacy norms changed the perspective of the creditor banks in terms of their preferred asset composition. There was a natural tendency to minimise risks on the part of the lending banks. This led to the holding of government bonds and other assets relating to the OECD, which often was at the cost of new loans to the developing countries. The emphasis in the BIS capital adequacy norm on individual asset risk rather than the portfolio risk had thus the potential of raising the portfolio risk of unexpected default losses. However, developing country loans could in principle provide a hedge to the bank portfolio since returns on these were often negatively linked to returns on other loans, specifically to advanced countries. With covariance among loan risks low between the internationally held assets with the OECD and the LDCs, the diversified loan portfolios could thus turn out to be eventually less risky for the creditor banks. As pointed out in a recent study, '...optimal risk weights should incorporate how addition of an asset to a portfolio increases the risk of the portfolio. Thus the regulation focuses on asset variances, ignoring the covariances'.[54]

It was often the case that loans were rationed out, especially to developing countries which were considered less creditworthy. This was due to the 100 per cent risk weight applied equally to *all* LDC borrowings. However, risks other than loan losses (for example, on interest rate, exchange rate and so on) and the position risk in traded equity securities was ignored in the BIS manual of capital adequacy, thus protecting the creditworth of assets held within the industrialised area. Finally, the use of 'book value' accounting at historical practices ignored the changing asset and liability prices, thus missing out the state of a bank's cushion against unexpected losses. Even credit to the OECD, as has been argued, shrank as it was difficult for banks to float equities when their markets weakened after 1990 and the non-performing assets increased. This led banks to limit, in general, asset growth and to charge higher margins, in particular for assets carrying higher risks.[55] For reasons as above, the capital adequacy norm of the BIS, as has been argued, was inadequate to judge the credit standing and hence the asset risk of banks properly. Also, the mandate on capital adequacy and the provisioning for loan losses both had a bias against new loans, especially in the direction of the developing countries.

Capital adequacy standards set by the BIS for its reporting banks posed a greater threat to the financial system with the stock market crash of 1987 in the advanced economies. In June 1989, the Technical Committee of the International Organisation of Securities Commission (IOSCO) adopted a report on capital adequacy of securities firms. Instead of suggesting a common framework, it proposed some basic principles of what was considered desirable. It emphasised the liquidity as well as solvency aspect of firms. It also demanded information from security houses on the losses and so on, while recommending that each security firm's asset should exceed the sum of the risk-based requirements.[56]

Creditor banks also sought to minimise the loan losses by means of *debt sales* in its secondary market at discounts. As mentioned earlier, in the US this was started by the smaller and regional banks which found it hard to provide for loan-loss provisioning. Deviating from involuntary lending the TNBs started using a case-by-case approach by mid-1980s. By the end of the decade, debt trade as a voluntary approach was officially incorporated in the US proposals for the Brady plan in 1989. During 1987–88, the large US money-centre banks unloaded substantial stocks of third-world debt in the market. As a consequence, for Citicorp alone, third-world debt exposure was cut by $1.2 billion during 1988. This was substantial as one recalls that the nominal size of the Latin debt held by the Citicorp stood at $9.9 billion (which was 90 per cent of the bank's primary capital) at the end of 1987. The official value, however, was much larger than its market value at $6.7 billion. Debt exposure to Latin America for the four major US money-centre banks was till substantial and it ranged between 80 and 126 per cent of their primary capital in 1987.[57] According to estimates provided by the Wall Street Journal, debt trade in 1988 amounted to $15 billion or more.[58] In terms of an alternate source, debt trade during 1985–89 was of the order of $26 billion.[59] The magnitude of debt trade which included swaps, as estimated by the World Bank, was even larger at $50 billion and $60–80 billion respectively for 1988 and 1989. Demand for debt selling at discounts came primarily from the MNCs operating in the developing areas, and from those LDC governments which showed interest in debt-equity swaps and direct buy-backs at a discount. However, all these hardly left any buoyancy in the secondary market for LDC debt which continued to slump with record lows for debt prices. Debt held by Argentina continued to sell at as low as 20 cents (1988) and 11.5 cents (1989) per dollar.[60]

With debt prices touching a record low in their secondary markets, debt trade started contaminating the asset holdings of banks with large exposures. These included the money-centre banks in the US and large banks like Barclays, Lloyds and Midlands in the UK.[61] Occasional efforts at large loan-rescue operations (for example, the Morgan–Mexico deal) with large third-party purchases pushed up debt prices temporarily and helped banks, which held back debt to avail the benefits of free-riding! With small banks' willing to trade debt, the large banks were willing to participate, sometimes only on a confidential basis in debt sales.[62] The secondary market prices of debt held by the major borrowers, however, continued to drop during 1986–88. This acted as a disincentive to potential buyers and the discount on third-world debt thus failed to work as a 'giant exit bond'[63] or an incentive to pump in new money on the part of the creditor banks.

As for the impact of buy-backs which were often organised by the debtor governments, the impact on debt prices was similarly rather marginal. This was because of the restrictive clauses of the syndicated loan agreements, especially with their negative pledges seeking to 'eliminate discrimination among creditors through pledging of assets'. In terms of the 'cross-default' clause and the negative pledge, the creditors enjoyed equal rights in terms of their access to debt servicing at times of debt crisis. Also, any pre-payment of a rescheduled debt by the debtor was to be followed by a similar pre-payment of the entire debt on a pro-rata basis. By this token debt-equity swaps between creditors and debtor governments/MNCs were tantamount to pre-payment. Provisions as above, along with the cross-default clauses often proved a source of a legal deterrent for the debtors to buy their own debt. In Chile (where the swaps initiated by its government were prominent), large measures of amendments and waivers were used to overcome such problems.[64]

2.3.7   The Japanese banks

It is interesting to view the Japanese reactions to the debt crisis separately. This is because Japan, despite its large current account surpluses, had very little stake in third-world debt till the closing years of the 1980s. This is all the more surprising since the financial position of Japanese banks improved considerably as a consequence of the falling dollar rate after the Plaza agreement. That Japan's world view was very different, was evident from the statement of the country's Prime Minister Takeshita in 1988, that a global approach to third-world debt can be initiated with deposits of official reserves of debtor countries with the creditor country, thus absolving Japan the risks of a debt default.[65] Japan also initiated the famous Okita recycling proposal in the 1980s and the more recent Miazawa[66] proposal to redress the third-world debt, none of which was popular with other OECD countries. The US, in particular, was opposed from the beginning to these measures and continued to emphasise the case-by-case approach at bilateral or international levels. Much of the opposition stemmed from a desire on the part of the US to retain its supremacy and control over third-world debt.

In Japan, financial deregulation and securitisation speeded up during the late 1980s, when the newly launched Euro–yen market started providing an opportunity to invest in dollar-denominated assets. The market enabled the Japanese corporations as well as banks to float the Samurai bonds for yen in the Euro-bond market, and then swap the yens for dollar to buy dollar-denominated bonds. The device aimed to achieve expansions in dollar-denominated assets held by the Japanese investors while avoiding any strain on the yen–dollar rate. But in practice a large number of the US financial agencies took advantage of the swap, effectively pushing up the dollar at the margin against the yen. While these measures were not officially permissible in terms of the MOF regulations, the global market created the potentials for making yen a key currency, while filtering the process of transactions in order not to weaken it in terms of dollar.[67] Financial intermediation in Japan picked up, both with deregulation and with the country's financial surpluses reaching new heights by the mid-1980s. Since stock markets in Japan were not active in providing investment opportunities to the savers, most of the intermediation was done through banks, post-offices and pension funds, the first two harnessing about one-third of the Japanese savings by 1986. Funds collected by post offices were forwarded to the MOF, to be distributed at low interest rates and according to national priorities for domestic investments.

In Japan, financial deregulation and securitisation were supported by a close 'bank–business link' which prevailed as a result of the 'group orientation' of Japanese banks which included the close links between 13 city banks and 6 major industrial groups. The banks lent, through their overseas branches, to the client industrial corporation abroad. Thus, despite the legal separation of commercial and investment banking in terms of Article 54 of Securities and Exchange Law of Japan, '... in contrast to the Anglo-Saxon pattern of financial markets, bank–business links prevailed as a result of the group orientation of the Japanese banks'.[68] In Japan, security houses had a role which was one of a mediator rather than an investor. Four major security houses, which dominated Japan's financial market, were vertically linked to their smaller cohorts in the security market and to the banks, hence defying the basic role of equity-linked financial intermediation. Thus in Japan, finance and industry supported each other with a complementary role, both in terms of domestic and overseas investments. A high degree of concentration, in industry as well as finance, supported the group affiliation in lending. Large corporates at home and their subsidiaries abroad were dependent on affiliate private financial institutions which provided 27.8 per cent of their investment finance in 1986, a pattern which continued till the mid-1990s. As for the smaller corporations, funds were supplied mostly by the government affiliates like the post office banks or the life insurance funds.[69]

Competition from the Japanese banks in the international capital market became effective only by end of the 1980s, as restrictions on foreign exchange transactions were substantially removed in the country. As a consequence, overseas banking was substantially deregulated while the Japanese City banks established new overseas branches and entered into joint ventures abroad.[70] The process was reinforced by the changes in the yen–dollar rate after the Plaza agreement. It is, however, interesting that the amity between finance and industry, as observed in terms of overseas expansion of the Japanese banks, did not prevail within the country. Thus, the security houses resisted the repeal of the segregated commercial and investment banking laws within the country, because of their fear that the banking lobby would swamp them.[71] However, as pointed out above, there was unanimity between the two groups on targets of pushing overseas activities. For Japan, problems of an impending crisis through an overlap between the banking and the security sectors did not surface until the late 1990s. This was because the top 13 city banks had close links with the six major industrial groups within the country. The '...group-orientation forged close bank–business relations...with banks following the customer in foreign lands where they lent to corporate subsidiaries having common affiliation to business groups'. Simultaneously, the MOF exercised a certain degree of discretionary authority by means of its access to a major part of domestic savings in Japan, channelled through the post-offices. In Japan, the 'financial pyramids' operated with own cohorts 'of small security firms which were closely knit with major banks'. Thus, the 'quasi-market' and 'customer-based' relations between banks and corporate borrowers worked in the context of industrial groupings as well as the forged links between Japanese financial institutions and their multi-national enterprises abroad. These also included small firms, which were relatively dependent on private sources of funds.[72] The legal separation of banking, security houses and insurance companies which was in accord with Article 65 of Japanese Security and Exchange Law, was thus least operational in practice in Japan. At the same time, the affiliation, at the level of business groups dominating overseas operations of both industry and finance, worked to eliminate competition between banks and security houses abroad. Growth of finance in Japan during these years was matched by expansions in the operation of domestic and industrial corporations – both of which explain the ascent of Japan as an industrial economy during the 1970s and 1980s.

The situation, however, changed drastically during the 1990s, both with the problems transmitted by the closer links with the world financial markets in general and the onset of the financial crisis in Asia.

2.4 Securitisation of the financial flows – non-bank sources of profits for banks

Looking at profits earned by the banking industry during the late 1970s and 1980s, one is struck by the 'carnival' of record profits, generous dividends and rising share prices of bank equities which was prevailing in the shadow of a major threat to the financial system.[73] A paradox as above, however, did not last long, as we have already pointed out. The anomaly which prevailed during the early years of the debt crisis can in part be explained, as mentioned earlier, by the rise in loan-loss provisioning which automatically secured a hike in the post-tax income and profits of banks in the 1980s.

Concentration in the international banking industry, as mentioned earlier in this chapter, was rather high from the beginning. It is, however, interesting to note the relative performance of banks, with small banks outperforming the larger units, both in terms of the capital/asset and the profit/asset ratios. As opposed to the large banks which remained 'over-exposed' in terms of third-world debt, the smaller units were protected with their superior performance. The phenomenon, captioned as an 'inversion of pecking order' in the Banker Magazine, characterised the potential fragility of the financial institutions in industrial economies. However, the ability of large banks to provide for loan losses probably 'lifted the system by its bootstraps', with effective support to profits on shareholders capital rather than the interests of the potential borrowers.[74]

With banks operating in the security sector, a steady source of non-interest income was there to prop up bank income and profits. A marked reduction in the operating costs of banks, especially in Japan, was another factor which helped. However, the ability of banks to handle assets other than interest yielding loans was initially rather limited, especially in the US and Japan both of which were formally on segregated banking practices. In the US, the Congress was found defending the Glass-Stegall Act of 1933 till the end of the

1980s. But as pointed out earlier, in reality most banks were violating and bypassing the rules by transacting business which was recorded as off-balance sheet deals. These transactions covered the deals in derivatives which, however, could be treated as permissible financial instruments. In essence, these derivatives reflected attempts on the part of bankers to hedge against market risks, on loans selling at discounts in the market and on securities held as assets. The relatively higher risk of marketised loans often made the bank portfolios swing in favour of securities as preferred assets, which of course had its own hazards and risks. Typical of the risk-hedge derivatives were the NIFs, forward deals, futures, options and swaps, mostly designed as hedge against risks. The derivatives used by banks also included leverage finance involving the issue of junk bonds used for leverage buy outs (LBOs). Banks also were lending on the basis of short-term Euro Commercial Papers (ECPs). The rising popularity of all these non-interest bearing activities with banks was evident in the growing share of non-bank sources of income to banks in the OECD by mid-1980s.[75] Thus in 2001, most money-centre banks in the US were found to '... produce about a third of their income from net interest margins on traditional intermediation activity, a third from fees and commissions from arranging financing and about a third from what is called proprietory trading, primarily from exploiting international interest rate differentials'.[76] Thus, it was not just an accident that mainstream research in the area of finance was directed to optimal hedging techniques during the period, especially with the much acclaimed formulations like the Black–Scholes theorem[77] on put-call parity in option trading. We will dwell in the next section on the limits of these prescriptions as a means of avoiding financial instability.

As mentioned earlier in this section, non-banking assets which included securities constituted a major source of profits for banks by late 1980s. Thus, with financial deregulation, the distance between banks and security houses in terms of their operation in the international capital market narrowed considerably, with banks earning income from security holdings and security houses operating as sources of credit. Securitisation of banks, as mentioned above, generated problems, especially in terms of enforcing the prudential legislation.[78] This was more so because securities were less homogeneous and prone to both credit and market risks as compared to bank loans. As it was pointed out, '... diversification, not least the banks' involvement in securities activities and new financial instruments has made banks vulnerable to . . . market risks'.[79]

Holding of securities made the banks vulnerable to *three* types of risks: first, the 'position risks' due to changes in the value of securities in which banks had an non-hedged position; second, a mix of a currency plus country risk, 'primarily with internationalisation of bank assets' and third, '. . . the interest rate risk arising out of maturity mismatches on interest-bearing assets'. Banks also held large amounts of OTC type off-balance sheet assets which were out of the net of the regulatory mechanism. Moreover, the competition between banks and security houses had increased the need for a harmonisation of these practices between banks and security houses at an international level.[80] In absence of a common approach, financial stability was thus at stake, with problems in the security sector spilling over to the banking sector.

2.4.1 Securitisation, financial derivatives and capital flows

Trade in securities under uncertainty warrants the search for instruments which hedge against risks. The fact that financial derivatives today dominate the international capital markets is explained by the rising uncertainty and the related risks as are witnessed in the latter. As pointed out in an analysis of derivatives, '. . . the explosive use of financial derivative products in recent years was brought about by *three* primary forces: more volatile markets, deregulation and new technologies'.[81] The turning point can be traced back to the early 1970s when the major currencies started floating in the market and risk-management products like the forward contracts were developed by banks and other financial institutions to hedge currency risks. Removal of interest rate controls in terms of Regulation Q in the US and the steep rise in prices following the oil price hikes intensified the volatility, not only in the currency market but also encompassing the international capital market which was already integrated.

Beginning in the 1980s, the advances in information technology offered newer methods to deal with risks in the financial market. Also, the simpler instrument of forward contracts were supplemented by futures which were standardised by exchange clearing houses. These could, in principle, be supposed to ensure anonymous trading in competitive and liquid markets. However, since the future contracts are marked to market daily, the counterparty risk (that the other party would fail to meet the contract) is enhanced automatic-ally.[82] Around 1980, swap deals were also initiated. These were in the nature of forward-based derivatives '...which oblige the two counterparties to exchange a series of cash flows at specified settle-ment dates in the future'. With interest rates as well as exchange rates subject to changes in the market, swaps were used to hedge against these fluctuations, often designated as swaptions when exer-cised through an option.[83] These financial innovations were devised to protect the agents from the potential losses which are more pronounced with uncertainty and the greater degree of risks in liberalised markets.

It has been argued in the literature that the derivatives provide an opportunity for the transfer of risks, from the risk-averse to risk-neutral agents in the market. The consequence, as has been argued, may be a rise in efficient allocation of resources. From a market-oriented perspective, '...the derivatives thus offer the free-trading of financial risks'.[84]

The theoretical justification of using derivatives by financial agents thus comes from the claim that these instruments are supposed to provide a better allocation of economic risks. A systematic argument was provided by the 'state-preference' model of Arrow and Debreu[85] which pointed out that derivatives provide the opportunity of 'completing' the capital market. In terms of this argument, with unconstrained trading in securities, the financial agents can achieve the desired allocation of risks in terms of the distributions of the 'pay-off' across the respective 'states' (of trading in the market), thus implying an unconstrained Pareto-efficient allocation of risk. Options (or other forms of derivatives) are thus welfare-increasing instru-ments, as has been pointed out in the literature.[86]

Delving further into the economic theory behind the functional role of derivatives, we use the following quote from a study: '...As a matter of fact, the inter-temporal nature of financial decisions implies *uncertainty*....Risk is therefore an inherent characteristic of financial decisions....In order to achieve an unconstrained Pareto-efficient allocation of these risks within a market system, capital markets must provide sufficient opportunities to trade and price the various kinds of risk'.[87] From this, it is thus imperative that derivatives are expected to provide an *outlet* for the pricing of risks and their allocation amongst different agents trading with each other.

As it has been argued, derivatives significantly reduce the cost of diversification and leverage. This is because the global risk positions and portfolios can be traded as a 'single' financial product when traded as derivative, say as options. Since investment in terms of derivatives involves a fraction of the cash instrument representing the underlying securities, these facilitate diversification of a given amount of liquidity across several assets, while reaping the benefits of *leverage* in terms of potential gains or losses. In terms of the Black–Scholes–Merton formula for option pricing, the pay-off of an option can be *replicated* by a levered position in the underlying risky asset (for calls) or in cash (for puts). Thus, diversification and leverage are supposed to be the two key functions provided by options and futures. While operating as 'static' portfolio strategies, these instruments substitute for dynamic operations. In such cases, the proportion of the various assets in the portfolio is dynamically adjusted according to changes in the underlying variables as interest rates, stock prices and so on.

There remain *two* aspects of derivatives which are critically important in their functioning. The first relates to the pre-condition that the market is subject to risks and uncertainty. As put in the same study, '...in a perfect market with no transaction costs, no frictions and no informational asymmetries, there would be no benefits stemming from the use of derivative instruments'.[88] The second aspect is related to the 'informational aspect' of derivatives, which is the essence of the prevailing uncertainty and risks. However, in order that the theory of option pricing permits the '...replicating of options with dynamic trading in the underlying asset classes', it is necessary that the underlying asset structure *continues to prevail*. In other words, 'The true stochastic process followed by the underlying asset, and especially its volatility, must be known *ex ante*'. Arguments as above become apparent, as one examines the option pricing formula of the Black–Scholes model where the rise in the call premium caused by a rise in stock prices (known as the delta) would be higher when the variance of stock price movement (the probability distribution of which is known ex ante) is also higher.[89]

Assumptions, as above, of full knowledge regarding the probability of stock price movements, which are supposed to be subject to a normal probability distribution, sound untenable in reality. As an example, one can cite the case of the 1987 stock market crash or the more recent Asian currency crisis of 1997 followed by more recent turmoils in Mexico (1994), Russia (1998) and Brazil (1998). In all these cases, dynamic adjustments on the part of investors by taking positions seemed futile and too late in the face of the sudden and fast movements in the markets. In other words, assumptions regarding the path of the stock price movements, subject to a normal distribution, turn out as untenable when the market moves fast and especially, in an unpredictable manner.[90] The process also involves a 'reflexive' pattern, where the realisation of expected events in the market (profits, asset prices, call premiums on options and so on) is influenced by the subjective biases of the actors in the market (which include the seller/buyer, lender, investor and so on). We have discussed the above aspects in Section 1.3.4.

Despite the theoretical underpinnings which justify these financial innovations, the desired results, both in terms of a better allocation of risks amongst investors and the related stability as well as real growth, hardly seem to have been realised. Indeed, the volatility in financial markets, especially in advanced economies where derivatives have been much in use, has rather been on the increase since the initiation of these innovations. Nor can one witness an improved growth record in these economies during the same period. Critiques of the mainstream position also point out that derivatives, by concentrating capital in short-term speculative transactions, divert money from long-term investment. It is also pointed out that derivative trading destabilises the cash market by increasing the volatility of its fundamentals (such as interest rates, exchange rate of currencies and so on). Finally, the rampant and wide-scale use of these instruments with the failure to prevent the stock market crash in different parts of the world leads to the view that these risky instruments generate systemic disruptions in the market.[91]

Emphasis on financial derivatives as instruments of policy in the financial markets explains the fact that transactions in financial derivatives, as estimated, were around $20 trillion in December 2000, which is more than double the size of current US GDP. These oft-quoted figures are related to the '...notional principal which does not change hands but is simply used to calculate payments'. Of the $20 trillion worth of derivatives currently floating around in the financial markets by December 2000, as much as $15.66 trillion are reported to be off-balance sheet transactions in the currency market. The latter include $13.32 trillion short-term (less than one year) dollar denominated currency swaps and forward contracts. The rest consist of options, mostly short-term, amounting to $2.33 trillion. Derivatives are also prominent in the equity-linked derivative contracts. Thus, the sum of OTC derivatives at the end of December 2000 was at $1.98 trillion, which was a multiple of the flow of equities in the world economy as a whole. In contrast to the foreign exchange market, where forwards and futures were more important, options at $1.53 trillion dominated most of the $1.98 trillion of OTC derivatives used in the equity market.[92] More recent estimates of securitisation for the US banks indicate significant variations across large and small banks. Thus, of the ten largest securitisers among financial service providers in the US at the end of 2001, proportion of securitised assets varied from 170 per cent (MBNA), 100 per cent (Country-wise credit), 17.8 per cent (ABN Amro Bank), 12.1 per cent (Citibank) and 6.4 per cent (Deutsche bank).[93]

Use of derivatives in the global capital market, which has expanded noticeably over the last few years, raises the question as to whether the outcome had been conducive in terms of financial stability and real growth. In particular, one needs to critically examine, not only the logical but also the historical validity of the claim that the use of derivatives as instruments of hedging against risks and uncertainty has been conducive to financial stability and growth. If we look at the record of global financial flows since the dominance of these derivative instruments, which started by the mid-1980s, it does not require much effort to observe that financial instability (or to be more specific, fragility) has been on the increase since then. While financial flows, which include the more stable FDIs as well as the rather volatile bank credit and equity flows, have both been on the uptrend, the latter has been combined by unpredictable swings, as happened during the bank credit crisis of the early 1980s. Credit cycles have also been manifest, during the more recent years, in security markets where the swings are equally prominent. Use, as such, of the derivatives has thus been of limited use, if at all, in arresting these upheavals.

2.5 Boom and bust cycles of credit under financial liberalisation: Asia during the 1990s

This section aims to provide an example of the implications of financial liberalisation with a reinterpretation of the recent boom and bust credit cycle in Asia. Our analysis relies on an explanation which is different from what has been viewed as the 'disordered-fundamentals' explanation in mainstream economics or the alternate interpretation of a pure 'banking panic' scenario. In our judgement, problems in troubled Asia during the late 1990s need to be traced back to factors which encompass *both* its real and financial aspects. A reference to the decelerating real sector of these economies is thus crucial in understanding the fragile performance of finance, a boom in which continued well into the first three quarters of 1997 despite a slump in real activities by the end of 1996.

This is not to discount or minimise the overwhelming presence of the in-built instabilities in SE Asia's financial system which was bred by the wide-ranging deregulation of finance in these countries during the 1990s. As the financial boom continued in the face of the sluggish real activities during 1996–97, the financial sector became over-sensitive to a potential collapse in asset prices which eventually came about at the end of 1997. Deregulation of financing in SE Asia, which initiated the financial innovations and also increased the trans-border as well as domestic credit flows in these countries, was responsible for the vulnerability in the financial markets. The monetary authorities eventually failed to control such situations despite their efforts.

Interpretations of the Asian economic crisis in the mainstream literature have glossed over, in our judgement, the following aspects:

- The *first* relates to the problems in the real sector which surfaced at least a year before the financial crisis actually broke out. These disorders included, in addition to their rising CADs, decelerations in terms of growth rates of exports, imports and of GDP by 1996. The slump in real activities was also reflected in the reduced personal consumption in these countries, which dried up a major source of demand in the domestic economy. Finally, decelerations in the real sector performance of these economies resulted in steep declines of property prices, reflecting an end to the construction boom in these economies.
- A *second* aspect of the SE Asian crisis relates to the financial deregulation in these countries, which provided the space for financial innovations with unrestrained flows of credit which continued even when the real sector was stagnant or decelerating. The

following aspects, in particular, deserve a mention: (a) Expansions in the domestic financial sector which continued till the end of 1997. In the meantime, domestic credit flows were generated, both with external borrowings and financial innovations at home, as long as there was a sustained flow of demand. Much of these flows were directed to the high-profit speculative financial ventures which had little, if any, links to the stagnating real sector activities within these countries. (b) As is typical with the boom and bust credit cycles, the lull in the real sector failed to provide a signal to the rising credit flows until the boom in the financial sector actually busted by the third quarter of 1997. The end came with dips in stock prices, exchange rates and depletion of officially held reserves, along with a severe liquidity crunch within the respective economies. Thus, the financial crisis appeared at the end of a phase with large and uncontrolled credit inflows in the liberalised financial regime of these countries during the 1990s, much of it consisting of short-term external borrowings. (c) This brings us to the third aspect of the financial upheavals in these countries. These include the unsuccessful damage control measures on the part of the national monetary authorities which were designed to arrest the downslides in their currency and capital markets. Measures as above included the floating of currencies and the steep hikes in domestic interest rates, none of which were adequately effective to control the upheavals in the deregulated financial markets. The reason behind was the wide-ranging speculations and uncertainty which plagued these deregulated financial markets, thus creating a situation where the respective financial agents failed to respond to the corrective measures offered by monetary authorities. An analytical interpretation of this has been provided earlier in Section 1.4.3 in terms of the 'impossible trilemma'.

- The crisis seems to have subsided by 1999–2000, leaving behind a trail of untoward consequences which may reappear in future. Of the explanations for the recovery, as have been offered from different circles, a major factor seems to be the recovery of the US economy. Also, with the restructured financial scenario, fiscal-monetary policy in these crisis-ridden economies of Asia has assumed an accommodating role, permitting domestic credit expansions at moderate to low real interest rates. The move also goes with the closer integration of their (domestic) financial sector with international credit markets where interest rates have already come down considerably. Finally, it probably indicates a post-crisis realisation on the part of the IMF which is no longer hung-up on fiscal-monetary tightening in these countries of Asia. The pattern marks a stage of recovery in the credit cycle, which is subject to reversals, especially with added degree of vulnerability, both in terms of real sector performance as well as the financial flows.

The changing economic scenario in the Asian economies documents the pattern of a boom-bust credit cycle, as pointed out in Appendix 1B. The initial credit boom and later its continuation in the face of deceleration in the real economy respectively characterise Phases I and II of the credit cycle. The reversal of the financial boom along with the continuing deceleration of the real sector characterises Phase III with a financial crash which is followed by a recovery, as prevails at the moment.

2.5.1 The pattern of the boom and its collapse in SE Asia – the events

Similarities in the pattern as well as the timing of domestic growth, financial deregulation and the collapse of the real as well as the financial sectors justify clubbing the three countries of the ASEAN (Thailand, Indonesia and Malaysia) along with South Korea. This, however, is, not to undermine the singularities of each country. Deceleration in exports, GDP and other real variables in these economies began in 1996, thus recording a reversal of the forces which brought an end to the expansionary phase of the 'miracle years'. With the depreciation of the Japanese yen as well as the Chinese yuan vis-à-vis the US dollar, which effectively was the link currency for the ASEAN, export competitiveness of the products from these economies got a jolt (Tables 2.9 and 2.10). The other explanation of the slump in export markets of these economies included the generally sluggish demand in export markets from the OECD which was going through a recession. Tendencies, as above, were aggravated by a tendency for real wages in these Asian economies to rise relative to productivity, especially in Malaysia (Table 2.10). Indications of a slump in the real sector of the economy were visible in reduced levels of consumption demand by mid-1996, which thus started much earlier than the crisis of 1997, especially in Thailand and South Korea.[94] In Thailand, one witnesses a sharp drop in new car sales or in the sales record at 38 top retail stores of Bangkok by the second quarter of 1996 (Table 2.11). Contraction in the growth rate of output as took place in these countries was also contributed by measures towards a tightening of monetary and fiscal policy, as

Table 2.10   Wages and value added per worker in US dollar

	1980		1990		1993	
	Value added	Wages	Value added	Wages	Value added	Wages
Thailand	5675	2543	13613	3523	17184	4661
Malaysia	8198	2257	10881	3240	14400	4148
Indonesia	3497	743	4245	925	4949	1128
South Korea	9545	2837	33184	9353	43961	12269
Japan	30912	11522	79823	26368	106510	37854

Source: UNIDO, *Industry and Development*, 1995, PP. 174, 177, 207, 215.

Table 2.11   Weakening of personal consumption: annual percentage changes – Thailand and South Korea

		New car sales in Thailand	Retail sales		
			Bangkok 38 stores	All Thailand	South Korea
1996	Q1	11.3	0.9	NA	10.9
	Q2	3.1	−2.9	NA	10.1
	Q3	3.6	−14.4	NA	11.2
	Q4	−1.8	−16.8	NA	9.4
1997	Q1	−8.8	−14.7	NA	6.4
	Q2	−19.9	−24.4	NA	6.5
	Q3	−48.7	NA	−8.0	5.6
	Q4	−73.5	NA	−7.3	0.3
1998	Q1	−70.7	NA	−12.3	−9.9
	Q2	NA	NA	NA	−10.3

Note: Standard deviation of percentage deviation of regression on a time trend.
Source: World Bank, *Global Economic Prospects*, 1998–99, pp. 68, 90.

reflected in the high spread between the local deposit rates and the libor in these countries other than in Malaysia. This in turn provided incentives to the local agents to borrow abroad. Fiscal policy in these countries was far from profligate, as can be seen from the regular surpluses in their budgets which were maintained on an average over 1992–96. Thus, in none of these countries, a profligate fiscal budget can be held responsible for the financial crisis which ensued. However, the conservative monetary-fiscal policy which prevailed, remained ineffective in these countries, and it was not possible to control the rising credit flows in these economies which went up much faster than M2 during the 1990s (Table 2.12).

The continuing rise in credit flows despite the real stagnation, and especially, despite the monetary tightening in these economies, can be interpreted in terms of what has been described earlier in Chapter 1 as the 'finance' motive of liquidity demand. In terms of this motive, credit could be generated by means of financial innovations, much of which were facilitated by deregulation. The resulting flow of credit was demand determined and as such not subject to exogenously determined monetary restraints.[95] The role of credit flows in meeting the liquidity needs of the private sector was evident in the rising leverage ratios of the corporate sector in all these countries. The process worked, as corporate debt was 'validated' in the market, with financial innovations generating credit flows to meet the high-profit high-risk speculatory demand for financial assets which often had no real counterpart in the economy. Finance, under such circumstances, got dissociated from real spheres of activities in the economy. By 1996, the median value of foreign debt ranged between 70 per cent of firms' equity in Indonesia and 80 per cent in Thailand to 150 per cent in Korea. Moreover, short-term foreign debt ranged from about 40 per cent of equity in Indonesia to nearly 100 per cent in Korea[96] (Table 2.13). Compounding the problems, ratio of short-term debt held abroad was also generally moving up. These expansionary developments in the financial sector naturally had little effect on the decelerations in the real sector for the respective countries, which were signalled by 1996 with a drop in the respective GDP growth rates in 1996.[97]

2.5.2 Changing flows of finance in the Asian economies

We now draw attention to the changing pattern of financial (credit) flows in the four Asian countries mentioned above. The pattern

Table 2.12 Macroeconomic changes: annual percentage changes

	1990	1991	1992	1993	1994	1995	1996	1997
Indonesia								
Annual growth in domestic credit	58.3	18.9	14.1	21.0	NA	NA	NA	NA
Annual growth in M2	44.2	17.5	20.2	20.2	27.6	29.8	NA	NA
Credit to private sector as % of GDP	46.9	46.2	45.5	48.9	53.7	55.8	NA	NA
Foreign liability of banks as % of GDP	11.0	8.6	10.3	10.9	9.6	8.5	27.7	NA
Malaysia								
Annual growth in domestic credit	18.0	18.5	29.2	14.8	29.5	NA	NA	NA
Annual growth in M2	12.8	14.5	19.1	14.7	24.0	20.9	NA	NA
Credit to private sector as % of GDP	71.4	77.0	111.4	115.0	129.5	NA	NA	NA
Foreign liability of banks as % of GDP	7.3	9.0	13.0	8.8	6.5	NA	18.5	NA
South Korea								
Annual growth in domestic credit	NA	22.4	11.7	18.4	14.7	19.4	NA	NA
Annual growth in M2	17.2	21.9	14.9	18.7	15.6	15.8	NA	NA
Credit to private sector as % of GDP	65.3	65.4	65.6	69.2	69.4	74.8	NA	NA
Foreign liability of banks as % of GDP	6.5	7.7	7.6	8.0	10.1	12.1	14.7	NA
Thailand								
Annual growth in domestic credit	26.8	15.5	18.0	26.8	23.1	14.0	NA	NA
Annual growth in M2	26.7	19.8	15.6	12.9	17.0	12.2	NA	NA
Credit to private sector as % of GDP	83.1	89.1	98.6	128.4	138.8	100.0	NA	NA
Foreign liability of banks as % of GDP	6.4	6.0	6.9	20.3	24.3	23.3	15.0	NA

Source: M.K. Rakshit, *Money and Finance*, January 1998, pp. 35–41; ADB, *Asian Development Outlook*, 1997; IMF, *International Financial Statistics*, 1996; *World Economic Outlook*, 1997; World Bank, *Global Development Finance*, 1998.

Table 2.13   Short-term debt in Asian countries at end of 1997 ($ billion)

Short-term debt to	Total debt	Official reserves
Indonesia	24	160
South Korea	67	300
Malaysia	39	55
Thailand	46	107

Source: IMF, *International Financial Statistics*.

seems to reflect the three distinct phases of credit cycle mentioned earlier in Chapter 1. These include: *first*, a period when flows of finance supplemented real growth, a pattern which continued through the 1980s and till the mid 1990s. Flows of external finance supplemented the productive process during these years. The *second* phase, however, is marked by flows of finance flowing along alternate channels which were related to speculative activities in these economies; in particular, during 1996 and the first half of 1997 (or even later) when real growth had already tapered off. With external finance continuing to flow to these economies, it was directed to the speculatory spheres of secondary stocks and property markets which had no contribution whatsoever in terms of productive activities. In its *third* phase, one witnesses an abrupt end to the financial boom as the affected countries experience sharp declines in exchange rates, capital flights and liquidity crunches. We will provide, in what follows, a commentary on the failed responses, on the part of the national monetary authorities, especially in the context of the financial deregulation. As pointed out above, the sequential pattern in the boom-bust cycle of credit in the crisis-torn economies of Asia in the 1980s tallies with the analysis provided earlier in Chapter 1 on the credit cycles and on the post-Keynesian notions of 'finance' and endogeneity of credit. The underlying theory is of help in interpreting financial innovations, fragility and the eventual collapse of the financial system as actually happened in Asia.

Dominating policy in these countries since the mid-1980s, financial deregulation was prompted by a desire on the part of their monetary authorities to attract capital from overseas. In Indonesia, the drive was reinforced by the collapse of oil prices in 1982 while a similar downturn in primary goods markets contributed to the urgency for financial liberalisation in Malaysia. A pressure from the powerful industrial conglomerates in South Korea to make use of the international capital market was instrumental in Korea's plunge into the global financial market. The pattern was similar in Thailand where banks and industries were both keen to avail of the benefits of financial deregulation, especially with the setting up of the Bangkok International Banking Facilities (BIBF). However, in general, a desire to attract foreign capital (especially, the FDIs) worked as a major incentive to open up the capital market in all these countries.

For the Asian economies in crisis, much of their overseas debt were contracted by private banks and corporates. Unlike what the practice had been with other developing country borrowings, most of these privately held external liabilities were contracted without formal government guarantees. However, an implicit guarantee and compliance from the respective national monetary authorities, as mentioned earlier, eased the credit flows to these countries, rendering it profitable for the private borrowers to access large sums of foreign currency, and often at short maturities. The ongoing process, however, ended up with a serious mismatch between assets and liabilities when the crisis broke out in 1997. The slump in the OECD and the relatively lower interest rates prevailing therein made these borrowings mutually remunerative, both for borrowers and lenders. The lenders found it lucrative to hold financial assets in Asia, especially with the option of holding the assets in currencies linked to dollar.

For the Asian economies in distress, a deceleration of the real sector which started in 1996 had an impact on the destination of external finance flowing to these economies in subsequent years. As already mentioned above, incentives on the part of foreign investors to acquire financial assets in these countries did continue for some more time and was facilitated by deregulation in their financial sector. With the ongoing slump in the real sector, a large part of these flows were already deployed in speculatory ventures, covering property and stocks. The latter in effect was chasing the available financial assets (shares and so on) in the secondary markets, thus bidding up prices in stock markets. The impact was felt in the capital market of these economies in terms of the steep climbs in stock and property prices. Later, such hikes turned out to be a source of additional financial liability for the banking sector which suddenly found itself saddled with bad debts which were backed by collaterals at inflated stock and real estate prices. Much of these assets were also in the high-return high-risk category, as justified by the stiff rates of interest at which these were offered.

Stock prices relating to financial companies and the property market started tumbling down by the second quarter of 1995 in Thailand.[98] This did cause heavy damages to the asset value of banks. As a consequence, the share of non-performing assets held by both banks and the corporates went up sharply in these countries. In addition, indices for private investments and construction activities in Thailand started declining from the first quarter of 1996, while those for gross fixed investment fell in South Korea from the second quarter of the same year.[99] Estimates provided by the Morgan Guarantee, as cited in the World Bank report, indicate that credit against property amounted to 25–30 per cent of aggregate bank lending in Indonesia and 30–40 per cent in Thailand and Malaysia.[100]

It is apparent that the pattern of financial flows in the affected counties of Asia underwent changes which made for vulnerability. A large part of the credit flows, both domestic and foreign, were of a short-term nature. Much of the credit flowing into these economies proved unsecured, with values of collaterals against these domestic credit flows collapsing as prices of stocks and property crashed. The boom in credit during the upswing was based on financial innovations which made it possible to continue with an elastic credit system. Moreover, there was a serious mismatch between assets and liabilities, as short-term foreign borrowings continued to increase at the prevailing dollar peg. Since the latter was rated as overvalued by the market, those short-term external liabilities rose sharply relative to the official reserves in these countries. The rising stock of foreign liabilities mostly consisted of portfolio capital with short durations, an outcome which threatened the viability of the process when the soundness of the financial arrangements were questioned by international creditors.

2.5.3   On crisis management in the deregulated financial markets of the troubled Asian countries

The collapsed financial sector in the troubled economies of Asia in September 1997 sent shock waves to the global financial community. It was apparent that the value of stocks and property which had served as collaterals against credits advanced in these economies was grossly overpriced, which in turn was largely due to the increased flows of finance into the high profit circuits of both finance and real estate. An impending collapse was evident with profits already choked off in the real sector.

The crash in the stock and the property markets was nearly simultaneous with the slump in the inflow of external credit. When foreign creditors started repatriating credit, the drop in the new flows was even more drastic. The flight of capital exerted further downward pressures on the exchange rates of these currencies, which the monetary authorities in these countries found difficult to control, even with steep hikes in the domestic short-term interest rates. The viability of the financial flows was questioned by both domestic and foreign creditors, which finally resulted in a credit squeeze in these economies.

As it can be expected in terms of the 'impossible trinity' (of pegged exchange rates, open capital accounts and autonomous monetary policy), efforts on the part of the respective national monetary authorities to sustain CAC at the prevailing exchange rates turned out as unsuccessful. The stability of the external value of their currency was already suspect in the currency markets and the growing accumulation of short-term speculatory liabilities pushed the foreign exchange market to a point where it was wary of continuing with the prevailing nominal rates, especially with the limited ability of the monetary authorities to support the latter. Efforts on part of the regulatory bodies to restrain the flow of domestic credit by instituting monetary controls succeeded to bring about a slower growth in M2. The latter, however, did not have a proportionate effect on the flow of aggregate domestic credit, until the demand for credit shrank drastically by the last quarter of 1997.

The ongoing credit expansion to a large extent was due to the continuing optimism shared by the non-bank agents in the financial markets who remained, by and large, outside the net of the respective national monetary authorities. The outcome also reflects the fact that credit in an economy is after-all endogenous and demand-determined, a position which challenges the monetarist stance on the issue. The latter came to be questioned and was discredited only when the process met with a grinding halt.[101]

The inherent weakness of these currencies in face of a run on them was thus rather evident in the failed attempts on the part of the monetary authorities to support the ruling rates, initially, by depleting reserves and later, as currencies depreciated fast, by raising the short-term interest rates. The latter evidently was a bid to attract inflows of foreign (mostly bank and portfolio) capital. In a deregulated market where quantitative controls on capital flows are ruled out, interest rate remains the sole option for the monetary authorities to arrest further downslides in their stock prices and exchange rates. However, in a market where volatile expectations dominate the foreign exchange rate in terms of the future movements in the price variables, it often is the case that the market turns out to be unstable. In such situations, a hike in short-term interest rate may *not* be viewed as an once for all affair. Expectations of further hikes in interest rates can encourage sales of stocks at the prevailing price before it goes down further, with anticipated upward movements in interest rates. In such situations, capital outflows are likely to continue and be even more rampant as the monetary authorities try to arrest these with successive rounds of increases in the domestic interest rate. Strategies of monetary control, as were open to these Asian economies at the end of financial deregulation, were effectively confined to using of price variables alone, which include possible variations in the interest rate and exchange rates. We have provided, in Appendix 1C, a formal argument to analyse these probabilities and their implications.

In the troubled economies of Asia, hikes in short-term interest rates as well as the steep depreciations of national currencies proved counter-productive, generating unstable conditions in the foreign exchange and domestic stock markets within. Depreciation of national currencies and interest rate hikes was of an astronomical order, which in turn only generated expectations of further changes, in the same direction, and thus provided an impetus for outflows of capital from these countries. As for other remedial measures, unsuccessful brakes, in the form of caps on bank lending and so on, especially relating to the stock markets, were tried out by Malaysia. State takeovers and assistance to the industrial conglomerates, were tried out in South Korea. Finally, approaching the IMF for loans to overcome the liquidity crisis was tried out by all three excepting Malaysia. None of those, as recorded by recent history, proved successful in bringing out a solution. Rather the panic triggered off by speculators in the financial markets was reinforced by sudden closures of financial institutions saddled with bad asset profiles in Thailand and South Korea. Uncertainty in the market was also triggered off by IMF policies in terms of its bail-out programmes. Weakness of national currencies spread, with a contagion effect, across markets within the region, covering stocks, money and property.

Links between financial sector liberalisation, credit boom and banking crisis in East Asia have been unfolded in the growing literature on cross-country research. In a recent study of 53 countries during 1980–85, a strongly significant relation is observed between the probability of a banking crisis and financial liberalisation, the latter proxied by the removal of interest rate controls.[102] An outcome as above prevailed as national currencies started weakening in these deregulated financial markets. The impact was especially severe with the adverse performances of the real sector since an increasing portion of the financial flows was driven to ventures which were predominantly speculatory and short-term in nature. Finally, the uncontrolled accumulation of short-term external liabilities became disproportionately large in relation to the official reserves.

The second-round effects of the financial collapse in these economies included the sharp downslides in output, employment and wages between 1997 and 1999. The social impact of this narrates a tell-tale story of enormous deprivation and destitution which continued till 2000, an economic measure whose costs are difficult to arrive at. The high weightage of traded goods in the GDP of these countries made it especially difficult for these economies to recover from the ongoing real stagnation. It was difficult to recreate a niche in the global market for their export wares, even with the most drastic order of currency depreciation. This was due to the global pattern with an oversupply in products like semi-conductors which ignited the crisis in the export sector. Competitive exchange depreciation only ended up in pre-emptying of each other in a global market which itself was stagnating.[103] Also, the crash in the financial sector affected the real sector by dampening the domestic demand as originated from these sectors. Moreover, because of its dependence on imported inputs which was difficult to procure with the difficult foreign exchange situation, it became a problem for the real sector to continue with positive growth rates. It was thus natural that foreign investors showed a lack of interest in having fresh investments in this region. Finally, the financial performance of the industrial conglomerates, which, as in South Korea, was closely linked to the functioning of the financial institutions also aggravated the downslides of the real sector.

Recovery, as came about in the crisis-ridden economies of Asia during the year 2000, has been initiated by a combination of several factors. A major factor behind this was the recovery in the US, which generated demand for exports from East and SE Asia. It has been argued that the change in the US economic policy during the late 1990s, prompting it to assume the lead role of an engine of growth was conditioned by several factors. These include the terms of trade gains for the US and other industrialised countries, vis-à-vis the developing countries, both with drops in primary export prices and exchange rate depreciations in parts of Asia after the crisis.[104]

Simultaneously, monetary policy in these economies was accommodating, thus deviating from the earlier stance of the hikes in domestic interest rates during the period of economic crisis. Incidentally, this was accepted by the IMF, probably with the experience of the crisis years in the region. With exchange rates floating in the market, monetary authorities in these countries no longer needed to stiffen the interest rates in order to attract capital, as was done earlier. With employment and real wage rate returning to the pre-crisis level, demand in the respective domestic economies was doubly rejuvenated, first with the revived external market and second with the revival of domestic demand. This was reflected in the estimated contribution of domestic demand to growth which, in terms of BIS statistics, had distinctly improved by 1999. Exports of high-tech products comprised 58 and 34 per cent respectively of Malaysia and Thailand's total exports to the OECD countries.[105] However, despite the growth rates of GDP at 4.8, 8.5 and 4.3 per cent in the respective economies of Indonesia, Malaysia and Thailand during 2000, their current accounts continued to be in surplus, as during 1999. This was due to an absolute fall in domestic output during the slump and some degree of a shift to import substitution, both by the domestic and the foreign controlled firms in the economy.

One observes, in the present recovery of the crisis-ridden Asian economies, *two* major sources of vulnerability. These are related to the added degrees of dependence on the OECD in general, and on the US in particular, for the stability of their export revenue as well as equity prices.[106] Unlike what it used to be in the past, NASDAQ and the local equity prices are found moving together in most of these countries, with the correlation between the two working at

0.25 for Malaysia and at 0.32 for Thailand. Thus, movements in the equity prices of the emerging countries in Asia, Latin America and Central Europe (which included the transition economies) had been rather close in recent years.[107] It is therefore quite probable that growth and recovery in these areas may turn out to be non-sustainable as the wind of fair-weather prosperity blows away from North America, especially with shocks in the stock market which contributed an atmosphere of well-being with increased consumption spending in the country. The following years already confirm some of these apprehensions.

2.5.4 Summing up the Asian experiences

On summing up, the recent economic upheavals in SE Asia and even the more recent recovery confirm our hypothesis of financial deregulation as a contributing factor of instability. This is supported by the following analytical observations:

- First, that a financial boom which often follows deregulation in the financial sector, is potentially unstable and fragile unless it is matched by real sector expansions. This is because of the fact that financial expansions can continue as long as expectations regarding profits on these pure financial transactions continue to be self-fulfilling. The above, however, is difficult to ensure in an uncertain world, especially when the real sector is non-performing. Profits on financial activities in such situations are crucially dependent on *changes* in asset prices, as can only be sustained with uncertainty. Returns on these financial assets might even move up as risks rise with uncertainty. However, there will be no guarantee that such situations will continue. While the process described above is close to the panic-run interpretations of bank-currency market crashes, the origin of these developments can often be traced back to the poor performance of the real sector, as actually happened in Asia.
- Second, with deregulated finance, it is difficult for the monetary authorities to provide a package of policies which can avert a financial crisis. This can be explained by the following: first, the fact that credit expansions in the economy are often beyond the control of monetary authorities, especially with privately engineered financial innovations which are more effective under deregulation.

It fuels the spiralling of speculation in the economy, which is financed by the uncontrolled expansions in finance. In the absence of controls on the quality as well as the quantity of credit, it leads to mismatches, between short-term liabilities and long-term assets on the one hand and assets held in local currency against foreign currency liabilities on the other. Foreign currency reserves held by the monetary authorities against these liabilities often prove inadequate. A crash in the domestic financial market which ensues is capable of intensifying the problem, causing further reductions in the value of assets held by financial institutions (say in the form of collaterals) and reductions in official reserves of foreign currency as monetary authorities use the latter to support the exchange rate.

- A third aspect of the problem, which is interrelated, concerns the limited scope of monetary interventions in open, deregulated financial markets to manage a weak currency. As mentioned earlier, with financial deregulation, the variables which are open to official interventions include the managing of exchange rate and the domestic interest rate. Both, however, are subject to the influence of expectations which are shaped by the state of uncertainty in the market. Since monetary authorities enter the market as one among several agents who are active they have to outperform others in order to be effective. It may thus prove difficult to arrest a financial crisis when speculation is strong as well as adverse. Thus, efforts to arrest further attacks on a depreciating currency by raising the domestic interest rate proves self-defeating in attracting inflows of capital as long as there is an expectation of further interest cuts. An alternative, which relies on capital controls (or even monitoring and supervision) can only be tried out by departing from the regime of deregulation.

- Finally, we also point out that a recovery of the sort which at the moment is taking place in Asia, to the extent it rides on externally determined forces like export expansion and stock prices abroad spiralling in the upward direction, may not be sustainable unless it is backed by growth-rejuvenating forces from within.

Arguments which seem to follow from our analyses of the four Asian economies in distress suggest that the stabilisation as well as monetarist doctrines and policies advocated by the IMF seem to have been once more discredited by the recent crisis. It also follows that to make the remedial policies effective, efforts should be there to focus attention on the performances of the real sector, lapses in which stall all attempts to cushion the financial sector.

2.6 Concluding observations

Tracing the evolution of private capital flows across nations, from the time in post-war history when the boom was manifest during the early 1970s; one witnesses the dramatic changes, in terms of the rising volume and the changed pattern of these flows. The latter included the flows in newer directions, which now cover the developing countries; initially as bank credit and later as security-linked finance, as bonds, equities and even as derivative trading. The flows however, were concentrated in a few countries in the developing region, considered as creditworthy by the private credit rating agencies. As for the major part of international credit flows which remained concentrated within the OECD, these were increasingly dissociated from real activities in the region. This was largely due to the multiplying of pure finance-related activities which aimed to insulate the agents in the market from uncertainty, by using instruments of hedging of various sorts. Deregulation of the financial market made the use of these financial innovations both necessary as well as practicable for the agents in the market. Finance, under these circumstances, was guided by its own tribulations, an absence of which would have dampened its profitability!

Our observations indicate the need for surveillance of the market, preferably by the state, in order to avoid the pitfalls in a purely market-driven path of financial growth. As we would point out in the next chapter, this would be in the interest of global growth and stability.

3
Pattern of Global Finance and the Real Economy

We dwell further, in this chapter, on the de-linking of the real and the financial sphere of activities in the world economy. Some aspects of above have already been discussed in Chapter 1. This chapter seeks to look into the reality of such discrepancies, which has been apparent with the surges as have taken place in global finance and with its failure to regenerate real output; not only in the recipient countries, but also in the capital-exporting regions. The fact that financial flows do *not* necessarily succeed in generating output either in the donor or in the recipient countries demands further analysis, both with theoretical explanations and the observed realities. Problems as above are compounded by the asymmetry in terms of the deleterious consequences of a downswing in the financial flows which inevitably contracts the real sector activities.

Flows of private capital across international boundaries usually take place with the following possibilities: first, the flows may be related to over-savings in the capital-exporting countries; an outcome which is related to a deficiency of investment demand relative to available savings in the latter.[1] Second, such capital flows may reflect a decision on the part of investors in the capital-exporting countries to invest overseas, thus availing the higher risk-adjusted returns in the latter. Movements of capital across countries thus reflect a structural imbalance within nations, in terms of the availability and/or avenues of utilisation of investible surpluses.

Barring the regional financial flows within the East and South-Eastern region of Asia and the earlier interlude of recycling the OPEC surpluses by TNBs during the 1970s, sources of international financial flows over the last few decades have mostly been from the capital-rich industrialised nations of the OECD. Consistent with the large credit potentials as were available with financial institutions in these countries, flows of bank credit, primarily in the direction of the developing countries, swelled, seeking investment outlets with the help of financial intermediation. In the absence of international openings as these, the savings-rich and demand-deficient countries in the OECD were prone to slide back to a path of deeper recession during the 1970s, a problem which frequently recurs in mature capitalist economies.[2]

Flows of finance warrant a complement in real terms in the direction of the recipients. The process is best viewed as one of a *net* transfer of financial as well as real resources to the recipients. It can also be expected that such flows, provided those are put to productive use, would generate output and demand in the receiving economies, a part of which might even spill over as import demand for goods sold by the capital-exporting nations. International flows of capital are thus capable of generating and reviving global growth, an aspect which merits special attention.

As mentioned in the previous chapter, private capital flows across nations during the post-Second World War period were subject to a spurt during the 1970s when a handful of developing country borrowers in Latin America and Asia entered the international credit market. Loans were offered by TNBs which were recycling the newly created OPEC deposits. We also notice that the pattern changed dramatically by the early 1980s when new credit to the debt-ridden developing countries fell drastically, largely due to the waning of creditor confidence vis-à-vis the debt held by the developing nations. In the process, syndicated bank credits were substantially displaced by new instruments of financial intermediation in the global market for securities and derivatives. Developing countries, having very little or no access to the security market, were unable to reach out these sources of credit till the early 1990s by which time a handful of such countries had some degree of access. Net bank credit flows to the developing countries, declined from $25.4 billion in 1980 to (–) $11.5 billion in 1990, which settled later at annual averages of $5.2 billion (1994–95), $21.6 billion (1996–98) and dropping again at a negative sum of (–) $76.6 billion on an average during 1999–2000.[3] With the flow of net official assistance declining simultaneously, it is thus not difficult to explain the fact that net financial and real flows in the direction of most developing countries turned out to be rather small or even negative. As it can be noticed from the figures provided in Table 3.1, both bank credit and portfolio flows in the direction of the developing countries as a whole have been rather small or negative from the beginning of the 1990s, thus leaving FDIs to bring in the net flow of resources, the scale of which was not very impressive. The share of developing countries in the global flow of private capital, both in FDIs and others, was also rather small (which of late has declined further, as can be seen from Table 3.1). Thus, developing countries received less than 16 per cent of global FDI flows in the year 2000.

It may be relevant, at this point, to recall the transformations in private international credit flows over the last couple of decades, some aspects of which have already been analysed in Chapter 2. It is important to highlight the transformed character of capital flows, especially in view of their deleterious impact on the stability of the financial system. With deregulation of the financial sector which started in the mid-1980s, bank assets and as such the sources of bank profits were no longer confined to interbank transactions and other advances alone. Instead, bank portfolios included assets which related to transactions with non-financial institutions. Thus, non-bank sources of profits became rather important in bank balance-sheets.[4] However, finance as was advanced by banks to acquire those new forms of assets did not necessarily generate industrial activities; a fact which can be ascertained both from the large flows of bank loans advanced to these real estates and from the bank finance to meet mergers and acquisitions, in the OECD and in other countries. Off-balance sheet activities of banks, which had their origin in the diverse national tax regulations within the OECD, were much in practice along with the derivative financial instruments or the OTC operations on the part of the banks. Most of these financial transactions were in the nature of multiple claims which were backed by the same real asset. The practice continued despite the reluctance of governments, say in the US, to back mortgage and consumer finance-related securities. With deregulated finance at large, it was not unusual to see the emergence of successful 'financial boutiques', with small high-powered experts having contacts at top level which avoided the organisational problems of big investment banks.

Table 3.1 Financial flows in the direction of the developing countries ($ billions)

	1970	1980	1990	1994	1995	1996	1997	1998	1999	2000
New bank loans	7.0	57.0	43.1	63.9	84.3	102.1	111.3	114.4	16.1	39.2
Interest on bank loans	2.3	31.6	54.6	60.7	77.1	80.5	87.1	94.9	100.3	108.2
Net bank transactions transfers	4.7	25.4	–11.5	3.2	7.2	21.6	24.2	19.5	–84.2	–69.0
Portfolio equity flows	0.0	0.0	3.7	45.1	36.0	49.1	30.1	15.5	34.4	47.8
New FDI flows	1.8	4.4	24.2	90.0	106.9	131.4	172.5	176.7	185.4	178.0
Profit remittances on FDIs remmitances	5.3	22.7	17.6	24.9	26.5	30.0	31.7	35.2	40.0	50.2
Net FDI transfers	–3.5	–18.3	6.6	66.1	80.4	101.4	140.8	141.5	145.4	127.8
Aggregate net resource flows	10.82	74.54	99.31	221.9	260.1	310.8	340.3	334.1	264.9	294.8
Aggregate net transfers	3.15	20.19	27.07	136.3	156.3	200.2	221.4	203.9	124.6	136.3

Source: World Bank, *Global Development Finance*, 2001.

Moreover, credit to finance transactions relating to securities and derivatives in the secondary market (for example, using options, swaps and so on) often bypassed the circuit of real transactions, thus adding on piles of financial claims on the same real asset. Off-balance sheet activities and the OTC type of derivative instruments, including warrants, asset-based securities (ABS) and so on were widely practised by banks in a bid to supplement income. In fact, the bankers actually claimed that these operations were no less risky than the ordinary credit business in the 1980s![5] According to the BIS, it was a combination of excess liquidity with banks and the rather low transaction costs (especially with the advances in information technology) which played a role in diverting funds to the derivative market. In terms of one estimate, off-balance sheet activities of the US banks exceeded 700 per cent of their on-balance assets at the end of 1990. For the BIS banks as a whole, steep increases are observed in their off-balance activities.[6] As mentioned earlier, banks in the OECD were advancing money, since the 1980s, to finance real estate transactions and also to arrange for mergers and acquisitions for the corporate sector, both activities having special reasons to multiply in these countries where real growth was at a low ebb. At a later stage, the pattern as above relating to financial flows was replicated in the fast growing countries of Asia and eventually followed up by an economic crisis, which erupted in these economies by the third quarter of 1987. Clearly, the ordinary (or traditional) functioning of banks, which had closer links with the real sector, was in large measure substituted by the emerging pattern of non-conventional banking. These new forms of financial intermediation were in essence a response to the increasing market uncertainties, especially in the deregulated financial sector. *The outcome was a clear paradox where global finance survived through its own turbulence and not on the basis of the real sector activities.*[7]

Like in the rest of the market economies, the survival of the financial sector as a sub-system of the economy usually rests on the realisation of profits. Going by this criteria, financial intermediation has to dwell on the creation of debt by the other sectors. However, with the rather unimpressive record of real growth in the industrial economies since the 1970s, financial activities had been instrumental for a 'debt explosion' which was not backed by real transactions.[8]

3.1   Flow of goods and services: the North and the South

We document, in this section, the pattern and the magnitude of the current account flows as result from the ongoing capital account flows. We have considered the aggregate flows for the industrialised economies, henceforth North, and the non-oil developing borrowers, the South. We have not dealt with the oil-exporting countries in the developing region, which have exported capital during the oil boom period. We also have left out the transitional economies, capital flows in which direction have been of more recent origin.

We provide, in Table 3.1, the statistics relating to the *net flow of financial transfers*, defined as the current/capital account balance less net investment income flows. The sum, if *negative*, indicates an equivalent *inflow* of financial and real resources (at current prices) to the country group concerned. The figures, for each group, however, have been arrived at by adding up the country totals, which include the intra-regional flows within the respective area.

Contrary to what is expected, the relatively prosperous areas in the world economy (which include the industrial North) seem to have been *receiving* net inflows of financial transfers. The negative sum, as can be seen from Table 3.3, was at (–) $188.3 billion in 1999. The opposite seems to be the case for the non-oil developing economies, which of late have been *sending out* steady *net outflows* of financial transfers, with a positive sum which was as large as $141.2 billion during 1999 (see Table 3.3).

Analysing the flow of services which includes both factor income (investment income) and non-factor income, industrial countries as a group seem to be net exporters of services, as is indicated by the positive entries in column (3) of Table 3.3, The figure, however, includes large flows of direct investment income retained and re-invested abroad. If net flow of services excludes the investment income flows, exports of (non-factor) services on a net basis by industrialised countries also turn out to be substantial, as can be seen by comparing figures in columns (3) and (6) of Table 3.3. With their tendencies to incur merchandise deficits which prevailed during the 1980s and later reappeared in 1999, *the industrial area emerges as a steady net exporter of services and net importer of merchandise* during most of the recent period. The picture may shed some lights on the current debates relating to their ongoing domestic stagnation. This is

Table 3.2 Developing country share in global private capital flows as percentages of total

	1991	1992	1993	1994	1995	1996	1997	1998	1999	2000
Capital market flows	9.7	9.4	9.4	9.0	9.0	9.8	10.8	6.2	4.7	5.5
FDI flows	22.3	27.4	29.5	35.2	32.3	34.9	36.5	25.9	18.9	15.9
Total capital flows	11.8	12.4	12.6	12.8	12.4	13.2	14.4	9.9	7.6	7.6

Source: World Bank, *Global Development Finance*, 2001.

Table 3.3 Balance of international accounts, 1986–1999 ($ billions)

	CAB	MB	SB	IIB	CAB less IIB	SB less IIB
Industrial countries						
1986	−30.2	−11.4	26.5	4.1	−34.4	22.4
1987	−59.2	−30.0	21.1	4.3	−63.5	17.6
1988	−54.5	−8.4	6.1	7.5	−62.0	−0.7
1989	−79.8	−34.3	9.5	8.7	−88.5	0.8
1990	−113.0	−37.6	12.1	−2.2	−110.4	14.3
1991	−28.4	10.1	24.8	−9.0	−19.4	33.8
1992	−46.5	43.7	20.5	−20.5	−35.5	41.0
1993	43.3	100.1	38.2	11.3	32.0	26.9
1994	22.8	94.1	40.2	7.2	15.6	33.0
1995	58.4	124.6	39.3	11.0	47.4	28.9
1996	48.0	95.1	59.6	11.1	36.9	22.7
1997	83.1	99.1	63.7	31.1	52.0	32.6
1998	−32.9	28.1	48.9	15.0	−57.9	33.9
1999	−203.0	−109.0	42.6	−14.8	−188.3	27.8

118

Table 3.3 (Continued)

	CAB	MB	SB	IIB	CAB less IIB	SB less IIB
Non-oil developing countries						
1986	-12.7	4.8	0.8	-57.4	-13.5	58.2
1987	11.8	22.7	3.6	-58.6	8.2	62.2
1988	9.1	21.5	3.6	-60.4	5.5	64.0
1989	-4.7	8.9	0.9	-62.3	-3.8	63.2
1990	-2.7	-17.2	2.1	-62.8	-20.6	64.9
1991	-25.7	-27.1	5.0	-57.4	-20.7	62.4
1992	-42.8	-51.5	8.2	-57.7	-34.6	65.9
1993	-83.8	-67.1	-6.68	-68.2	-15.6	61.5
1994	-58.9	-50.8	-0.84	-66.3	7.48	65.5
1995	-93.9	-64.5	-9.17	-80.1	-13.75	70.9
1996	-101.0	-78.4	-1.76	-87.9	-13.52	86.1
1997	-83.4	-55.1	-7.07	-92.3	8.889	85.2
1998	-24.6	16.11	-7.9	-106.0	81.56	98.2
1999	35.82	85.83	-19.0	-105.0	141.2	86.3

Notes: CAB, Current account balance; MB, Merchandise balance; SB, Services balance; IIB, Investment income balance.
Source: IMF, *Balance of Payments Yearbook,* 2000.

Table 3.4 FDIs and cross-border mergers and acquisitions ($ billions)

	1991	1992	1993	1994	1995	1996	1997	1998
By purchaser firms								
World	85.27	121.9	162.3	196.3	237.1	274.6	341.7	544.3
Developed countries	79.9	99.1	134.1	163.0	212.0	239.1	299.1	526.7
Developing countries	5.1	22.3	26.8	32.3	24.4	32.8	40.8	16.3
Total FDI outflows								
World	NA	NA	247.2	284.9	358.5	379.8	475.1	648.9
Developed countries	NA	NA	207.3	242.0	306.0	319.8	406.6	594.6
Developing countries	NA	NA	39.7	42.6	52.0	58.9	65.0	52.3
By seller firms								
Developed countries	71.4	83.7	97.8	129.1	168.4	186.4	233.7	467.7
Developing countries	10.6	32.1	48.6	60.9	52.7	83.3	95.6	67.7

Source: UNCTAD, *World Investment Report*, 1999, pp. 483, 525–33.

especially so given the disproportionate weight of financial services-related factor income in aggregate service-export earnings, given that most of the former (for example, capital gains) do not contribute to GDP of the exporting nations. Nor do they have the same level of second-round multiplier effect as with other exports.

Net inflows of financial transfers for the non-oil developing countries, as indicated by the negative entries in column (5) of Table 3.3, have since 1997 been reversed, thus signifying *net outflows of financial and real flows from these countries*. This goes with the perceptible declines in the net merchandise deficits which has even turned positive by 1998. The developing countries, many of them large debtors, were paying out large sums as investment income payments on their past borrowings. Disregarding imports of these factor services (as are related to capital flows from abroad), the non-oil developing area as a whole emerged as net exporters of non-factor services, and net importers of merchandise in general. This can be observed from the respective entries in columns (6) and (2) of Table 3.3. The reversal in net financial and real transfers along with the merchandise balance since 1997 was a consequence of several factors. These include the rising investment income liabilities, the much reduced gross inflows of external finance and more crucially, the financial crisis in Asia and elsewhere, contributing not only to reduced external financial inflows but also to a dampening of import demand in the crisis affected region.

Observations as above can be used to arrive at the following generalisations:

- During the years between 1986 and 1990 and then again in 1999, *industrialised countries had been importing merchandise on a net basis. Hence, trade in merchandise has generally failed to contribute to domestic demand on a steady basis in the industrialised economies.*
- Net exports of services, which consist of both factor and non-factor services seem to have been substantial from these industrial countries. Evidently, it has been the *services sector which got a fillip from external trade in the industrial countries*, as can be judged by the data on net exports of services.
- However, a large part of these net service exports from the industrialised countries have been contributed by the net investment income from abroad with a large proportion retained as income earned abroad. These components, generating income in the financial

sector, are often treated as transfers (for example, capital gains) which do not contribute to GDP. The second round effect of these investment income inflows on the GDP has to be discounted for by leakages from the income stream as result from savings and imports out of such income. Analytical aspects of the latter are dealt with, later in this chapter, and in Appendix 3A.

- The above mentioned pattern of the current account for industrial countries gets reflected in the large share of rentier income (sum of interest, profits and property income) as a proportion of their GDP. In terms of a recent calculation,[9] rentier income share has been rising consistently over the last few decades in most countries of the OECD (Tables 3.5A and 3.5B). Thus for UK, which is still the citadel of financial capital, rentier income share (excluding capital gains and losses) rose, on an average, from 3.97 per cent during the 1960s to 14.16 per cent during the 1980s. If capital gains on transactions of financial assets are included, the share of rentier income was around 59 per cent of GDP during the 1980s as well as the 1990s. It is thus not unrealistic to conclude that the 'rentier effect' rather than 'trade effect', as defined earlier in Chapter 1, was the major contribution of international transactions (including capital flows) which prevailed in these countries.

- *As for the non-oil developing countries, trade has failed to fetch substantial transfers of financial and real resources from abroad.* This can be explained by the large investment income liabilities during the period, which reduced the CAD as could residually meet the merchandise deficits. Barring the more recent years, the developing region had been consistently importing goods on a net basis while continuing with net exports of non-factor services. Thus, we observe a distinct propensity, on the part of the developing countries, to import goods rather than non-factor services as far as the net capital flows made it possible. *This indicates the potential for these areas to provide global demand for merchandise, as and when the capital inflows net of investment income liabilities permit it.*

To dwell on the direction of international capital flows since the beginning of the 1990s, one observes a strengthening of the borrowing capacity for a handful of developing countries. Thus, governments as well as corporate borrowers in these countries have been able to raise funds, especially from the international bond market and even to

Table 3.5A Rentier income share (not including capital gains on financial assets) in GDP in some OECD countries, 1960–2000

Country	Years reported		Average decade share 1960s (percentage of GDP)		Average decade share 1970s (percentage of GDP)		Average decade share 1980s (percentage of GDP)		Average decade share 1990s (percentage of GDP)		Percentage change over the period 1960s/1970s and 1980s/1990s	
	Rentier income share	Non-financial sector profit share	Rentier income share	Non-financial sector profit share	Rentier income share	Non-financial sector profit share	Rentier income share	Non-financial sector profit share	Rentier income share	Non-financial sector profit share	Rentier income share	Non-financial sector profit share
Australia	1969–98	1969–95	6.67	12.66	7.92	8.10	14.50	5.24	12.97	7.91	76.55	–26.76
Austria	1987–99	1995–99	–	–	–	–	8.53	–	6.34	13.49	–	–
Belgium	1970–99	1970–99	–	–	11.69	11.66	21.81	12.92	21.28	14.66	84.36	18.30
Canada	1982–99	–	–	–	–	–	12.22	–	13.15	–	–	–
Czech Republic	1993–99	–	–	–	–	–	–	–	–0.64	–	–	–
Denmark	1970–99	1981–99	–	–	4.94	–	11.62	6.45	11.75	16.05	136.69	–
Finland	1960–2000	1960–2000	5.61	14.28	6.04	7.37	6.58	6.72	8.75	10.56	32.39	–.33
France	1970–99	1970–95	–	–	6.24	6.39	10.62	5.97	21.19	11.07	155.00	23.25

Country	Period										
Germany	1960–99	2.98	16.23	5.02	12.09	7.83	9.80	7.43	11.16	90.87	–26.02
Greece	1989–98	–	–	–	–	0.29	–	0.59	–	–	–
Hungary	1994–99	–	–	–	–	–	–	0.24	–	–	–
Iceland	1979–99	–	–	0.65	–	0.34	–	0.34	–	–47.11	–
Ireland	1995–98	–	–	–	–	–	–	2.72	–	–	–
Italy	1980–99	–	–	–	–	18.77	11.68	18.08	16.12	–	–
Japan	1960–99	9.00	11.96	12.30	9.02	14.27	9.91	11.22	8.25	19.69	–12.54
Korea	1960–98	–	–	4.70	7.32	8.63	7.93	–18.21	8.23	–201.90	9.90
Luxembourg	1975–95	–	–	6.14	6.14	6.43	6.43	12.41	12.41	53.31	53.31
Mexico	1979–99	–	–	–	–	1.52	–	6.74	23.92	–	–
Netherlands	1977–99	–	–	13.47	9.86	18.69	13.06	20.97	15.33	47.17	43.90
New Zealand	1990–99	–	–	–	–	–	–	7.71	–	–	–
Norway	1978–2000	–	–	6.03	10.74	10.45	12.44	9.56	15.20	65.60	29.31
Poland	1993–99	–	–	–	–	–	–	0.63	–	–	–
Portugal	1986–98	–	–	14.47	–	15.92	14.90	16.90	11.87	–	–
Spain	1985–99	–	–	13.61	–	12.53	8.70	13.21	9.22	–11.05	–
Sweden	1980–99	–	–	5.61	–	12.34	2.95	12.30	5.51	–9.47	–
Switzerland	1990–95	–	–	–	–	7.34	–	9.14	7.34	46.81	–
Turkey	1983–99	–	–	–	–	0.70	–	1.19	–	–	–
UK	1968–2000	3.97	14.82	6.33	13.45	10.85	15.83	14.16	15.95	112.13	16.19
US	1960–99	14.81	11.31	22.47	10.65	38.26	12.18	33.49	9.97	92.43	0.89

Source: Gerald Epstein, Dorothy Power, and Matthew Abrena, 'Recent Trends in Rentier Income in OECD Countries, 1960–2000' (mimeo), 2002.

Table 3.5B   Rentier income including capital gains on financial assets in some OECD countries

Country	Years reported	Decade average 1980s	Decade average 1990s	Percentage change over the period 1980s and 1990s
Australia	1989–98	35.02	33.81	–3.44
Austria	–	–	–	–
Belgium	1981–99	46.69	47.08	0.83
Canada	1982–98	34.16	34.66	1.46
Czech Republic	–	–	–	–
Denmark	1995–99	–	42.30	–
Finland	–	–	–	–
France	1981–97	37.73	26.53	–29.68
Germany	1981–96	22.51	25.86	14.87
Greece	–	–	–	–
Hungary	–	–	–	–
Iceland	–	–	–	–
Ireland	–	–	–	–
Italy	1992–99	–	39.69	–
Japan	1990–91	32.21	2.80	–91.32
Korea	1981–98	41.40	72.14	74.25
Luxembourg	–	–	–	–
Mexico	1989–99	–	98.95	–
Netherlands	–	–	–	–
New Zealand	–	–	–	–
Norway	1981–95	37.22	14.25	–61.71
Poland	–	–	–	–
Portugal	1996–98	–	48.77	–
Spain	1981–98	39.28	42.68	8.63
Sweden	1991–98	–	37.54	–
Switzerland	–	–	–	–
Turkey	–	–	–	–
UK	1981–97	48.96	46.24	–5.55
US	1981–99	58.94	59.19	0.43

Source: Gerald Epstein, Dorothy Power, and Matthew Abrena, 'Recent Trends in Rentier Income in OECD Countries, 1960–2000' (mimeo), 2002.

a restricted degree, from international banks (see Tables 3.1 and 3.2). The above, along with a drop in the real interest rates in the international credit market has led to a *revival of net financial inflows (transfers) to these select non-oil developing countries between 1991 and 1996*. Since 1997 however, the trend has reversed, with negative transfers of financial (and real) resources from SE Asia which got reflected in the statistics for the developing area as a whole (see Table 4.1). This happened with a combination of the declining gross inflows of capital and rising investment income liabilities on foreign debt and other investments. However, as it can be expected, the *distribution of net financial flows to the developing countries* as a whole (including the oil-exporting countries of West Asia) had been *rather uneven*, with West Asia and Latin America appropriating most of the inflows while Africa as a whole and other Asia experiencing negative financial (and real) transfers, especially after 1997. To be precise, Latin America started receiving financial transfers on a net basis only from 1992. A major factor behind this new wave of financial flows to Latin America was the restructuring of debt by the international financial community which started acting on the perception that very little of these sums could otherwise be recovered. Also some countries in Latin America received substantial inflows with the return of flight capital, which was based on a positive outlook relating to the economic performances of these economies.

As for the pattern of international capital flows which evolved since the mid-1980s, it reflected the changing portfolio decisions in countries with surplus finances. Thus, it was portfolio investments rather than bank lending which gained popularity, in countries with surplus savings during the period. In addition, the superior growth performance (relative to that in the industrial countries) made the developing countries relatively investment-worthy, especially for the institutional fund managers in these countries who were in control of vast amounts of household savings. Funds raised from the market, mostly as bond finance which have restored the positive net flows since the year 1990, were actually restricted to specific countries in Latin America. The scene, however, got a jolt with the Asian crisis of 1997 and the contagion effects later engulfing, in quick succession, some Asian countries (1997–99), Mexico (1994), Brazil and Russia (1998) and finally Argentina (2000–02).

Slow growth or stagnation of output as well as high rates of unemployment in the industrial countries seem to have continued over the past decade, as is indicated by an annual average of 1.1 per cent rate of output growth in the industrial areas during 1991–93. Performance of these economies has remained at a low ebb on average, with the exception of the US which of late has recovered to a moderate degree. Deregulated finance and fiscal-monetary tightening in the North were to a large extent instrumental in generating stagnation in the industrial countries which continued despite the boom in financial flows and the service-related sectors in these economies. The boom in services was most visible in the finance-related activities, as was to be expected from the wide-ranging deregulation in the financial sector and the integration of the international capital markets in the OECD (see also Table 3.5A for contribution of these services in GDP).

A rather anomalous picture, which conforms to the prevailing UN System of National Accounts (SNA), relates to the exclusion of the value-added services from the financial intermediation industry in final demand. This implies that a large part of the income originating in this booming sector remains unrecorded in national income statistics. While resolving these issues opens up serious methodological problems in the area of national accounts, the current practice probably has its own justification. This is in terms of separating out the transitory and speculatory financial gains and losses from final demand in terms of the capacity to generate output in an economy.

It is thus possible to explain the fact that the prevailing pattern of activities as well as capital flows in the international capital markets (with the major part remaining confined within the OECD), has failed to generate a proportionate flow of real activities and output in these economies. The explanatory factors, as pointed out earlier, include the heavy reliance of the industrial countries on financial services, much of the income originating from which (for example, with capital gains tax) remain outside the compass of national income calculations.

3.1.1 Monetarism in the North – the mainstream doctrines and the post-Keynesian critique

Attempts to control stagflation in the industrial countries initiated a regime of tight control over monetary and fiscal policies in the respective domestic economies which had been continuing over nearly two decades since the early 1970s. Stiff increases, in the rate of interest which resulted, were accepted, in terms of the received doctrines of monetarism, as an effective device to curb stagflation. Little, however, was the impact of these policies on financing of bank credit. This was because much of the credit demanded had its origin in speculatory financial activities which thrived with financial intermediation in deregulated markets.

On the whole, as it has been documented in Chapter 2, problems faced by the TNBs in third-world debt were largely resolved with active debt management policies on their part. This finally ended up both in reducing the third-world debt which was outstanding and also the flow of net credit to the developing countries.

Thus, debt management policies have often been guided by the interests of the most active partners in the debt process which include the private financial institutions in the lending countries. Even official agencies, both national and multilateral (which are largely dominated by the creditor governments), seem to have displayed a disproportionate concern to protect the dominant interest of finance. A major factor which worked behind such tendencies has been the reality that finance has for some time served as the main conduit of profit generation in the advanced economies. Efforts to avoid a collapse of the international banks have led the financial institutions and/or the regulatory authorities to refinance loans, to go for debt-equity swaps or for loan-loss provisioning. In none of these cases could new credit be advanced to the debtor nations since the gross credit advanced was actually compensating for the likely shortfalls in debt charges which were due from the borrowers. Possibilities of a pick-up in the volume of gross advances, at a scale which could ensure positive net flows at the end of meeting the debt charges, seemed to be rather remote, as can be confirmed from Table 1.4. Even the revival of credit flows with bond finance, especially for the borrowing countries in Latin America during the 1990s, has incurred much heavier debt burden because of the wider margin of spreads charged by the creditors.[10] Flows of FDI in the developing areas, which have drawn attention in the literature, have so far been inadequate to ensure a rise in the net flow of finance to most of the developing countries.

With the pattern of net financial flows as above, the supply-constrained developing countries have been forced to adjust downwards their real expenditure which in turn did restrain growth in these areas. The global implications of these adjustments have been adverse, not only for the developing countries but also for the industrialised countries which have lost, as a consequence, the opportunities of an expanding market in these areas. The dominance of finance in the world economy was thus manifest in the policies adopted to manage third-world debt, resulting in an widening gap between the performance of finance and the real sectors in the world economy.

In the advanced countries, policies concerning money and credit were influenced heavily by the received doctrines of monetarism, the central messages of which embodied the interest of finance in these economies. Characterised as 'Washington Consensus' in the literature, economic policy was geared to the liberalisation of financial markets, to achieve higher growth rates of output by means of efficiency gains. This allowed the rate of interest to be determined by market forces which, if higher, was expected to generate savings and thus additional investments as is implicit in terms of an 'enabling assumption'. Monetary policy was also targeted to achieve growth with price stability under financial opening.

Principles of monetarist doctrines have been qualified in the new Keynesian models which rely on asymmetric information and heterogeneity of bank assets. Postulating a set of perceived risks which are differentiated, these models seek to explain the widely prevalent phenomenon of credit rationing in the financial markets. Lendings, borrowings as well as acts of default or its absence are thus explained in these models as optimal decisions based on rational choices. All policies which tinker with the market – as for example, with deposit insurance or with the Central Bank actions as lenders of last resort – are disapproved in these models since these can cause moral hazard problems with distortions.[11] However, in reality such choices are often hard to be exercised uniformly by all agents in the market.

The mainstream neo-classical free-market paradigm as well as the new Keynesian analysis embodying the 'risk-adjusted rates of returns' have been questioned in the literature as improbable and unreal. The critics point out that neo-classical theory has failed to recognise the crucial role of factors like internal savings of corporates and the liquidity (credit) which is advanced on demand, for investment by the banking system as sources of finance. The latter involves liability management on the part of banks, which is lost sight of even by the New Keynesians. Liability management provides for the requisite elasticity of the credit system, thus reducing the effectiveness of monetary policy in controlling credit by regulating high powered money. Innovations in liability management allow banks to seek off-balance-sheet funding as well as loan commitments, an aspect which often leads to pro-cyclical variations in money and credit supply. With an access to liability management, especially with the whole-sale loan markets acting as provider as well as a repository of banks' discretionary funds, it was thus no longer necessary for banks to seek a cover under deposit insurance. Liability management by banks tends to create an endogenous source of financial crisis, especially at the peak of a cycle when debt becomes high in relation to equity. With the above possibilities, even monetary policy may act as a conduit for financial fragility, for example, when high interest rates affect genuine demand from less creditworthy but productive borrowers, while encouraging those who indulge in speculation. In contrast to the conventional approaches, a social construction of credit reveals its different use in an economy with financial volatility, much of which is linked to the high-risk speculatory ventures. While credit sets the liquidity constraint for growth, the sources of credit money in this alternative view are endogenous, and cannot be controlled by monetary policy. Ultimately, in a money economy, where 'money matters' (that is, money is never neutral), it is liquidity constraint and never an income (or savings) constraint that limits expansion before full employment. Urge to invest is thus not necessarily restrained by the high rate of investment. Thus, '... (finance) is best treated along with the animal spirits of the firms, as an element in the propensity to accumulate in the economy'.[12] Central Bank actions are thus clearly inadequate to control these sources of 'inside money' by using the standard tools of monetary control!

Analysis provided above can now be used to interpret the scenario relating to the flow of capital across nations, and especially, those between the advanced and the developing economies. As recorded in Table 3.1, the composition of global finance has gone through noticeable swings over the last two decades, with portfolio capital taking precedence over bank credit flows as well as the FDIs. Compared to other forms of capital flows, especially short-term portfolio capital, FDIs are considered desirable in terms of their potential for generating real activities. The argument of course, treats the FDI as entirely of the Greenfield variety, thus disregarding the sharp increases in the M&A types. We consider, in the next section, the implications of FDI flows as a channel of real transfers to host economies in the South and as an instrument for generating global growth by stimulating growth of output and demand in these capital-scarce economies.

3.2 On the implications of FDI flows – theory, history and policy

The ongoing wave of FDIs, from the industrialised North, has evoked mixed reactions from academics and policymakers in the home and host countries. Thus foreign investments, hitherto unquestioned, have of late been subject to criticisms from influential circles in capital-exporting countries, on grounds which include the job losses in the home countries. As alleged, these losses are typically suffered by unskilled workers who are employed in the production of labour-intensive manufactures in the host economies. The critics argue that exports of these products are facing stiff competition from cheaper varieties originating from suppliers relocated in the South.[13]

With FDI flows having their recent foray in the manufacturing sector of developing countries, a concern is there, both in literature and in public policy, about the implications of these flows for advanced economies. Thus, FDI abroad are held responsible for the onset of de-industrialisation in the home economy, inflicting losses in terms of jobs, output and export markets. Drawing attention to the strategic role of firms in determining a nation's export competitiveness, arguments are advanced for strategic trade, using market interventions by the state to bail out the domestic 'sunrise industries' in the export market. As opposed to this, there remain the critics who are concerned with the impact of FDI flows on host economies in the developing areas. As it has been argued by this school of thought, international distribution of gains from the FDI flows is subject to gross inequities and most of these gains are retained by the industrialised capital-exporting countries.

In the literature, one thus comes across positions which are polar opposites, with one school of thought championing the case for FDIs on grounds of global efficiency in production, as are achievable under Pareto-optimal market conditions. Success of FDI flows to instil higher growth rates is linked to the vital role played by the TNCs in terms of their access to finance, trade and technology across nations. Contesting this, opponents from *both* host and home countries question the merits of the FDI flows, on grounds which, however, are very different from each other. We would deal separately with these arguments later in this section.

Concerns in the North as are related advocate strategic trade and active industrial policy in these areas. These devices are considered useful to counter a process of de-industrialisation by strengthening, through protection of a non-tariff variety, the base of the 'high value' industries in home countries. The perceived conflicts between the microeconomic profit-maximising motive of the TNCs and the macroeconomic goals of output growth as well as employment in the North rely on the 'trade-diverting' impact of the FDI flows. The argument runs on a possible substitution effect which displaces industrialised country exports by cheap-labour manufactures from the developing economies. As held by these critics, FDI flows intensify the process by setting up TNC-subsidiaries in developing countries with cheap labour.

Arguments as above advanced in the North ignore, in our view, the 'trade-creating' effects of the FDI flows which may turn out to be expansionary in terms of North's output. As we would argue later, FDIs can create additional *demand* for exports from the capital-exporting country. With expansion in the recession-prone North constrained by demand, which at the moment is typical in the area, net exports of merchandise and non-factor services (by means of FDI-led demand originating in the capital-importing South) can have an expansionary impact in the North. However, since foreign investments abroad also generate a stream of investment income which lacks a counterpart in domestic output, one has to discount for the additional leakages in the income stream as are likely to result from these investment income inflows. Thus, the net expansionary effect of the FDI flows on output in the capital-exporting country would be proportionately less as compared to what might result from the trade-creating forces of a merchandise surplus. It should also not go unnoticed that FDI flows from countries have been instrumental to shift the terms of trade in their favour. This happens with tendencies, on the part of the TNCs, to rely on transfer pricing in intra-firm transactions, a tool commonly used in a vertical integration of the production process. A favourable turn in home country's terms of trade can induce growth in the demand-constrained capital-exporting countries with improvements in the merchandise surplus. Arguments as above can be supported in terms of a formal model which is provided in Appendix 3A at the end of this chapter.

Controversies as above make it important to look beyond, at a historical as well as an analytical level, and to analyse the implications of FDIs in terms of global growth. We delve into these aspects, starting with the early historical debates on overseas investments. This is followed by a survey of the contextual concerns as are currently relevant. Finally, the formal outline provided in Appendix 3A projects the short-run macroeconomic implications of the FDI flows for the home and host economies.

3.2.1   International capital flows in theories of imperialism

Early discourses on international investments can be traced back to late nineteenth century when flows of financial capital across nations had just begun gaining ground, for the first time in history, along with flows of commodities and gold. With the rise of banks and stock exchanges in the industrially advanced countries, a stage was set by this time for an unprecedented scale of international capital flows which later was interrupted with the onset of the First World War. Capital exports occupy a centre stage in what later came to be known as theories of imperialism. In terms of these theories, capital flows were the responses to difficulties experienced by advanced capitalist countries in finding investment opportunities in the domestic economy.[14]

A major difference, however, was there between alternate positions held on capital exports even in the theories of imperialism, especially when it concerned the possible impact on finance and industry in the capital-exporting countries. A fusion between domestic industry and finance was paramount in Lenin's account of imperialism in which capital exports were expected to fetch benefits, *both* for domestic industry as well as finance, especially as long as domestic industry remained competitive in external markets. In contrast, for Hilferding, the main proponent of 'finance capital', the extra-territorial identity of finance seemed to dominate domestic industry (and hence the nation state as a whole). The nationalism question however, soon became a rather contentious issue in debates amongst the contemporaries which included Rosa-Luxembourg.[15] The arguments have a parallel in voices currently raised, both in the advanced and in developing countries, against FDIs, on grounds of economic nationalism.

Commenting further on finance-industry links and their implications in terms of capital exports in the early theories of imperialism, links between the real and the financial sphere of economies had reasons to be relatively close around the time when these theories were originally advanced, compared to what it is today with the fragility of finance. This is also consistent with a clubbing together, in these early writings on imperialism between direct foreign investments and the portfolio types, despite the fact that overseas investment by this time was no longer confined to (direct) investments alone. Instead, portfolio finance, the newly acquired financial instrument of banks and joint-stock companies was quite often used for bond financing along with direct equity investments.

A failure to identify the institutional forms of capital exports probably also explain the differences between Lenin and Hilferding on the implications of capital exports for these advanced economies. While Lenin's model of imperialism and his observations there-in were very close to a Germanic model of bank–industry combine, Hilferding had in mind the role performed by stock markets of England and France as channels of overseas investments. It was thus logical for Hilferding to visualise scenarios where the finance motive was dominant. Capital exported overseas in such cases did not necessarily contribute to industrial growth in the country of its origin. Competition amongst capital-exporting countries to capture export markets for their home industry remained the central theme in Lenin's account of inter-imperialist rivalry among capitalist nations – an issue which seems to have surfaced again, in the current concerns in the North, over the impact of FDI flows in terms of their export-competiveness. Little attention, however, was paid in the classical literature on imperialism, to capital-importing countries in the periphery, which reflects an Eurocentric bias.[16]

3.2.2 Current concerns over FDI

Much has happened between the pre-war era of high finance and the current phase of history which has witnessed a varied and much larger flows of international capital. Volatility of portfolio finance has been responded, at level of policy, by proposals which range between a tax on windfall profits on currency conversions like 'Tobin tax' and safeguards to ensure a level playing field for direct investments as put forth by the OECD. As for the second, it is possible to identify *two* distinct positions on FDIs which are spelt out below:

- First, there prevails the euphoria that FDI always promotes effi-cient resource allocation on a global scale, especially when restrictions on trade and payments are minimised. The argument relies on the neo-classical free market paradigm as its starting point. For allocative efficiency to come about, it is accordingly of paramount significance that there has to be the requisite space for free international investments. Views as above had gained credence, in the liberalisation decade of the 1990s, and are supported by the story of FDI-led growth behind the 'Asian Miracle' of the 1980s.[17] An urge to replicate the 'miracle' led the World Bank and other multilateral financing institutions to press for a quickening of the pace of liberalisation in other developing countries. Currently, the WTO is engaged in pushing a multilateral investment guarantee scheme which, as claimed by its proponents in the European Commission and other groups of advanced economies, would ensure a level playing field for foreign investors, against the prevailing discrimination in host countries.[18]
- Contrasting the picture of global harmony, concerns are expressed over the FDIs, both from the capital-exporting North as well as from the capital-importing South. Issues questioning the impact of these flows on the host and home economies thus open up an area of mayhem, with contending pleas from the host as well as the home economies to regulate the FDI flows in their respective national interest. Challenging the faith in a regime of unbridled trade and investment flows, the critics question the universality of the virtuous cycle of growth and prosperity. This is opposed to what is claimed in terms of the unquestioned virtues of the FDI flows. Paradoxically enough, the two positions, while polar opposites of each other in terms of their specific con-tention against the free flow of FDIs, converge in terms of their mutual concern for the respective national economy. While the opponents from the North attack the FDI and the related trade flows as being responsible for de-industrialisation in their domestic economies, a parallel voice of concern from the South stresses the point that these flows of FDIs are in fact detrimental to their

economic sovereignity as well as development. One witnesses, in these critiques, a revival of economic nationalism. Economic nationalism has thus been a response to the forces unleashed by a liberal global economic order, with implications for policy which however takes different routes depending on whether it champions the case for the developed or the developing nations.

One can identify, in above positions, two distinct world-views on FDI flows. The first is a picture of harmony, one where these flows exist for the global good. The other one manifests a cynicism as well as a concern, regarding the flow of FDIs and their impact. As pointed out above, the voices of dissent from both North and the South arise from a sense of strong economic nationalism, which of late has seen a revival and official sanction. This is rather paradoxical, especially in the industrialised countries of the North, which in principle continue to champion the case of free trade and investment at international fora.

3.2.3 More on FDI opponents in North

For opponents of FDIs in the capital-exporting countries of the North, these flows of overseas investments are held responsible for the loss of output, jobs and export markets in their domestic economy. Thus, the flow of investments overseas is viewed as a 'relocation' of (rather than addition to) global investments. Accordingly, the new pattern of trade as results from these FDI flows is considered to be demand displacing in terms of the goods produced by the home country. Thus, tendencies on the part of the transnationals to invest abroad, especially in the cheap labour economies of the South, are strongly disapproved by an influential lobby in the North today, linking these up to the ongoing processes of de-industrialisation in the home economies. As a sequel, there is a tendency in economic literature and policy today to rely on what is described as a 'strategic trade', a tool for achieving export competitiveness. Thus, Lester Thurow's 'The Zero Sum Society' (1980) offered, to the USA, 'a vision of how to fix America's problems – by shifting resources from "sunset" to "sunrise" industries'.[19] The arguments were strengthened in Robert Reich's popular writings urging the US to support its 'high value industries' and to upgrade technology in the traditional sectors. Think tanks in Harvard Business School and at the Berkelay Round-table approved of aggressive industrial policy while the media

'... kept up a steady drumbeat of concern about the issue of US competitiveness throughout the 1980s'.[20] It took, however, a considerable length of time before the Democratic party in the US officially
accepted, under Clinton administration, the 'industrial policy' idea in
terms of the strategic trade theory.[21] Outside the government, political
stalwarts like Ross Perot continued to warn about the job movements
to Mexico under NAFTA. Flows of FDIs to the South were openly
attacked in Europe as the EU also decried the rise of manufacturing
production and trade in the low wage countries of the South which,
in its view, had a competitive edge over products from the high wage
industrialised countries.[22]

Tracing back the conceptual background of above arguments, the
early technology gap – Product Life cycle (PLC)[23] models of the 1970s
hinted that technological advantage enjoyed by the hi-tech high-
export sector in the most advanced economy was likely to erode over
time. This was expected since new products were imitated by other
advanced countries and eventually standardised at plants set up
overseas with the help of the TNC subsidiaries. It was thus possible
to predict a decline, over time, in the flow of merchandise exports
from the capital-exporting countries and substituted by FDI flows
from industrialised countries. Explanations offered in the literature
on the 'flying geese' paradigm highlighted the sequential links
between trade and direct investment flows between the North and
the South.[24,25]

In terms of the above view, a paradigm shift has taken place in the
production structure of the capital-importing countries of the South,
which threatens North's industries. The latter relates both to the
labour-intensive products from the South and also to the skill- and
capital-intensive products which were hitherto monopolised by the
North. Thus, the comparative advantages of investments (which
initially arose from the strong linkage effects) within the North are
no longer sustainable over time, especially with transport costs as
well as the costs of accessing information steadily falling with new
technology. Also, the widening wage differentials continue to reduce
the relative costs of manufacturing in the South. However, it is
expected that the relocation drive could eventually favour the North as
wages start catching up in the fast growing economies of the South.[26]

Concerns expressed in the North over the deleterious effects of FDI
flows to South on North's exports have been further strengthened by

the observed 'skill mismatch' in these areas. In terms of this argument, workers displaced in the North (as a consequence of competition from the Southern products) typically include the unskilled or semi-skilled, an outcome which adds to the excess supply of the low skill workers in these countries.[27] Aspects as above make it important that the North continues to maintain its relative advances in technology and exports, if necessary by using strategic trade and investment policies, which openly deviate from principles of free international trade and investments.

A concern as above in the North on the role of FDIs in relation to the national economy is similar to the notion of inter-imperialist rivalry in earlier literature. However, the current debates focus more on the possible rivalries between transnational firms rather than across nations, especially with the domain of the transnational firm transcending those of nations. One can here analyse the identity of the TNCs, which remain the channels for the FDI flows. Thus, the transnational firms can shed off the colour of their national origin, especially when they are powerful enough in relation to the host country governments. As argued in some quarters, the Ricardian paradigm of comparative advantages among nations needs to be replaced today by an alternative paradigm where a nation's competitive strength is determined not only by its own exports but also by the performance of its subsidiary firms located abroad. Accordingly '...the traditional foundations of industrial policy – to support national companies – is no longer relevant: what is good for General Motors in France is as good for the French economy as what is good for Renault'.[28] Recognising the dominant position of the TNCs, all nation states are even advised to accept, for global good, the global strategy of the multinationals on world trade and investments. Views as above even question the prudence of strategic industrial and trade policies of the North and also any attempts on the part of the South to contest the terms set by the multinationals.[29]

Voices raised in the North against FDI outflows, especially to the industrialising areas in the South, have prompted the use of subsidies and dumping as policies to sustain exports from the North. At the level of theory, these policies are backed by the principles of strategic trade. With oligopolistic firms controlling major trade shares in the global market, the final impact of FDI flows on the host and home economies is sometimes interpreted in terms of strategic trade behaviour, not just on the part of the TNCs but also by the home as well as the host governments.

The host country, however, is often at a disadvantage in terms of bargaining power.[30] Use of export subsidies (and its substitute, the dumping of exportables in foreign markets) is thus related to the ability of firms to discriminate between markets. This is done by charging relatively higher prices in the domestic market where it wields monopoly power. It has been pointed out that in terms of a partial equilibrium framework, the optimum level of subsidy (at which a domestic firm's level of profits is at its maximum) is inversely related to the numerical value of the price elasticity of foreign demand for exportables. The optimum level of subsidy is thus expected to move up, as demand abroad is more elastic, thus allowing the firm to generate more revenue through price cuts.[31] Strategic behaviour also has a role to play in setting the terms at which the TNCs finally choose to operate in the host economies.[32] While the use of subsidies has been recommended in this literature as a means to encourage aggressive export strategy by TNC subsidiaries which face competition abroad, firms in reality are capable of using a similar strategy even in the absence of subsidies. Transnational firms also use 'transfer pricing' to operate along the vertically integrated international network of their own firm-level organisations, thus bypassing the market channels. Such practices include the use of dual pricing across countries. This has been characterised as an 'internalisation' process, with firms reducing transaction costs by making use of the non-market channels *within* the organisation.[33] It is not difficult to see that since the foreign-controlled firms normally have an edge over the local firms and the host country governments in terms of bargaining strength, the resulting exchanges tend to be unequal. On the whole, gains from international trade and investments as arise from the functioning of the TNCs in the host economies thus tend to be unequal, with the major share accruing to the more powerful.

It is also observed that inflows of FDIs to developing countries have sometimes been responsible for terms of trade losses to these countries, the major part of which originates in the manufacture–manufacture trade. This aspect of North–South trade has been highlighted in several recent studies.[34] Attention has also been drawn to the simultaneous drop in the double factoral terms of trade, which indicates a relative decline in labour productivity, valued at product prices fetched by the same group of countries in international trade.[35]

None of the above observations, however, offers a convincing explanation of the forces behind these tendencies. To explain the slide in the manufacture–manufacture terms of trade as are faced by the developing countries, one also needs to go back to the firm-level behaviour of the TNCs, which, as already pointed out above, demonstrate a tendency to practice price discrimination across international markets. Firms are thus inclined to use what has been described in the literature as 'internalisation',[36] a process that in effect avoids using market channels. Internalisation covers, in addition to subcontracting of semi-finished products, cross-border flows of finance, technology and managerial skill. It often proves cost-effective to limit these transactions within the firm, a practice that may be responsible for a lowering of the prices of manufactured products exported by the TNC subsidiaries located in the developing economies. Thus, price-discrimination, which is a part of the 'internalisation process', provides explanations of the recent experiences of the manufacture-exporting countries in terms of declines in their net barter terms of trade.

Arguments in the North on grounds of job losses and so on ignore, in our view, the 'trade-creating' effects of the FDI flows which may have an expansionary effect on the home country's output. It can be argued that FDIs can generate demand for output in the capital-exporting country. When expansion in the North is constrained by demand which currently is the case, increased exports of merchandise and non-factor services, with additional demand originating in the capital-importing countries of the South, would generate an expansionary effect for the North. However, as mentioned earlier foreign investment-income inflows generate a stream of investment-income inflows as well, which lacks a counterpart in terms of domestic output.[37] Operations of foreign-controlled firms add to the external liabilities of the host country to meet royalties, dividends, technicians' fees and so on, to the home country. And the outcome is an inflow of investment income. As pointed out in Chapter 1, these may make it difficult for the home country to sustain net outflows of capital, which support demand in recession-prone economies. Income inflows from past investments abroad also generate leakages in the form of additional savings and imports which reduce the income effect of additional exports, if any. We have dwelt on these aspects in Appendix 3A at the end of this chapter. As pointed out, one has to recognise the leakages in the income stream that result from these income inflows. Thus, the net expansionary impact of the FDI inflows on the capital-exporting country would be relatively less as compared to what might result from the trade-creating effects alone.

We already have drawn attention to the fact that FDI flows have often been instrumental to turn the terms of trade in favour of the home countries. This happens, via intra-firm transactions, using transfer pricing, a tool commonly in use with vertical integration of the production process. Improvements in home country's terms of trade, brought about by the FDI flows, can then contribute to output growth in the demand-constrained capital-exporting countries by augmenting the merchandise surplus. Arguments as above can be formulated in terms of the model provided in Appendix 3A at the end of this chapter.

3.2.4   The voice of the South

Recognising the inequities, which are inherent in the international division of labour, the New Left in the US and elsewhere has pointed at the possibilities of 'uneven development'[38] and the 'underdevelopment' of the periphery.[39] However, the classical notion of uneven development as is caused by concentration of investment in metropolitan areas (with a division of the world into advanced industrial and backward primary producing territories) is today a thing of the past. Exporting manufactures and receiving substantial inflows of capital (including the FDIs from abroad), a large number of developing countries today have reached the status of semi-industrialised middle income nations.

Sceptics however have continued to question the universality of the virtuous cycles of FDI-led growth, especially as far as the developing economies are concerned. Fearing an infringement of national sovereignty, particularly with the entry of powerful foreign firms into the domestic economy, the critics point at the perilous consequences. This in particular is related to the displacing of domestic firms by foreign ones, with contingent external liabilities in way of imports and income payments. In terms of this view, FDI inflows can have a harmful effect on the balance of payments as well as on the growth of output and employment in the host economies. Sentiments as above run high in political debates between the conservatives and the radicals in the South on the entry of multinationals to the developing countries.[40]

Arguments, about the worth or otherwise of FDI flows in generating growth in the world economy remain inconclusive in absence of an assessment in terms of the current realities. As a sample observation, we can cite the findings in a recent UNCTAD report on FDI and its implications. It reports the rather small contribution of the foreign-controlled firms on the trade balance of the host economies. While for China, Hong kong and Malaysia, exports by the affiliates were respectively at 40.9 per cent (1997), 35.4 per cent (1997) and 51 per cent (1994) of their aggregate, the performance looks less striking when one compares the *net* trade balance of affiliates, which is negatively affected by the high import content. Thus, for China, the foreign affiliates maintained a negative trade balance of (–) $2.82 billion in 1997. The negative balance moved up to (–) $4.86 billion for 1991. For Mexico also, the trade balance contributed by the affiliates was a negative sum of (–) $6.90 billion in 1993. However for Brazil, Malaysia and Taiwan, the positive trade balance of the affiliates contributed to improve their overall trade balance, which was negative. Looking at other dimensions of FDI flows, primarily as repatriated earnings from the host countries which are retained in the developing area, the ratio of these remittances to total FDI inflows averaged 31.3 per cent over 1986–89, as reported in the same study. Thus, while paucity of data prevents a generalisation, it remains true that these firms, especially with their high import content, large remittances of profits, royalties and so on, did not necessarily improve the BOP of the host economies.[41]

As mentioned earlier, the global pattern of FDI flows has changed drastically in recent years, with M&A type of flows taking precedence over the Greenfield varieties. On an average, the share of the take-over purchases by firms in the North had been as large as 73.09 per cent of aggregate FDI outflows from the region during 1993–98. As for the inflows, M&As had a 29.3 per cent share of aggregate FDI inflows to the region over the same period.[42]

It however, remains true that among the developing economies, the high growth economies were also the largest recipients of inflows of FDI, especially as compared to the low growth host economies. In other words, host economies, which received heavy inflows of FDI, were also growing faster. The share of those external inflows, however, has been rather small as a proportion of the aggregate investments in these areas in recent times. In most countries, the share of FDI in aggregate investment had been less than 10 per cent on an average during 1991–97. As for their impact on domestic investment, only a handful of countries in the developing area experienced a 'crowding-in' effect during 1970–96. The rest had a 'crowding-out' or at best a neutral effect over the same period.[43] Treating FDI as a dependent variable, the changes in which are explained by growth rates of GDP in host countries, with one or two-year lags for the period 1970–96, the results turn out to be significant only for developing countries in East, South and the SE Asian region. Otherwise, for most other countries, FDI flows can be treated as an exogenous variable.[44] Evidently, the high growth in these regions worked as a pull factor in terms of the FDI flows. From above, it can be argued that the high domestic growth rates in some developing countries provided incentives to foreign investments, not only as export platforms but also as large potentials of domestic markets.[45]

Much of what has been pointed out in this section contest the conventional wisdom in terms of an unquestioned faith in the global benefits from FDI flows. There also are reasons to dispel judgements against FDIs which are conceptually unfounded, both in outright condemnations of or uncritical persuasions for FDI. Much of the current debate, however, hinges on the firm-level microeconomic aspects of FDI impact, thus neglecting the macroeconomic implications of these flows on the home and host countries.

To complete the analysis, we now turn to the macroeconomic significance of these flows, which are worth examining, especially in terms of the analytical content of these arguments, which follows.

3.2.5   The macroeconomic effect of FDI flows in the short run

The short-run macroeconomic impact of FDI flows on output in home and host economies can be analytically traced at *two* levels: first, in terms of their direct impact on balance of payments of the respective economies; and second, in terms of the effects on investment and output, which include both the direct and the indirect (or second round) impact of these flows.

As it has been mentioned above, with FDIs operating through the parent–subsidiary network of firms set up as TNCs, flows of intra-firm trade have of late assumed a much greater degree of significance than it used to be earlier. It is the growth of intra-firm trade that is primarily responsible for what can be described as the 'trade effect' of these flows on the home and host countries. This happens, first, with the relatively higher trade propensity of the multinational firms operating in the host countries, and second, with non-market transactions between parent and subsidiary firms which are vertically integrated. The first of these two effects is visible in the trade balance of the TNC subsidiaries operating in the host countries, some estimates of which have been provided earlier in this section.

Transactions, both at the intra-industry and inter-firm levels, are often conducted at internalised transfer prices. As pointed out earlier, these transactions may have a tendency to adversely affect the terms of trade of the host countries. The adverse impact of those losses, if any, on the trade balance of the host country often tends to be compounded by propensities, on the part of the TNC firms, to have a higher import-intensity (which, as mentioned above, includes both intra- and inter-firm trade). As a consequence, there results a higher trade deficit with a demonstrated tendency on the part of the TNC subsidiaries to have import intensity, which is higher than those for the domestic firms are. Damaging effects, if any, as are inflicted by FDI flows on the BOP of the host country, are expected to have an exactly opposite effect on home country's BOP which is bound to be favourable.

There also remain other macroeconomic effects that include the demand-displacing effects of FDIs on home country's output. With the higher import intensity of foreign firms and their crowding-out effect on firms of domestic origin, it is relatively difficult to figure out the overall effect for the domestic economy, in particular, in the absence of detailed empirical analysis.

Commenting on the first round effect of the FDI flows on BOP of the host and the home country, the effects are bound to be in opposite directions, since the trade surpluses as well as the additional investment income generated by FDIs for the home country are matched by trade deficits and added investment income liabilities for the host country. As for the second round consequential effect of these changes on output, the impact of the trade surplus in the home country will be expansionary for its output as long as capacity remains under-utilised in the economy. As mentioned earlier, account has also to be taken of the leakage from these investment income inflows in the form of savings and imports which do not contribute to domestic output in the home country.

The above-mentioned repercussions of the FDI flows on home country's output can be further reinforced/counteracted by changes in demand in the host economy. The outcome would depend on whether the latter experienced a worsened or improved trade balance as a consequence of these flows. A positive reinforcing effect would come about if the additional capacity created by the TNC firms in the host country, matched by additional demand for its products, generates export demand for the North.

TNC investments with FDI flows can also have direct supply-creating effects in the host economy. However, the impact may be stalled when the export drive of the transnational firms causes intersectoral transfers within the economy, which result in net declines in aggregate investment therein.[46] We have provided, in Appendix 3A, a formal model, which supports the arguments in this section.

3.3   Assessing the overall impact of financial flows on the real economy

This chapter has made an attempt to gauge the impact of international capital flows on the capital-exporting and -importing nations. The observed volatility in the financial flows made us look afresh into the implications, especially from the angle of its growth-generating capacity on a sustainable basis. This led us to consider the Greenfield FDI flows as the potential source of real growth, not only in the host countries but also in the home economies. Thus, advanced nations which are demand deficient can benefit from these flows only when the trade-creating effects of these flows are strong, both with capacity created and output generated in the capital-importing countries. However, the expansionary effects of positive trade effects in home economies are beset with the leakage in the income stream, in terms of savings and imports out of the additional income. These will tend to be higher as the rentier-effect predominates the trade-effects if any (see Tables 3.5A and 3.5B for OECD statistics). Arguments as above on the macroeconomic implications have also been spelt out in Appendix 3A.

On the whole, links between financial flows and the real economy are not as simple or direct, as it may seem. The arguments and analysis provided above reflect the changing scenario, both with the dominance of finance in the advanced economies and the new paradigm of political and economic premises as are appropriate to what has been described as 'finance international'.

We now turn to the possible impact of FDI flows on output in the home and host countries. As mentioned above, these can be related to the 'trade-effect' (that is, the change in trade balance for either country) and also the 'rentier-effect' (the related leakages from income stream of the home country due to the additional savings as well as imports as are generated from FDI-related investment income inflows to the home country). As has been argued earlier (and also in terms of the model in Appendix 3A), the net expansionary impact will depend not only on whether the trade effect of FDI is positive but also if the related improvements in investment income do not turn out to be *contractionary* in terms of the leakages of savings and imports generated therefrom. The outcome is as results from the opposite effects of the trade and investment income-related flows. Expansions of 'rentier income' from FDI flows is thus beset with problems in a demand-constrained country which exports capital, opening up problems which can only be offset by the added impetus to domestic investment as are simultaneously provided by the trade-effects of the FDI flows. To be positive on a net basis, the 'trade-effect' of the FDI flows on North's GDP should be able to compensate for the leakages as are due to the higher savings and imports arising from the investment income inflows from these flows. The positive 'trade-effect' of the FDI flows for North can further improve by the favourable terms of trade effects, if any, of these flows.

Empirical observations on the 'trade-effect' of the FDIs are possible to calculate by looking at the trade propensity of the foreign affiliates of TNCs as compared to the average trade propensity in the respective host country. This, if positive, can have an expansionary impact on GDP in the home country. The 'trade-effect' of FDI flows in the home country's GDP has been estimated in studies which are available by calculating the trade intensity of the TNC subsidiaries in the host economies. According to estimates of the UNCTAD, foreign affiliates have been responsible for a large part of export sales from the host countries in the mid-1990s. One of the largest contributions to exports came from the foreign affiliates of Singapore, with their share exceeding 60 per cent of total exports from Singapore since the mid-1980s. Similarly, the export share of Malaysia and China was at 51 and 41 per cent respectively during 1994 and 1997. In general, in most of the emerging economies, the foreign firms were responsible for a significant part of their export business.

However, those firms were also large importers, a fact which was responsible for their *negative* contribution to trade balance in some of these countries, as mentioned above. Thus for China and Mexico the above was true. This can be witnessed in the consistently high shares of the subsidiary firms in total imports of these countries. Import share of the foreign-controlled firms was 49 per cent in China in 1997, 26 per cent in Malaysia in 1994 and 23 per cent each in Brazil and Mexico respectively in the years 1997 and 1993. The impact turned down as negative in terms of the trade balance for the subsidiary firms for China at (−) $4.8 billion and $2.8 billion in 1991 and 1997. For Mexico, the trade balance for these firms was also negative at (−) $2.96 billion in 1990 and $6.90 billion in 1993. While the negative trade balance of the FDI-controlled firms implied a corresponding foreign exchange loss and a leakage from the output generation process for the host countries, the opposite happens with equivalent trade surpluses for the rest of the world which often consists of the home countries of FDI flows. However, the empirical studies as are available do not suggest any definite pattern in terms of the net trade effect of the subsidiaries operating in the host countries. It is thus difficult to arrive at a conclusive argument on the trade effect of FDI operations for the home or the host economies.[47]

As for the home countries, the trade effect, even when positive, needs to swamp the negative effects of the leakages related to the rentier effect of additional investment income inflows. There are estimates of repatriated earnings on FDI flows. These are the investment income flows corresponding to FDI flows from the home countries. Estimates by the UNCTAD for the years between 1991 and 1997 are available. It is found that for the developing countries, the repatriated earnings on an average comprised almost one-third of the FDI inflows over 1991–97. (Of the different regions, Africa once again leads with the share of these earnings at three-fourth of FDI inflows.) The sum of repatriated earnings from the host countries in the region provides the sources of investment income to the home countries which are mostly the developed countries. Investment income inflows from FDI flows within the industrial area is also substantial at 40.9 per cent of FDI within the area.[48] Facts as above open up, once again, the issue of the 'rentier effect' of FDI flows and their impact on output in the demand-constrained home economies.

Empirical studies on the impact of FDI inflows on investments in the host countries can be considered in terms of a crowding in (CI) and crowding out (CO) effect. Looking at the empirical observations as are available, for the years between 1976 and 1985 as a whole CI was strong in Africa. However, it tapered off to a weak CI by 1986–96. In Latin America, the impact has been consistently of a CO pattern, which however has weakened between the two periods. Most of Asia showed strong CI effects in both sub-periods, while in West Asia the impact has changed from CI to CO.[49] The mixed results relating to the impact of FDI as a catalytic agent which has strong CI effects make it relevant to test whether FDI should be treated as an exogenous or an endogenous variable in the host economies. A test, conducted in the same study[50] reveals that domestic growth rates do not explain the flows of FDI, thus rejecting the hypothesis that it can be treated as an endogenously determined variable. However, for SE Asia, the results are different when the lagged values of FDI flows are also included (along with lagged values of GDP growth) as determining variables. We interpret the observation as an indirect evidence that capital inflows, and especially those which are on a long-term basis, have a tendency to follow a trodden path. Accordingly, these tend to respond favourably once the critical minimum flows have been forthcoming to the host economy. On the whole, FDI inflows seem to operate as an exogenously determined variable in the host economies, thus making it a function of the externally determined economic environment.

Despite the mixed outcome, the end result makes for a case for a flow of finance, in particular of FDIs, from North to South. This is especially true as one considers the relative stability in the observed flows of FDIs as compared to other forms of capital flows, and especially, the portfolio.[51]

FDI flows as reported, include, in addition to those which are of the Greenfield variety, the flows to finance M&As which have been increasing as a proportion of the total FDI flows. To net out, one needs to deduct the latter from the aggregate flows, especially because the implications are very different in terms of the impact on both host and especially the home countries.

As mentioned earlier, critics of FDI outflows from the advanced countries often point at the job-losses in these economies from the relocation of manufacturing processes to host economies. In our judgement, they fail to notice the demand generating potential of these flows for the capital-exporting country. Indeed, a situation may arise when the related investment-income flows enjoyed by the rentiers in the home countries dampen aggregate demand in its domestic economy, largely due to the related expansions in savings and imports. The above observation indicates the need to monitor the impact of direct investments, especially in terms of their impact on aggregate demand in the capital-exporting nations with their ongoing tendencies for recession. The opposite influence of the 'trade' and the 'rentier' effects of FDI flows in terms of demand in the capital-exporting countries typically reflect the conflicts between industry and finance in the advanced capitalist countries. However, there remain other areas of FDI operations, especially with the pricing by the TNC firms and the resulting terms of trade losses for the capital-importing countries, which do not deliver gains from FDIs to countries on an equal basis. Aspects as above need to draw attention, in academic debates as well as in public policy, while discarding the prevailing preoccupation with the 'skill-mismatch' lobby for new protectionism in the industrialised countries of the North.

Appendix 3A

A model of North–South flows in FDI

Of late, output in the North has been predominantly demand constrained. This is explained by the current recessionary trends in the industrialised economies, where demand shortfall operates as the major explanation for the observed unutilised capacity. In South, import-dependence has been growing over time, both with the direct influence of the TNC-controlled firms to rely on import-intensive technology and with the ongoing process of import-liberalisation in these countries. Capacity expansion and utilisation in specific sectors of these economies are often constrained by the foreign exchange bottleneck. Observations as these justify the assumption as in the model below, of a demand-constrained North and a supply-constrained South.

An analysis of the macroeconomic impact of FDI flows on the domestic economy demands a specification of the factors, which affect its growth. We have assumed that output growth in the capital-exporting countries is constrained by demand, while for the capital-importing countries such growth faces the limits set by supply.[52] The assumptions are consistent with the ongoing tendencies in the global economy. We assume, for simplicity, that the industrial region, which exports capital (henceforth North) consists of a single country. Similarly, the capital-importing region (henceforth South) is treated as a single unit. In either part of the world, the level of output Y is determined at $Y = Y_{min}$ (Y^s, Y^d) where Y^s and Y^d stand for the respective levels of GDP which are constrained by supply and demand. In the North, where $Y^d < Y^s$ FDI flows contribute to domestic output by generating *demand*, while in South these flows help to release *supply* to raise output, since $Y^s < Y^d$.

Let us start with the components of North's GDP (Y), measured in units of North's output, which are both consumed domestically and exported abroad. North's GNP can be found by adding net investment income flows (Z) to its GDP.

Thus

$$Y + Z = C(Y, Z) + I(Y, Z) + X(Y', F, p_x) - pM(Y, Z, p_m) \qquad (3A.1)$$

where consumption (C), investments (I), exports (X), imports (M), net capital flows from North (F) and net investment income (Z) are all measured in units of North's output. Both consumption and investments are positively linked to GNP which is the sum of its GDP and investment income.

GDP in South (Y') and its exports (which are imports for North) (M) are both recorded in units of South's output. Prices in North, of exports and imports are respectively expressed, in a common currency, as p_x and p_m. Defining 'p' as p_m/p_x or the terms of trade for the South, imports of North in units of its own output can be found by multiplying the volume of imports, measured in units of South's output, by 'p'. For simplification, we assume that p is initially at unity. This also implies that $p_x = p_m$.

In Equation (3A.1), there is an implicit assumption that exports from North (X) are *positively* linked to the size of net capital flows (F) from the country. This follows the logic as well as the observed fact that TNCs operating abroad help to increase the home country's exports to the host economy. Thus, F is assumed to consist of FDI flows alone which are capable of generating a positive 'trade effect' in North. The positive impact works on output via net exports from the country. However, flows of FDI also generate investment income (Z) that can cast a dampening influence on North's output, by generating leakage from the income stream in the form of savings and imports. These repercussions can be classified as the 'rentier effect' of FDIs in the home country, generating income against past investments. Aspects as above of FDI flows are usually left unnoticed in the literature.[53]

In Equation (3A.1), we also have introduced the standard consumption and investment functions both of which depend on the changes in the GNP, which include net factor earnings/payments. Investment is subject to the standard acceleration principle with changes in GNP affecting, via consumption, the demand for investments.

As in the capital-exporting North, the South is also likely to experience the impact of FDI inflows on its own output, which, in terms of our assumption, is supply, constrained. We assume, for simplicity, that the level of South's GDP (Y'), as reported in Equation (3A.1), incorporates these supply-augmenting effects of FDI on the latter.

Let us now make an attempt to assess the impact of FDI flows on North's GDP. Of the two routes by which FDI flows seem to influence North's GDP, a positive effect would entail from the 'trade-creating effect' while there can be a negative repercussion via the 'rentier effect' which originates from the investment income inflows.

We get, from Equation (3A.1), the following expression by using total differentials, and using subscripts to indicate the partials of the respective functions,

$$dY + dZ = C_y dY + C_z dZ + I_y dY + I_z dZ + X_{y'} dY' + X_F dF$$
$$+ X_{px} dp_x - M_y dY - M_z dZ - M_{pm} dp_m - M dp \qquad (3A.2)$$

where all the partials, other than X_{px} and M_{pm}, are positive.

Rearranging

$$dY(1 - C_y - I_y + M_y) = dZ(I_z - M_z + C_z - 1) + X_{y'}dY' - Mdp$$
$$+ (X_{px}dp_x - M_{pm}dp_m) \, dY(S_y + M_y - I_y)$$

$$= dZ[(I_z - S_z - M_z) + X_{y'}dY' - Mdp$$
$$+ (X_{px}dp_x - M_{pm}dp_m)] \tag{3A.3}$$

As for the sign of the LHS in (3A.3), by Keynesian stability $(S_y + M_y) > I_y$ always. Accordingly, dY will be positive when the RHS is also positive. Of the four terms in the RHS, the first term within the first bracket would be positive when

$$I_z > (S_z + M_z)$$

The condition is met with a stronger demand generating effect of investment income inflows as compared to the leakage through additional savings and imports. As for the second term, it is always positive because of the favourable income effect of expansions in South's GDP (Y') on its (North's) imports (exports). As for the third term, it will also be positive since dp by assumption is negative. The latter follows from our assumption that FDI flows worsen the terms of trade of South. Finally, the fourth term, to be positive, requires the condition

$$(X_{px}dp_x - M_{pm}dp_m) > 0$$

It may again be recalled that since the South is likely to face losses in its terms of trade (p), we have $|dp_x| > |dp_m|$ or $|dp_x| < |dp_m|$ according to whether price movements are positive or negative. However, since X_{px} and M_{pm} both have negative signs, the sum in brackets above will be positive only when

$$\frac{|M_{pm}|}{|X_{px}|} > \frac{dp_x}{dp_m}$$

Since the RHS in the above inequality is assumed to exceed unity, it is necessary (but not sufficient) that the ratio of the above partials in absolute terms is also greater than unity. On the whole, the conditions are not difficult to be met since the price-elasticities for products imported by the industrialised North are likely to be higher than that for the developing South.

Putting together, dY which captures the final effect of FDI flows from the North on its GDP would be *always* positive (unless the price effects rule it out) as long as $I_z > (S_z + M_z)$. The condition, to repeat, is met when the expansionary effect of Z in North on its investment exceeds the additional leakage via savings and imports. However, in case the condition is not fulfilled, the RHS can still be positive when the negative impact of investment income (dZ) on North's GDP (dY) is outweighed by the positive effects generated by the trade-related effects captured by the remaining terms. The expansion in North's GDP (dY) would be larger with (a) FDI-induced expansions in South's GDP (Y') and the related expansion of North's exports ($X_{y'}$) are higher; (b) the loss (gain) in the terms of trade of the South (North) (dp) is larger. This is because, a drop/rise in p would reduce/increase the value of imports of North (Mdp), measured in units of its own output; (c) the rise in import prices (dp_m) and the price-response for imports (M_{pm}) are both higher and the increase in export prices (dp_x) and the price-response of exports (X_{px}) lower. Results as above indicate the possible benefits the North can get from overseas direct investments in terms of expansions in its GDP.

The final increase in North's GDP seems to be favourably influenced by factors which include the favourable impact of FDI flows in the supply-constrained South. While the above aspect of FDI flows indicates an area of mutual gain for both North and South, such gains to North's output can only happen by depressing the terms of trade of the South, which reflect an opposite picture of conflicting interests.

We plot, in Figure 3.1, North's GDP (Y) against its savings (S), imports (M) and investment (I) all of which move up as Y rises. This is indicated by the positive *slopes* of II and SM schedules in Figure 3.1, respectively provided by I_y and ($S_y + M_y$). Since I, S and M are also positively influenced by investment income inflows, the schedules start from the y-axis. Finally, SM has a slope which is less than that of II since, as mentioned above, by Keynesian stability ($S_y + M_y$) > I_y.

At each level of North's GDP (Y), inflows of investment income (Z) raise, as can be seen from Equation (3A.2), the level of the three variables I, S and M. This is reflected in the *shifts* of both II and SM in the figure, which result from an increase in investment income.

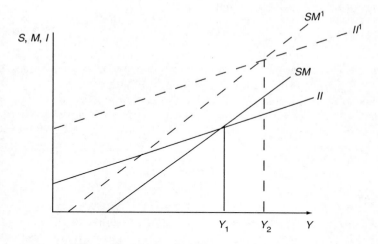

Figure 3.1   Leakages from income with capital flows

Comparing Y_1 and Y_2, it is obvious that Y_2 can exceed Y_1 only if the shift in II (which is equivalent to $I_z dZ$) exceeds that in *SM* (equivalent to the sum $S_z dZ + M_z dZ$). The observation is consistent with the conditions, worked out above, which makes for a positive value of dY/dZ.

We now get back to net exports (X) of the North which can, from balance of payments, be viewed as follows:

$$\dot{D} = X + iD \tag{3A.4}$$

where D is the stock of outstanding foreign investment (or foreign assets) of the North fetching an average rate of return 'i'. For simplicity, we assume that investment income flows are the only form of service transactions between the North and South.

Equation (3A.3) captures what can be described[54] as the 'rentier' and 'trade' effects of the flow of overseas investments for capital-exporting countries. While the rentier-effect relates to the flow of investment income or services (iD) in Equation (3A.3), the trade-effect is indicated by net exports of goods (X) in Equation (3A.4).

The trade-creating effect (α) of $\dot{D}$ on X can be spelt out as

$$X = \beta + \alpha \dot{D} \tag{3A.5}$$

From (3A.3) and (3A.4), when $\beta = 0$

$$\alpha = 1 - i/r \tag{3A.6}$$

where 'r' is the growth rate of gross capital exports $\dot{D}$, while Equation (3A.5) captures the conflicting rentier and trade interests in capital-exporting countries. Conflicts in the capital-exporting countries make it interesting to inquire whether exports of capital from the lender nations further trade/rentier interests in the domestic economy.
Let

$$\dot{D} = (\theta_N + \theta_S)\, \dot{D} \tag{3A.7}$$

where θ_N and θ_S are the respective shares of capital flow $\dot{D}$, which goes to country groups respectively described as North and South. It is further assumed that the North consists of the rich industrialised borrowers with higher propensities of importing services (consisting of investment income payments), while the South includes the developing borrowers having a propensity to import goods rather than services.
Let

$$\alpha = A + \dot{D}\left(\frac{\theta_N}{\theta_S}\right) \tag{3A.8}$$

where A is a constant and $\dot{D}' < 0$.

Substituting the value of A from Equation (3A.6) and rearranging

$$i = r\left[(1 - A) - \dot{D}\left(\frac{\theta_N}{\theta_S}\right)\right]$$

or

$$i = r\left[K - \dot{D}\left(\frac{\theta_N}{\theta_S}\right)\right] \tag{3A.9}$$

where $K = (1 - A)$ is also a constant.
Now

$$di/d\left(\frac{\theta_N}{\theta_S}\right) = -r.\dot{D}' > 0$$

It is evident from above that a distribution of international capital flows which favours the rich industrial country borrower of North would, in the lending area, further the rentier interests and hence harms (or at least be neutral to) the trader interests. The opposite would be the case when the South, consisting of the developing country borrowers gets a larger share of international capital flows.

It is now possible to see how a link can be forged between the trader-interests in capital-exporting countries and the interests of the developing country borrowers which has a natural propensity to import goods rather than services. We introduce here a notion of real transfer (RT) which is measured by import surplus in goods alone. (This definition of real transfer deviates from the definition provided elsewhere in this volume since we are now assuming that net flow of *all* services is zero.)
Thus

$$RT = M - X = I - S \tag{3A.10}$$

or

$$RT = (kg - s)Y$$

or

$$g = (RT/Y) + s)/k \tag{3A.11}$$

'k', 'g' and 's' in the two equations respectively indicate the capital-output ratio, GDP growth rate and savings rates in the economy receiving inflows of real transfers (RT).

Equation (3A.11) makes it evident that countries as above are dependent on net capital imports from overseas for their domestic growth. Simultaneously, the process instils a harmonious pattern of growth in the world economy, one where the trading interests (the real sector) in lender countries grow along with borrowing economies, creating a market space for goods from the former. It is not far-fetched to argue that the above opens up a plea for diversion of capital flows in the direction of the developing country borrowers.

4

Global Finance and Development

With current flows of private finance reaching out the developing areas, our analysis would remain incomplete in the absence of a close look at their impact on development. The pattern of financial flows to these countries was drastically changed by the early 1970s, as concessional loans from official sources started tapering off and were substituted by flows of bank credit from private sources. Unlike the official loans which used to be distributed relatively evenly across countries, the flow of private credit was directed primarily to a handful of middle-income countries in Asia and Latin America. As we have pointed out in Chapter 2, by the early 1970s, international banks in the West were already facing a dampened credit demand in home countries. Flushed with liquidity which augmented further with large OPEC deposits from the oil-rich Arab countries, banks in the West thus had to seek out borrowers from outside, if they were to remain in business. The middle-income developing countries, in turn, used the opportunity to avail of the credit which was cheap in terms of the low or even negative real interest rates at which these were offered. While these borrowings were mostly publicly guaranteed, the proceeds often added to private wealth, contributing little, if at all, towards national benefit in terms of growth and employment in these countries.

Drastic changes in the scene were there during the early 1980s, when new credit advanced to the developing countries dropped sharply. These developments included the following:

- First, the large developing country borrowers were on the verge of default. This happened due to an erosion of the perceived creditworthiness of these borrowers in the international credit market. Incidentally, the responses on the part of creditor institutions included the refinancing packages which sought to avoid interruptions in debt servicing. This had a favourable impact on the market value of debt held as assets by the creditors. However, little, if any, of these refinanced loans were available to the debtors for purposes other than loan servicing and repayments. Refinancing was generally offered by banks only if the borrowing country agreed to follow the fund-approved norms of conditionality. In effect, the debtors had to accept much harsher loan terms in exchange for the refinanced credit, largely to keep themselves solvent in terms of debt-compliance.

- The second aspect of the changes in the direction of global finance which took place during the 1980s was the steady expansion in the security sector of the private international capital markets. This was simultaneous with the fleeting reforms in financial markets within the OECD, which at one stroke removed the barriers between banks and stock exchanges, thus permitting a much wider scale of activity in the security sector. With controls on capital flows virtually extant in these countries, an expanded market for these financial transactions was thus created within the OECD itself.

- As for the sources of external finance for the developing countries, these also changed perceptively in the process. Thus, by the 1990s, private capital flows other than bank credit, both with portfolio and direct investments, turned out to be significant sources of borrowings. As during the 1970s, a handful of countries, this time in East and SE Asia, came up as emerging markets for foreign private capital. Like what happened with bank loans earlier, these new flows of finance to the developing countries turned out to be unsustainable. This can be witnessed from the credit cycles, which have been common in these countries over the last three decades. Problems as above were compounded by the virtual convertibility of currencies in a large number of these developing countries. Thus, partial or complete CAC was initiated in the major borrowing countries of Asia and Latin America.

Developments as above led to a situation where external finance that reached out to the developing countries failed to support a sustained growth process. This can be witnessed from the dismal growth record in Latin America, especially since the debt crisis began during the early 1980s. To explain the related lapses in terms of development as well as debt sustainability which came about during this period, one needs to go beyond the standard critique which points at the role of external agents (banks/creditor governments/ IMF in any order) in *causing* the debt crisis. At the other extreme, there is the view of mainstream economists who blame corrupt governments and the lack of transparency in financial institutions in the developing countries as being solely responsible for the coun- tries' failure to develop and remain accountable in the international credit market. None of the above, in our view, provides a complete picture of what stalled development in these capital-importing economies. We deal, in the next section, with the debt crisis of the 1980s.

4.1   The failed debt process of the 1970s and 1980s

To understand the dynamics of the failed debt process in countries which borrowed heavily in the 1970s, one needs to unfold the dialectics of the underlying alliances between the ruling elite in the borrowing countries and the concerned foreign lenders. We have documented, for the three major debtors in Latin America (Argentina, Brazil and Mexico), the pattern of internal–external alliances which evolved in the process, both during the debt build-up of the 1970s and in the crisis of the 1980s which followed. This, however, is not to discount the role of exogenous shocks which include the crash in commodity prices, the upward movements in dollar rate and the rise in interest rates in world financial markets which fuelled the crisis.

Let us consider, first, the debt build-up of the 1970s when TNBs were lending heavily to these countries. As mentioned, one needs to look closely at the internal–external alliance and its nemesis in the borrowing nations;[1] both in terms of low-growth performance and the difficulties encountered in sustaining net credit flows. Ironically, problems in accessing credit flows continued despite the fact that these countries had been complying with the schedule of debt servicing. We also discuss the responses as came up, with creditors willing to offer refinancing packages which were generally anchored to the fund-approved loan conditionalities.

As it has been pointed out in Chapter 2, profitability of banks was restored in the process of bank-restructuring which started with the debt crisis. The banks however, eventually exited from the third-world loan market by the mid-1980s when securities came up as far better financial options, especially with the end of segregated banking in deregulated financial markets. The initial resistance along with the moves to defy on the part of some of the borrowing nations, which expressed a desire to announce default (or short of it, cap the interest payments), was met with stiff creditor reprisals. The process ultimately gave way to compliance on the part of the debtor countries, thus setting a pattern which was similar in most of the developing countries which borrowed heavily from private banks.

The debt build-up in Latin America during the 1970s included seven of the world's 11 most heavily indebted countries at the beginning of the 1980s. International debt of developing countries increased from about $75 billion in 1970 to about $322 billion in 1978, which amounted to an annual increase of about 20 per cent over the period. This, of course excludes short-term debt held for less than one year, in accord with the standard practice in OECD statistics.[2] Debt in different countries of Latin America generally swelled under dictatorial regimes with identifiable and infalliable alliances between overseas foreign lenders and the oligarchical regimes within.[3] In the region, Brazil, Argentina and Mexico were saddled with the largest debt liabilities. All three were close to default by the early 1980s and for all these countries (as with others in Latin America) foreign borrowing had very little impact on their respective growth record.[4]

4.1.1 The pattern of alliances in Brazil

The Brazilian model, considered by many to be a miracle, was one with ample foreign credit inflows, which was matched by high growth of domestic output and exports during the 1970s. A stage was set during the earlier decades – with dictatorial regimes enticing TNCs by tax incentives, infrastructure support and cheap sources of labour – which worked under strict control. Labour was cheap, with mass exodus of workers from coffee plantations in the country which were threatened by mechanised cultivation of soya. Labour in urban areas faced reprisals on protest, and strikes were banned by the ruling government. All efforts on the part of the authorities to regulate the free play of foreign capital in the economy met with stiff opposition. Thus, President Varagas committed suicide in 1954 in the face of a joint campaign by the export sector and the pro-American military group against nationalisation of industry. Again in 1964, President Goulart was deposed with a military coup, which was backed by the local bourgeoisie, all because of the nationalistic policy moves initiated by him.

Brazil was all set for the so-called 'economic miracle' by the early 1970s, with the military rulers encouraging foreign capital inflows. Borrowing abroad turned out to be cheaper for Brazilians with the floating rate of the LIBOR at around 7 per cent, a moderate spread and the exchange rate of the Brazilian peso subject to a crawling peg along with weekly adjustments to the PPP. Investment banks in particular were borrowing heavily in order to profit by re-lending at the domestic interest rate which was higher. The TNCs in turn were keen to take full advantage of the numerous incentives locally provided to the country, including those on exports. In 1974, President Ernsto Giesel announced a 'big leap forward' with mega projects which included the Trans-Amazonian Highway, Rio-Niteroi bridge and the Augra Nuel Power station. Foreign loans to state-run companies comprised half to three-fourth of total foreign borrowings and there emerged a network of alliances between these state-run companies and the TNCs. Loans, however, were more often used to meet the debt services and also to bridge the supplier credits. Thus, of a sum of gross borrowing amounting to $74 billion during 1974–79, only $11 billion was left to finance investments, after using $56 billion for debt servicing and $7 billion leaving the country as capital flight! Ironical as it may seem, foreign capital financed only a quarter of domestic investments during these years, and savings at domestic origin was providing for the major part of financing domestic investment.[5] It has been argued that much of Brazil's borrowing during this period was unnecessary as well as unproductive. In the process, the TNCs continued to erode Brazil's external accounts, contributing to imports as well as investment-income liabilities.

As foreign debt was fast piling up, flow of new credit to Latin America virtually stopped, pushing the major borrowing countries in the region including Mexico close to default. As it happened with other large debtors in Latin America, Brazil's move to default was hijacked by creditor banks keen to avoid a run on themselves. Banks poured in a sum of $2.8 billion in the third quarter of 1983 as new loans to Brazil. Earlier than that, a steering committee formed by creditor banks under the leadership of Morgan Guarantee rescheduled $4.7 billion of Brazilian debt with high spreads over the Libor on privately held debt at 2.1 per cent. For public debts, the spread was even higher at 2.5 per cent. There was also a commission of 1.5 per cent which made the borrower receive $98.5 out of each loan of $100 which, however, had to be paid back and serviced in full. Debt servicing at floating interest rates amounted to a substantial sum on debt outstanding for Brazil, which stood in 1983 at $97 billion.[6]

The IMF played a major role in the debt-financing process of banks. This was largely to avoid default, by co-financing along with stiff conditionality. However, despite the difficulties in meeting debt liabilities, Brazil refused to accept conditional loan packages as were offered during the initial years of the debt crisis. Even President Sarney, backed by a conservative government which was in power, announced a number of measures to combat the crisis. These included the suspension of interest payments beyond $5 to $6 billion a year on foreign loans (which amounted to 2.5 per cent of Brazil's GDP); the Cruzado plan of a deflationary package to contain inflation and to improve the BOP; a plan to swap 50 per cent of the external debt to bonds and a move to nationalise banks. None of these proved palatable to the powerful elite in the country which also shared the interests of the creditor banks. Ultimately, Sarney had to retreat by lifting the moratorium on debt along with a scrapping of other measures. Earlier, the Cartagena declaration on the collective debt moratorium in Latin America in 1985 had failed as Brazil insisted on leading a separate debt front. Finally, all disputes were settled in favour of the creditor banks and Brazil accepted the juris-diction of the New York courts on the matter. The country had to pay all legal costs, including the daily allowances for the lawyers. In general, Brazil and other Latin American borrowers were forced to accept rescheduling by the creditor banks for whom the deal worked out as far more profitable (with commissions, spreads and floating interest rates) than the eventuality of default! That the country even-tually retreated to the conventional path of structural adjustments was not just because the Fund succeeded in pushing its dictates but also because the move had tacit (or at best, permissive) compliance of the local bourgeoisie.[7] Creditors in turn succeeded in legitimising the debt as civilian governments took over in most countries of Latin America, thus avoiding possible turnarounds by the dictatorial military regimes which were also responsible for the initial build-up of the debt.

4.1.2   Failure of debt-led growth: the case of Argentina

As for Argentina, the other major borrower in Latin America, it was a similar story as to how a path of debt-led growth can turn out to be non-viable. The failure, however, again had less to do with the political set-up in the country and more with its economic upheavals. Thus, over the preceding three decades Argentina had moved back and forth; from the dictatorial government run by military junta in the 1960s to the conservative civilian government under Peron of the early 1970s and then again to the dictatorial military regimes during 1976–83, which were followed by a return to elected civilian governments since then. President Raul Alfonsin, who came to power with a civilian government in 1983, was supported by the Radical Civic Union (or the VCR party). He was also assisted by Raul Prebisch as one of his economic advisors. Alfonsin and his left-to-centre party could thus be expected to lead the country to a path of self-reliant development, especially after the debt crisis. However, populist movements against Alfonsin's radical measures led to his overthrow in 1989 by his Peronist rival, Carlos Menem. Peron ruled as president for more than a decade till December 1999.

Argentina, which was one of the three largest debtor countries in the world during the early 1980s, had a wealthy middle class with upcoming urban centres which bore testimony to its prosperity. Thus an explanation of the current crisis in Argentina is not complete without a reference to past policies, of a nation swamped by flows of capital from overseas on one hand and a failure to make use of those in a productive manner on the other. To explain the lack of development as well as a lack of debt sustainability, one needs to go beyond the standard explanations which range between the role of external agents (the banks/creditor governments/IMF in any order) to blaming the corrupt governments in these countries as solely responsible for such failures. None of these, as stressed earlier, provide a complete picture of what actually happened in connection with these loans in the borrowing countries, a position which applies with equal explanatory power to the ailing economy of Argentina at the moment.

To come to grips with the reality,[8] we need to look back and identify policies which had sown the seeds of future problems in the country. Large flows of bank loans came to the country between 1976 and 1983 during the military regime. These investments turned out to be a profitable venture for bankers with the domestic interest rate at 20 per cent which was much higher than interest rates abroad at around 4 per cent. Despite such incentives, capital inflows started waning off by the late 1970s, largely due to the debt difficulties which were already showing up in Argentina and in other countries of the sub-continent. To attract capital inflows, Argentina announced a dual exchange rate in terms of which a devalued peso was used exclusively to encourage trade in goods and services, while using a higher rate for capital account transactions. By 1978, the exchange rate was unified again and was fixed at an overvalued level, thus emulating the Chilean pattern of economic strategy. The peso turned out, as a consequence, to be one of the most overvalued currencies by the end of the decade, offering little incentive to exporters while providing cushions to the residents who had been freely building up dollar assets abroad. It implied easy money for the local elite, especially with CAC which by now was nearly complete. However, the overvalued peso inflated the debt burden in local currency when it came to repayments or debt servicing. While large borrowings by both the government and the corporates went on, capital flights continued at an equal pace. Thus, during the first quarter of 1981, $10.8 billion was borrowed from abroad while a sum amounting to $10.1 billion fled the country. The pattern followed a 'bicycle' principle, with dollars borrowed abroad finally having their way to foreign banks as private deposits. The process led to dips in the official reserves which fell sharply to $6.25 billion in 1980–81, as compared to the previous peak at $10.5 billion in 1979.

A change of guard, when President Alfonsin was sworn in as the civilian head of state in 1983, had little long-term impact on the situation. Finally, the initial resistance of the rulers in Argentina to follow IMF diktats petered off, not withstanding the interim support from neighbouring states of Mexico, Venezuela and Brazil to help control the crisis. Foreign banks started putting pressure on Argentina and the crisis was sought to be defused in March 1984 with bridging loans of $100 million each from the oil-producing countries, Venezuela as well as Mexico, and $50 million each from non-oil producing neighbours which included Brazil and Columbia.[9] With hindsight, it is less clear as to whether the move towards debt redressal on the part of other countries in the region was a gesture of debtor solidarity, especially on the eve of Cartagena Conference in 1985, or whether it was simply a measure of compromise vis-à-vis the creditor banks by effectively bailing out the borrowing countries. The collapse of the debtors' cartel at Cartagena in 1985 nearly coincided with the capitulation by Argentina which had already accepted loans from IMF in mid-1984 under stiff conditionality. The step was welcome to the elite in the country and especially to the dominantly conservative Peronists who took over under the leadership of Carlos Menem in 1989. The return of the Peronists was in large measure a consequence of the resistance by big banks and other vested interests which were opposed to Alfonsin's proposals for nationalising banks.[10] Menem's policies included the fixing of the peso at a one dollar peg in terms of a currency board arrangement. Simultaneously, the tight fiscal-monetarist policies of the earlier military regimes in the country were reinstalled with interest rate hikes and fiscal cuts. Efforts to manage hyperinflation thus swung the pendulum to deflation and prices started falling sharply, with little demand in the economy. No respite could be offered by the monetary authorities who had lost the power to expand money supply in terms of the strictures of the currency board. The crisis deepened over the next few years with steady contractions in output, soaring unemployment and large withdrawals of peso/dollar deposits by residents, who were apprehensive of an end to the currency board and an impending devaluation of the peso.

Peronists continued in power during the next decade or so, which was followed by the quick turnover in the office of the President in Argentina. Five Presidents beginning with President Rua of the same party came and left in less than a fortnight since December 2001. This reflected both a political and an economic turmoil much of which owed its origin to the economic policies of the earlier regime which left the country with a staggering $141 billion of external debt by this time. As President Eduardo Duhalde took over in 2002, these steps were followed up by a set of draconian policies under the banner of 'new economy measures'. These included the re-introduction of a dual exchange rate system, and the conversion of all bank assets and liabilities denominated in dollar to peso. The measure ended the previous anomaly in the Rua regime of differentiating peso deposits and advances in terms of dollar conversion. President Duhalde made an effort to stem the outflows of dollars with a decree on bank withdrawals, which, however, was met with stiff opposition, not only from the elite in the country but also from the working classes many of whom had lost their jobs. The Supreme Court of the country had earlier passed a judgement disapproving the ceiling on bank withdrawals by the public. The Duhalde administration in turn sought to maintain and re-institute the freeze with the legislature (the Congress) impeaching the court.

While the measures implemented by President Duhalde were not immediately accepted by the IMF as satisfactory, Argentina was expecting a loan of $15–20 billion from the Fund. The 'new economic policy' announced in February 2002 by President Duhalde was in effect an effort to win back the international financial community, especially the IMF and the TNBs. Floating the peso had not met with a sharp decline in the exchange rate, since Argentinians just lacked the requisite liquidity to sell pesos and buy dollars. Fiscal cuts and monetary tightening had already been recommended by the Fund. If devaluation and floating of the peso would fail to work, there was even a talk of an official dollarisation of the country. At the moment, those within the country who enjoyed in the past the so-called prosperity of Argentina are waiting to feel good again, with renewed opportunities to launder money and to enjoy the best lifestyle that can be afforded. The alliance between the ruling oligarchy and the international financial agencies continues to prevail in the process.

Argentina in 2002 was still reeling under the pressure of its part-defaulted $141 billion debt, the protests on the reinstituting of capital account controls (which imposed ceilings on withdrawal of the privately held dollar deposits with its banks), the aftermath of an end of a decade-long currency reserve system and a currency peg (which was at par with the dollar), and finally the high level of unemployment and the severe recession. Circumstances as above led to mass reactions with violent protests in the country. The popular protests had gathered momentum in December 2001 as President de la Rua announced an austerity programme in terms of which drastic

cuts in all official spendings were to follow. By then, official expenditure was already reduced by nearly $1 billion over a period of less
than six months since Rua had taken over at the end of 1999. In particular, the cut in wages paid to workers in state-run concerns by 13
per cent along with other cuts on expenditure under social heads as
well as in pensions combined with steep increases in taxes infuriated
the public. The anger flared up as Finance Minister Domingo Cavallo
announced a further drop in the estimated public spending by
$7 billion in the budget placed for 2002, to meet the payments due
on foreign loans. Resignations of the President and his Economy
Minister were repeated, in quick succession, over the next fortnight
as four more Presidents came and left. In the meantime, the country defaulted in part on its $141 billion loans, while the peso was
de-linked from its dollar peg in terms of the currency board system
which prevailed over a decade.[11]

4.1.3   Bailing out Mexico in the interest of the creditors

Mexico with its oil reserves turned out to be an attractive destination
of foreign capital during the 1970s. With large flows of bank credits
flowing in, it provided a soft option for President Lopez Portillo in
terms of policy making during the early 1970s. Minister Jorge Serrano's
mega-plan to set up a refinery in the Gulf of Mexico was amply
funded by the huge borrowings which started in 1977. However,
with crude prices reversing the up-trend during the early 1980s,
Mexico was faced with serious BOP problems, especially in terms of
meeting the loan charges. In the meantime, the overvalued peso
initiated a climate of export stagnation, along with an erosion of
investor confidence abroad. The lack of confidence in the prevailing
exchange rate of peso also led to a situation where the domestic
residents resorted to large-scale capital flight. A financial crunch was
experienced by Mexico in August 1982 as it was having severe problems
in servicing foreign debt. As for the creditors, the responses came in
the form of a co-financing package which was offered by the IMF.
Offers were also made of short-term bridging loans by the BIS and by
creditor governments including the US. Mexico did not want to
decline these offers, especially after its proposal for a collective front
for a moratorium was turned down by Brazil and Argentina.[12] As for
the terms of refinancing the loans, the interest rate offered was as
high as 13 per cent, following the prevailing pattern of terms in the

loan-refinancing packages. Attempts on the part of the US to resolve the debt crisis included the Baker (1985) and the Brady Plans (1989). As pointed out in Chapter 2, these plans targeted Mexico as the principal debtor. The BOP crisis was already acute in Mexico since 1994, while the US went on making special efforts to defuse the crisis, especially with its high stakes in Mexico, both for trade and investment.

4.1.4   Other debt-ridden countries in Latin America

The narrative of debt and under-development in Latin America would remain incomplete if we do not refer to the experiences of at least three other countries in the region. The three countries are Chile, initially under Allende and later under Pinochio, rebellious Peru under Alan Garcia and Cuba under Fidel Castro.

For Chile, the major copper-exporting country, seeds of the peril of debt started with the overthrow of Allende by Pinochio in a military coup in 1973. This was followed by a reversal of all economic policies which were earlier initiated in the Allende regime to revive the economy. Pinochio adopted the Brazilian model of opening up the economy with free inflows of foreign loans. Policies were framed by the 'Chicago boys' (known as 'piranhas') in Chile, who framed the Economic Recovery Programme, with techno-military alliance. Chile's foreign debt went up steadily, from around $3 billion in 1970 to $35 billion in 1987. With corruption rife in the economy, the Chilean banks usually lent to companies, which were mostly within the same corporate group. The money borrowed by the latter was usually spent on speculation in property or sometimes to buy companies at cheap prices by taking advantage of the government's stage-managed privatisation programme. It was reported that General Pinochio himself spent a huge sum of $18 million in building his private mansion.[13]

The reverse (negative) flow of capital which was typical in other debt-ridden countries started even earlier in Chile as it could be recorded for the year 1977. By 1982, when the debt crisis hit Chile, the country's external debt was at 90 per cent of her GDP. Pressures on the government by creditor banks led Pinochio to float the peso in the market, where it dropped from a rate of 47 to 60 per dollar. While the country accepted the dictates of the IMF and foreign banks, loans were rescheduled at 2.16 per cent spread and 1.25 per cent commission which were enjoyed by the banks. By August 1982, the country's official reserves started falling at an alarming rate with capital flight on a massive scale. In the same month, the Central Bank of the country took over the privately held 'bad loans' worth $1.5 billion, thus assuring the creditors that privately held debts could be nationalised. Meanwhile, foreign banks were selling these 'bad' Chilean debts in the market – about 70 per cent of which were sold at discounts ranging from 30 to 40 per cent. With IMF mounting its pressures on the Chilean government, the latter followed the Fund-approved austerity programme, and despite the fact that there was an ongoing recession in the country.[14] The story thus continues, with a similar pattern as in the rest of debt-ridden Latin America.

4.1.5   The overall picture in indebted Latin America

On the whole, the accumulation of debt by the developing countries during the 1970s and 1980s ended up in a catastrophe for the region, contributing to added vulnerability on the one hand and worsened domestic economic condition on the other. Policies of deflationary adjustment,[15] as advocated by the Fund, was a major factor in directing policy. While much of the debt was originally contracted by the military rulers along with the tacit compliance by the powerful local elites, it had little, if any, developmental impact within the respective countries. With the piling up of external liabilities, both with greater dependence on imports and servicing of foreign loans, these countries fell into a typical debt trap, with new loans contracted to meet dues on past loans! In effect, the process amounted to one of a Mynskian ponzi finance, with borrowings which were unsustainable in the absence of their appropriate use in the borrowing country. Difficulties experienced by the debt-ridden countries to service past loans alerted the creditor banks, which responded by negotiating refinancing packages, often with IMF support, and in a bid to avoid possible suspension of debt servicing, leading to eventual defaults. With a change in regime from military to civilian rule in most of these countries, the debt-related liabilities were formally owed by elected governments rather than by individual military rulers. However, from the beginning, debt privately contracted was always publicly guaranteed, thus making even the military government responsible for the country's foreign currency liabilities.

Options to default, when it came to the crunch during the mid-1980s, were systematically annulled by policy makers in the debt-ridden countries. Deviating from the text book models of optimal borrowing, the outcome was not because the new loans (net of all debt-related payments) actually exceeded the debt charges.[16] Often the flow of new loans turned out to be miniscule as compared to the huge debt-related liabilities which had to be provided for. Thus, borrowing countries did not refrain from default because the new loans were substantially larger than the debt charges. Instead, the funds, as reached these countries, were mostly spent on meeting the debt-related liabilities which hardly left any amount for the domestic economy.

Governments in debtor countries lacked the political support from within to come to terms with default. The alternative chosen included the refinancing packages, with austerity programmes as were consistent with the Fund dictates on structural adjustment programmes. There resulted, as a consequence, a stream of outflows towards debt servicing which were often provided for by the trade surpluses which were generated by compression of imports and GDP. As we have argued in Section 1.4, these *negative* net financial and real flows dampened growth in the supply-constrained borrowing economies. As interest and exchange rates both started floating, the compounded debt liabilities soared up in foreign currency. This was because the interest rates in the credit market moved up, while the liabilities in local currency also went up along with repeated depreciation of local currency in terms of dollar. The burden in real terms became even heavier as commodity prices slumped in world markets, moving the terms of trade against the borrowing countries. The description above fits in the experiences of the debt-ridden countries in the 1980s, which faced the *triple squeeze* of higher interest rates, depreciating currency and adverse changes in terms of trade.

As the debt crisis deepened a large number of creditor banks moved out of the debt business and shifted to securities as an attractive form of assets. Paradoxically, these moves were not explicable in terms of the standard debt models in the literature as long as debt continued to be serviced by these trade surpluses, which in effect fulfilled the 'solvency' criterion. In reality, the lenders exercised caution, not just by stiffening the terms of lending, but more crucially, by rationing the quantity of loans. The curtailing of new loans was due to '...an increasing divergence in the lender's and borrower's expectations as to the prospects of returns on investments financed by borrowing'.[17] As the confidence in the stability of assets held as debt waned off, the lenders tried to minimise potential losses by getting rid of these assets and were quick to move to securities or other derivative products. Those strategies worked better with deregulation of financial markets.

However, the emphasis on liquidity as a major criteria of creditworthiness often made it obligatory on the part of the debtor governments to accumulate reserves, even with borrowings which in effect turned out to be much in excess compared to what was needed to prove creditworthiness. Borrowings, as mentioned earlier, proved costly with stiff loan terms along with spreads and commissions. On top of it, the borrowing country had to comply with the strictures of the loan market which included tight fiscal and monetary policies and wide-ranging reforms towards liberalisation of capital markets by the country. Building up these reserves with borrowed finance often turned out as incompatible with developmental goals.

It has been pointed out that the debt-distress of the 1970s and 1980s in the developing countries generated a state of *dependence* on the part of these countries, with foreign capital inflows instrumental in reducing savings propensity and increasing the propensity to import.[18] While observations as above are perceptive, cross-country analysis, as in these studies, misses out the essence of debt-dynamics. The latter encompasses the underlying dialectics of alliances between the ruling elite in the borrowing countries and the lenders' cartel, comprising of the creditor banks which have close contacts with the IMF.

As for the strategy adopted by the private lender institutions, it all worked as a 'containment policy', with options exercised to exit from the third-world loan market while avoiding losses. Despite a demonstrated aversion to third-world debt on part of banks, deals were struck by the same banks in order to improve the returns on these financial assets. This happened with stiff commissions, high interest rates (which were subject to spreads) and other benefits as could be achieved through refinancings.

4.2 The emerging economies and the recent pattern of capital flows

As the debt crisis in Latin America affecting the major creditor institutions was somehow resolved by the end of the 1980s, the pattern of global finance went through a drastic change. As with the earlier boom in bank credit, private finance in the direction of the developing area was concentrated in a handful of countries, described as 'emerging economies'. However, unlike what happened with the loan-push scenario of the 1970s, when recession in the OECD made the developing countries the favoured and lucrative destination of surplus funds with banks, the more recent trends indicate a different pattern. It shows a tendency for international capital flows to remain confined within the OECD, or at most to flow to the transition economies in eastern Europe. The new pattern with securities as major vehicles of financial flows have been rather uneven, especially with developing countries lacking in general the requisite institutional set-up as well as the investment climate as is considered appropriate by creditors. While gross flows of publicly guaranteed bank loans have continued, bonds have come up as new instruments of debt-creating finance to these countries. Non-guaranteed finance has been a major component of the above. Finally, there exist the non-debt creating flows, including FDI and portfolio, which of late have provided major sources of finance to the newly Emerging Economies of Asia and Latin America, especially for countries which have initiated partial or complete liberalisation of financial markets.

While these new forms of financial flows continued to reach out to the developing countries, their impact in terms of the *net* contributions on externally available finance has been rather limited. Flows of debt-creating finance (bank loans and bonds) in the direction of some of these countries came to a near standstill with successive eruptions of financial crisis in countries and regions like Mexico (1994), SE Asia (1997), Brazil (1998), Russia (1998) and Argentina (2001–02). Even FDI and portfolio investments, the flow of which have been neither buoyant nor stable to developing countries as a whole, failed to ensure steady net inflows. Despite the continuation of the gross inflows, (especially from bonds, FDIs and portfolio flows) *aggregate net financial transfers*[19] to the developing countries have turned *negative* since 1998. A region-wise break-up indicates a similar picture, with only two areas including the HIPC group as a whole and sub-Saharan Africa fetching net positive financial transfers by 2000. The sum had been too small to warrant a positive financial transfer for the developing area as whole. The rather dismal picture as above can be witnessed in the statistics provided in Table 4.1 and in Figure 4.1.

The overall pattern as emerges from this indicates that the integration of the developing countries with the financial market has been

Table 4.1 Net transfer of financial resources of developing countries, 1993–2000 ($ billions)

	1993	1994	1995	1996	1997	1998	1999	2000*
Developing countries	66.2	34.3	39.9	18.5	−5.7	−35.2	−111.2	−169.8
Africa	2.5	5.1	6.0	−5.1	−3.3	17.0	6.3	−14.5
Sub-Saharan excl. Nigeria and South Africa	19.2	3.7	10.1	12.2	12.9	13.1	16.4	15.8
Eastern and Southern Asia	10.0	1.9	22.9	24.6	−28.8	−127.7	−125.8	−102.9
Latin America	14.7	18.1	−1.6	−1.3	20.8	42.0	7.9	−1.6
Western Asia	39.0	9.2	12.6	0.2	4.9	33.5	0.4	−50.8
Memo: HIPCs	13.0	10.7	11.8	11.9	13.6	16.5	12.8	9.2

*The net transfer of financial resources comprises the net capital inflow less the net outflow of investment income; it finances the balance of trade in goods and non-factor services and net private outward transfers (largely worker remittances).

Source: UN, *World Economic and Social Survey*, 2001, New York, pp. 40–1.

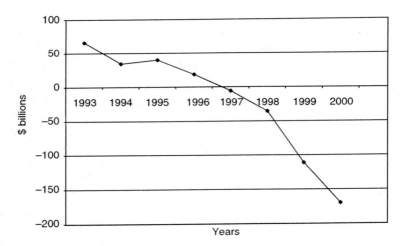

Figure 4.1   Net financial transfers to developing countries

at the cost of a regular 'drain' or transfer of financial resources from the region to creditors which include the private agencies in the advanced countries. The picture disputes the conventional wisdom relating to the universal benefits of financial liberalisation, not only in terms of an absence of positive *net* flows of finance but also in terms of the related erosion of their national autonomy, relating to fiscal and monetary matters.

4.3   On capital account convertibility in developing countries

Mainstream advocates of financial liberalisation and CAC rest their arguments on both macroeconomic and micro-theoretic benefits as are expected of these policies. In the context of the developing countries, the following include some of the claims regarding the benefits, as pointed out in the literature: first, the macroeconomic efficiency in terms of savings–investment balance along with allocation of global savings to ensure its full utilisation as well as maximum returns. In the process, the world's financial and currency markets are expected to be unified, with interest rates and exchange rates at equilibrium levels.

- Efficiency is also expected in terms of micro-level portfolio management, both temporal as well as spatial, for rational agents in the credit market which include the lenders and borrowers. The process is expected to maximise, as well as smoothen, the respective returns and consumption for lenders and borrowers over time.
- As we have pointed out in Chapter 1, in these rational expectation models of capital markets, uncertainty is either ruled out by assumption or is treated as ergodic and as such predictable. Thus, full knowledge is shared by all agents in the market. Accordingly, knowledge never remains private, and speculation in these situations is equivalent to arbitrage. We have offered earlier in Chapter 1 a critique of these aspects.
- Capital account liberalisation is also expected to increase investment in capital-scarce (developing) countries. Prudent macroeconomic policies in capital-importing countries are expected to end fiscal profligacy. CAC may also bring an end to porous and corruptive capital controls in the capital-importing countries. Measures to liberalise capital flows are also expected to end capital flights while encouraging inflows of capital to these countries.

As against the above claims, critics point at the problems as are likely to emerge with full CAC. There is thus a case for advocating caution in the implementation of such measures. The following include some of the critiques to the efficient market hypothesis and its implications in terms of policies towards full CAC:

- A major criticism relates to the assumptions underlying the efficient market hypothesis, and in particular those relating to the treatment of uncertainty. Thus, knowledge in the credit market is recognised as imperfect as well as asymmetric, with consequences which include credit rationing.[20] As it has been pointed out in other critiques, knowledge or information relating to uncertainty is bound to be subjective and as such are non-ergodic. This explains the recurrence of herd behaviour or contagion which relates to what Keynes had described as 'animal spirits' ruling the stock markets. Arguments as above have already been discussed in Chapter 1.[21]
- Critiques also point at the much-discussed trilemma which are often faced by policymakers in developing countries, in trying to implement CAC. Problems are often faced in trying to simultaneously maintain *three* goals which include a fixed or adjustable exchange rate peg, a national monetary policy and an open capital account. It is pointed out that with a configuration as above, it is only possible to achieve two of the three specified targets.
- It has also been argued that in absence of international tax compliance, there can also be a corrosion of the national tax base in these countries. Thus, there can be capital flights from a high tax country while corrective measures towards tax compliance may in turn adversely affect fiscal autonomy. Developing countries may also face a downturn in their growth rates with newly opened capital accounts, both with capital flights and rise in debt-related liabilities. As pointed out in the literature, CAC in absence of sequencing and proper regulatory measures, can lead to greater degrees of uncertainty, which causes volatility in asset prices, exchange rates and capital flows. These are often caused by abrupt changes in flows of short-term capital as well as in portfolio investments. For developing countries, the thinness of their capital markets magnifies the amplitude of the fluctuations, in asset

prices and in the volume of asset transactions, with consequences which are both harmful and difficult to control by means of national efforts on the part of the state. Fluctuations in the NER, the RER, in interest rates and the related swings in the volume of capital account transactions thus turn out to be costly in terms of the damage inflicted on these economies.

- Problems as above also generate parallel swings in the current account, which impacts real demand and output in these economies. A cut in the volume of net capital inflows reduces the capacity of the capital-importing country to meet its CAD, with resulting cuts in net imports. This is especially due to rising investment-income liabilities on past loans, which in a supply-constrained economy adversely impacts the country's investment and growth rate. This is especially true when the capacity of the country to withstand the reversals of capital flows is limited. At another extreme, surges in inflows of capital and the related upward movements in the NER may adversely affect the trade competitiveness of the country, especially when RER moves upward as a consequence.

- We now look at the possible impact on the flow of capital, which under CAC are guided by market managers. In absence of adequate information, they are subject to herd mentality which generates contagion effects, which in turn transmits systemic risks across global financial markets. Implicit insurance to foreign investors by Central Banks of borrowing countries in terms of a fixed or a band spread for exchange rate variations often encourages favourable market sentiments. As a consequence, credits become easy in the domestic economy which, however, is capable of encouraging risky investment projects. Unrestricted inflows of capital may also lead to other mismatches in the borrowing economies, with short-term borrowing abroad by local banks to finance long-term advances in the domestic economy. When a financial crisis sets in, the developing country typically attempts to bridge the BOP deficit by borrowing abroad, at high spreads over the interest rates prevailing in international markets. A part of the latter may be used to revamp the reserves, which are sometimes invested in foreign bonds at rates of return which are comparatively lower. Foreign borrowings at adverse loan terms reduce further the net proceeds of these receipts, as are left to finance imports of goods and non-factor services. Finally, expectations of further changes in the exchange rate and interest rates are capable of generating cumulative movements in these variables which tend to be destabilising.

Arguments as above on the benefits as well as costs of CAC for the developing countries need to be substantiated by analytical reasoning as well as documentation of facts. As for the analysis, we would like to revert to the discussions offered earlier in Chapter 1 on the futility of monetary control in arresting a speculative run on exchange rate under CAC. As is typical with the opening of capital accounts in countries with weak currencies, situations emerge which correspond to the 'impossible trinity' of fixed (or managed) exchange rates, national monetary control and open capital accounts. While exchange rate movements may stabilise when expectations are subject to a regressive probability distribution function, the reality tends to be very different. The assumption of a regressive probability distribution of expectations regarding exchange rate movements eliminates, by assumption, all deviations from what is viewed in the market as the equilibrium rate of exchange. Expectations in the foreign exchange market are, in reality, moulded by adaptive and even extrapolative probability distributions, especially with financial panic.[22] In such an event, movements away from the prevailing exchange rates tend to be cumulative and self-reinforcing.

As for the empirical observations relating to the developing-country experiences on the impact of CAC, there exists, in the literature, a mixed finding on the outcome with complete or partial liberalisation of capital flows. One may mention studies where capital controls are found to be a causal factor in countries behind higher inflation.[23] Studies have also shown that CAC *cannot* be associated with observed improvements in the indicators of economic performance which include inflation, per capita GDP growth and investment as a share of GDP. Thus, in one of the major studies, an index of capital account liberalisation has been constructed by relying on the number of years during which the capital account had been free of restrictions. These indices are then used to plot a scatter to display the relationship of CAC to the economic performance of 100 countries for the years 1975–89. The findings are rich with countries chosen from the developed as well as developing areas. It indicates that '....There is *no* evidence in the data that countries without capital controls have grown faster, invested more, or experienced lower inflation'. (italics added). The results are arrived at by controlling other determining variables which include initial per capita GDP, initial secondary enrolment date, an index of the quality of government institutions and regional dummies for East Asia, Sub-Saharan Africa and Latin America.[24] In more recent studies, CAC has been held responsible for currency crises in a large number of developing countries.[25] It has been observed that '...the risks associated with capital account liberalization in developing countries are much higher than in high income countries'.[26] The argument is based on the following observations:

(a) the marginal creditworthiness of developing-country borrowers has been associated with a much greater volatility in capital inflows to these countries;
(b) pro-cyclical behaviour of capital flows to developing countries, particularly in times of strain.[27]

These observations have been substantiated in the study with detailed statistical exercises.

In terms another recent study, IMF statistics bears testimony to the following observations over 1975 to 1997, '...there were 168 exchange rate and 54 banking crises in a representative sample of 22 industrial countries and 31 developing nations. Moreover, for this sample, there were 32 recorded instances when a country was supposed to be suffering from the combined impacts of both currency and banking crises'.[28]

Inadequacy of financial flows to the developing regions has created a situation where these flows have turned negative on a net basis. Figure 4.1 bears testimony to the fact that these flows (calculated as capital account balance less investment income payments) had dropped from $75 billion in 1993 to a negative sum of (–) $175 billion in the year 2000, when we consider the developing area as a whole. Weak social safety nets have contributed to a rise in the number of people living below poverty line, as observed for Latin America during the 1980s. Thus, '...greater economic volatility in Latin America (compared to OECD countries) worsened income distribution significantly. And, after controlling for lower economic growth and educational attainments, raised the percentage of the region's total in poverty by about 7 percentage points'. Again '...in sharp contrast to industrial countries, few if any developing countries have effective social security and unemployment insurance programmes to mitigate the effects of recession'.[29]

The observed inadequacies in the banking and financial institutions in developing countries and the obvious hurdles in getting a quick-fix by implementing reforms and legislations make a case for a gradual and sequenced approach to capital-account liberalisation. The above has been stressed in a large number of recent studies, especially after the recent crises in the developing countries, in order not to be drawn into what is viewed as a 'black hole'. It is thus considered advisable to take measures of CAC as are appropriate in terms of the quality of bank regulation in the country.[30] In terms of an unofficial study, about a third to one-half of capital inflows to the developing countries went out as capital flights during recent years.

The advocacy of CAC for stability and growth is thus beset with problems, especially when practiced by developing countries, which have very little ability to withstand speculative runs on their currencies and capital flows.

As opposed to capital account convertibility, there remain the possibilities of using capital account controls, which was the basic tool of BOP management in a large number of developing countries during earlier years. Of late, the experiences of Chile (1990–98) and Malaysia (1997–98) are often cited as examples of successful management and control of capital account in recent decades. To avert excessive capital inflows of a short-term character in the year 1990, Chile introduced a 20–30 per cent URR. (Unremunerative Reserve Requirements) on all foreign borrowings (excepting trade credits) including short-term portfolio capital flows. In addition, there was a minimum stay requirement for both portfolio and direct investments along with minimum regulatory requirement for all corporate borrowings. All private banks in the country were required to report capital transactions to the monetary authorities. The measures did not dampen inflows of capital as can be witnessed from the increases in the flow of capital which rose from 7.3 per cent on an average between 1990 and 1995 to 11.3 per cent during 1996 and 1997. Controls over movement of capital were, however, lifted by the Chilean authorities in 1998 when these flows fell sharply, largely in response to the global financial crisis which started in Asia in 1997.[31]

Malaysia, which similarly faced the 'impossible trinity' or trilemma of having to cope with open-capital account, an exchange
peg with dollar and national control over monetary policy, reacted
very differently from the neighbouring countries to come out from
the impasse of 1997. Faced with the crisis, Malaysia did not want to
float its currency and hike domestic interest rates as was done by its
neighbours. Instead, controls were re-imposed on capital flows in
1998 and for this purpose, all non-residents were asked to return
ringits held by them, to the monetary authorities at the official rate.
Moreover, offshore dealings in ringit were proscribed with immedi-
ate effect. Also, non-residents were not permitted to repatriate
capital before the expiry of one full year. As for residents, capital
exports on their part were officially discouraged and penalised.
These restrictions on capital inflows however, left out three categories of finance which included trade credits, long-term portfolio
investments and FDI. With domestic interest rates pitched at a level
which provided incentives to domestic investors to borrow at home,
growth rate in Malaysia revived by 1998, rising above the previous
year by 5.8 per cent. This was remarkable as compared to the
negative growth rate of GDP in the country at (–) 7.4 per cent during
the preceding year.[32]

It has been pointed out that with CAC, the poorer countries having
no access to private sources of international capital hardly had any
positive benefits. Those with a GDP above the threshold minimum
faced a trade-off between larger inflows of capital and instability.
As for the concentration of flows, the top 12 among the emerging
market countries of Asia and Latin America received 75 per cent of
capital inflows to the region in 1996 which amounted to 4.5 per cent
of their aggregate GDP and 20–30 per cent of export earnings in the
same year. The pattern of volatility can be witnessed from the record
of fragile capital flows for SE Asia and South Korea during the troubled
years of 1997–98. According to statistics provided by the Institute of
International Finance at New York, the $118 billion inflow to the
region in 1996 dropped sharply to $38 billion by 1997.[33]

To complement these observations on the aggregate pattern of
capital flows to the developing countries since the beginning of the
1990s, we now provide a taxonomy which relates to countries which
have been most affected by the massive flows of capital and its
fluctuations during the period. Countries faced with financial crises,

Table 4.2 Beneficial impact of capital account convertibility

Countries in crisis	Efficiency in portfolio management		Larger capital imports for borrowing countries	Financial integration		Fiscal-monetary discipline
	Lender	Borrower		Stable exchange rate equilibrium	Stock prices at global parity	
Mexico 1994	?	No	Yes	No/Yes	No	No
SE and East Asia 1997	?	No	Yes	No/?	No	No
Brazil 1998	?	No	Yes	No/?	No	No
Russia 1998	?	No	Yes	No/?	No	No
Argentina 2001–02	?	No	Yes	No/?	No	No

in a chronological order, cover Mexico (1994), SE Asia (1997), Brazil (1998), Russia (1998) and Argentina (2001–02). Their experiences with the open capital account during the period are summed up in Table 4.2.

It is rather evident from this taxonomy, dealing with countries in distress, that CAC did not turn out to be what usually was proclaimed by its advocates, not just in terms of the impact on the capital-importing nations in the developing region but also for creditors. The impact, as pointed out earlier in Chapter 3, has been adverse for the global economy as a whole, which was denied a path of stable expansion.

Notes

1. Changing Pattern of International Capital Flows: Some Theoretical Insights

1. Robert Merton, *Continuous Time Finance*, Oxford, 1990. F. Black and M. Scholes, 'The Pricing of Options and Corporate Liabilities', *Journal of Political Economy*, 1973.

2. See, for a survey and critique of the optimum borrowing models, Lance Taylor, 'The Theory and the Practice of Developing Country Debt: An informal guide for the perplexed', *Journal of Development Planning*, vol. 16 (1985), pp. 196–200. Sunanda Sen, *Trade and Dependence: Essays on the Indian Economy*, Sage Publications. New Delhi/Thousand Oaks/London, 2000, pp. 132–6. Byasdeb Dasgupta, *Recent Theories of Third World Debt and its Management: An Assessment*. M. Phil thesis, JNU, New Delhi, 1991, pp. 53–86.

3. Jeffrey Sachs, 'LDC Debt in the 1980s: Risks and Reforms' in P. Watchel (ed.), *Crisis in the Economic and Financial Structure*, Lexinton Books, 1982, pp. 197–243. Richard N. Cooper and Jeffrey Sachs, 'Borrowing Abroad: The Debtor's Perspective', in G.W. Smith and J.T. Cuddington (eds), *International Debt and the Developing Countries: A World Bank Symposium*, Washington, 1985, pp. 21–60.

4. In terms of the solvency criterion, it is necessary that

$$\Sigma(1+r)^{-i}\,TB_i = \sum_{i=0}^{\infty}(1+r)^{-i}D_0$$

where r and TB_i respectively refer to the real interest rate and trade balance in period i. The condition ensures that debt accumulated at the end of the ith period is cancelled through trade surpluses and the country is left with no more than the discounted value of initial debt (D_0). The solvency criterion also satisfies an equivalent fiscal self-sufficiency in the borrowing country over time.

5. Dragoslav Avramovic *et al.*, *Economic Growth and External Debt* (Baltimore, Johns Hopkins University Press, 1964). Mario Henrique Simonsen, 'The Developing Country Debt Problem', in Smith and Cuddington (eds), op. cit.

6. Cooper and Sachs in Smith and Cuddington, op. cit., pp. 21–60. Paul Krugman, 'International Debt Strategies in an Uncertain World', in Smith and Cuddington (eds), op. cit., 1985. Jeremy Bulow and Kenneth Rogoff, 'A Constant Recontracting Model of Sovereign Debt', *Journal of Political Economy*, vol. 97, 1989.

7. Jeffrey Sachs, op. cit., 1982; Cooper and Sachs, op. cit., 1985.

8. With the social welfare function (*U*) of the borrowing country depending on the consumption level of the country as a whole (*C*), the maximising function can be specified in terms of a two-period model. This implies that the borrower seeks to maximise the discounted stream of consumption over two time periods, using a time rate of discount which reflects pure time preference. The function can be specified as follows:

    $$\max\ U(C_1, C_2) = U(C_1) + U(C_2)/(1 + \delta)$$

    such that $U' > 0$ and $U'' < 0$.
    where δ is rate of pure time preference, while C_1 and C_2 respectively refer to consumption in two time periods. Loans in a two period framework are thus extended in period 1 and paid back in period 2.
9. Ibid.
10. Paul Krugman, op. cit.
11. Krugman in Smith and Cuddington, 1985, op. cit.
12. Ibid.
13. In terms of a bargaining model of recontracting, debtors can foreclose lender reprisals by offering an one-time pay-off to the latter. Logically the size of side payments would be as large as the size of the entire amount of outstanding debt if the latter is below a critical sum (Nash bargaining solution). Alternatively the pay-off may be less while the margin (the shortfall) would go up when the penalty conditions (for example seizure of assets and so on) are more stringent. This of course assumes that the players act subject to self-confirming or neutral expectation in order to arrive at the Nash game equilibrium. See John F. Nash, 'Non-Co-operative Games', *Annals of Mathematics*, no. 45, 1951, pp. 286–95. See also Bulow and Rogoff, op. cit., 1989.
14. Ibid.
15. Lance Taylor, op. cit.
16. An earlier version of the arguments in this section was published earlier. See Sunanda Sen, 'Swings and Paradoxes in International Capital Flows', *Cambridge Journal of Economics*, vol. 15, June 1991, no. 2, pp. 179–98.
17. The formal aspects of arguments in this section are provided in Appendix 1A. See also, S. Sen, op. cit., June 1991.
18. R. Luxembourg, *Accumulation of Capital*, Routledge and Kegan Paul, 1951. V.I. Lenin, *Imperialism, the Highest Stage of Capitalism*, 1916 (Progress Publishers 1970 reprint).
19. John Maynard Keynes, *A General Theory of Employment, Interest and Money*, Macmillan, 1936.
20. E. Domar, 'The Burden of Debt and National Income', *American Economic Review*, no. 34, 1934, pp. 798–824.
21. R. Hilferding, *Finance Capital*, T. Bottmore (ed.), Routlege and Kegan Paul, 1910. V.I. Lenin, op. cit. See also, J. Coackley and Laurence Harris, 'The Industry, the City and the Foreign Exchanges', in L. Harris, J. Coackley, M. Crossdale and T. Evans (eds), *New Perspectives on the International Financial System*, Croom Helm, London, 1988.

22. R.E. Rowthorn and J. Wells, *De-industrialisation in the British Economy*, Cambridge University Press, 1987.
23. Richard Cooper, *Economic Stabilisation and Debt in Developing Countries*, MIT Press, 1991, p. 49.
24. Gary Dymski, 'The Social Construction of Creditworthiness: Asymmetric Information and Trivialization of Risk' (mimeo), October 1994.
25. Paul Davidson, *Money and the Real World*, 2nd edn, 1978, London, Macmillan.
26. E.F. Fama, 'Efficient Capital Markets: A Review of Theory and Empirical Work', *Journal of Finance*, 2001. See also E.F. Fama, Efficient Capital Markets II', *Journal of Finance*, 46(5), 1991, pp. 1575–617.
27. Ronald I. McKinnon, *Money and Capital in Economic Development*, 1973; Shaw, *Financial Deepening in Economic Development*, OUP, New York, 1973.
28. Steven Pressman, 'What do Capital Markets do?: And What should we do about Capital Markets?', *Economies et Societés*, Serie M.P. no. 10, 2–3, 1996, pp. 193–209.
29. Jeffrey Sachs, op. cit., 1982; Richard Cooper and Jeffrey Sachs, op. cit., 1985.
30. Bulow and Rogoff, op. cit., 1989.
31. Gary Dymski, op. cit.
32. Ronald I. McKinnon, op. cit.; Shaw, op. cit.; Richard E. Caves and Harry Johnson, *Readings in International Economics* (Articles by Swan, Mundell, Corden); Maxwell Fry, Money, Interest and Banking in Economic Development, 2nd edition, Baltimore, 1995.
33. Paul Davidson, 'Thoughts on Speculation and Open Markets', in Paul Davidson and Jan Kregel (ed.), *Full Employment and Price Stability in a Global Economy*, Edward Elgar, 1999, pp. 91–2.
34. Ronald Mackinnon, op. cit.
35. J. Stiglitz and A. Weiss, 'Credit Rationing in Markets with Imperfect Informations', *American Economic Review*, 1981.
36. See K.J. Arrow, 'Alternative Approaches to the Theory of Choice in Risk Taking Situations', *Econometrica*, vol. 19, 1951, pp. 403–37, cited in Amit Bhaduri, 'Micro-foundations of Macroeconomic Theory – A Post Keyenesian View', in A. Bhaduri (ed.), *Unconventional Essays*, OUP, 1993, p. 133.
37. See Dymski, op. cit., for an exposition of these arguments.
38. See David Dequech, 'Different views on uncertainty and some policy implications', in Paul Davidson and Jan A. Kregel (eds), *Improving the Global Economy*, Edward Elgar, London, 1995. See also Andrea Terzi, Financial Market Behaviour: Rational, Irrational or Conventionally Consistent? in Davidson and Kregel (eds), 1999, pp. 109–22. T. Lawson, 'Probability and Uncertainty in Economic Analysis', *Journal of Political Economy*, 1988, pp. 38–65.
39. *The Collected Works of John Maynard Keynes*, vol. XIV, 1973, London, Royal Economic Society, p. 114.
40. J.M. Keynes, 'The General Thoery of Employment', *Quarterly Journal of Economics*, February 1937.
41. Paul Davidson, 'A Technical Definition of Uncertainty in the Longrun Non-neutrality of Money', *Cambridge Journal of Economics*, September

1988; 'Is Probability Theory Relevant for Uncertainty? A Post-Keynesian Perspective', *Journal of Economic Perspectives*, vol. 5, 1991, no. 2, pp. 129–43.

42. G.L.S. Shackle *Keynesian Kaleidics: The Evolution of General Political Economy*, Edinburgh University Press, 1974.

43. R. Shiller, 'Human Behaviour and the Efficiency of the Financial System', *Working Paper*, no. 6375. NBER, January 1998. R. Shiller, 'Stock Prices and Social Dynamics', *Brookings Papers on Economic Activity*, no. 2, 1988, pp. 457–98.

44. Kenneth A. Froot, David. S. Scharfstein and Jeremy S. Stein, 'Herd on Street: Informational Inefficiencies in a Market with Short Term Speculation', *Journal of Finance*, September 1992, pp. 1461–81.

45. Paul Davidson, 'Thoughts on Speculation and Open Markets', in Paul Davidson and Jan Kregel (eds), *Full Employment and Price Stability in a Global Economy*. Edward Elgar, 1999, pp. 91–2.

46. Ibid.

47. Gary Dymski, op. cit.

48. George Soros, *The Alchemy of Finance Simon and Schuster Inc.*, New York, 1987.

49. Ibid.

50. Ibid., pp. 17–18.

51. Soros, op. cit., p. 17.

52. Ibid., p. 83.

53. Ibid., p. 84.

54. David Dequech, op. cit., pp. 100–1.

55. David Dequetch, op. cit.

56. Keynes, *The General Theory of Employment, Interest and Money (1936)*, Macmillan, 1964 edition, p. 315 and Keynes, op. cit., 1936, p. 48 cited in Michael Anderson and Arthur H. Goldsmith, 'A direct test of Keynes's theory of investment: assessing the role of profit expectations and weight', in Paul Davidson and Jan A. Kregel (eds), *Improving the Global Economy: Keynesianism and the Growth in Output and Employment'*, Edward Elgar, 1997, pp. 63–78.

57. Robert Boyer and Daniel Drache, *States against Markets*, Routledge, London, 1997.

58. Anderson and Goldsmith, op. cit., p. 64.

59. Ibid., pp. 67–8.

60. Ibid., p. 72.

61. David Dequech, 'Different Views on Uncertainty and Some Policy Implications', in Paul Davidson and Kregel (eds), op. cit., 1997.

62. Gary Dymski, 'Money as a Time Machine in the New Financial World', in Philip Artesis (ed.), *Keynes, Money and the Open Economy*, Edward Elgar, 1996, p. 89.

63. Ibid., p. 99.

64. J.R. Hicks, *Critical Essays in Monetary Theory*, OUP, 1974.

65. Hilferding, op. cit.

66. Laurence Harris, 'Financial Markets and the Real Economy', in S. Sen (ed.), *Financial Fragility, Debt and Economic Reforms*, Macmillan Press Ltd, Houndsmill, 1996.

67. See also, Sunanda Sen, 'On Financial Fragility and its Global Implications', in S. Sen (ed.), op. cit., 1996. See for this part of the argument, Sunanda Sen, 'Economic Turmoil in Asia: A Reinterpretation', *Economic and Political Weekly*, August 1999.
68. See for an early reference the 'finance motive' in J.M. Keynes, 'The General Theory of Employment', *Quarterly Journal of Economics*, February 1937. J.M. Keynes, 'Alternative Theories of the Rate of Interest', *Economic Journal*, June 1937. J.M. Keynes, 'The Ex-ante Theory of the Rate of interest', *Economic Journal*, December 1937. See also Stephen Rousseau, *Post-Keynesian Monetary Economics*, Macmillan, 1986.
69. Hyman Minsky, *Can 'It' Happen Again? Essays on Instability and Finance*, 1982. Paul Davidson, *Money and the Real Economy*, Chapter 7. Stephen Rousseas, op. cit., pp. 38–50.
70. Minsky, 1992, p. 65.
71. Steve Keen, 'The Chaos of Finance: The Chaotic and Marxian Foundations of "Mynski's Financial Instability" Hypothesis'. *Economie and Societé*, no. 10, 2–3/1996, p. 58.
72. Ibid.
73. Martin H. Wolfson, 'The Causes of Financial Instability', *Journal of Post-Keynesian Economics*, 1996.
74. Minsky, 1982, pp. 120–4.
75. Ibid. See also Steeve Keen, op. cit., 'The Chaos of Finance: The Chaotic and Marxian Foundations of "Mynski's Financial Instability" Hypothesis', *Economie and Societé*, no. 10, 2–3/1996, pp. 55–82.
76. Gary Dymski, 'Banking in the New Financial World: From Segmentation to Separation?' (mimeo), October 1998, pp. 1, 13–14.
77. Ibid., p. 5.
78. J. Stiglitz and Weiss, op. cit.
79. A.K. Bagchi, 'Fluctuations in Global Economy: Income, Debt and Terms of Trade Processes', in Sunanda Sen (ed.), op. cit., 1996.
80. See for the tensions of the jurisdiction of a nation state under globalisation, Gerry Epstein, 'International Capital Mobility and the Scope for National Economic Management', in Robert Boyer and Daniel Drache (eds), *States Against Markets: The Limits of Globalization*, Routledge, 1996.
81. Paul Krugman, 'The Eternal Triangle: Explaining International Financial Perplexity', 1998, www/mit/edu/krugman.
82. In terms of a recent study of interest rate policies in 1986 speculative attacks on currencies in 75 middle and high-income countries in 1960–97, interest rate hikes have not been successful to avert a speculative attack on currencies. See Kraay, Aart, 'Do High Interest Rates Defend Currencies against Speculative Attacks?' (mimeo), Washington, DC, World Bank, 1998. Cited in World Bank, *Global Economic Prospects*, 1998, p. 98.
83. John Grant, 'Productivity Slowdown and Financial Tensions', Thames Papers in Political Economy 1986, 1988, pp. 88–115.
84. An earlier version of this section was published as an article. See, Sunanda Sen, op. cit., June 1991.
85. E. Domar, 'The Burden of Debt and the National Income', *American Economic Review*, no. 34, 1944, pp. 798–827. Also E. Domar, 'The Effects

of Investment on the Balance of Payments', *American Economic Review*, no. 40, 1950, pp. 805–26.

86. Domar's model originally related to US direct investments and official loans to post-war Europe. In the slightly different context of the expanded portfolio investments during the 1980s, the ratio of interest (real and nominal) on international credit has been steadily rising with rising US demand for credit from the bond market. The rate of interest cannot, under these circumstances, be treated as an exogenously determined policy variable in the international credit market.

87. R.E. Rowthorn and J. Wells, op. cit.

88. $\alpha < 0$ implies that the import-substituting effects of foreign capital inflows in the borrowing country can be strong enough to overrule the trade-creating (α) effects of foreign investment.

89. Symbols in this section are defined as follows: Y, gdp; C, consumption; I, investment; M, imports; X, exports; D, outstanding debt at end of period; CAD, Current Account Deficit (absolute value); RT, real transfers (absolute value); i, rate of interest on past loans; g, domestic growth rate; s, average savings propensity; t, the subscript which refers to the time period.

2. The Evolving Pattern of International Capital Flows

1. Shelley Cooper, 'Cross-border Savings Flows and Capital Mobility in the G-7 Countries', *Bank of England Discussion Paper*, March 1991.

2. While the literature on the evolution of the regulatory apparatus for banks in this period is rather abundant, the present study makes use of the following sources: OECD, *Banks Under Stress*, op. cit., Richard Dale, 'International Banking Regulation', in Benn Steil (ed.), *International Financial Market Regulation*. John Wiley and Sons, Sussex, 1994, pp. 168–95.

3. E. Rodrigues and S. Griffith-Jones, *Cross-Conditionality, Banking Regulation and Third World Debt*, Macmillan Press, 1992.

4. W. Darity Jr, 'Loan Pushing: Doctrine and Theory', *International Finance Discussion Paper*, Washington, 1985.

5. Citicorp, Chase Manhattan, J.P. Morgan & Co., Manufacturer Honavar, Bank Syndicate and America Corporation.

6. Lance Taylor, 'The Theory and the Practice of Developing Country Debt: An Informal Guide for the Perplexed', *Journal of Development Planning*, vol. 16, 1985, pp. 201–2.

7. Michael Mortimore, 'Conduct of Latin America's Creditor Banks', *Cepal Review*, no. 37, April 1989.

8. Lloyds (UK), Bank of Montreal, Bank of Tokyo (Japan), Canadian Imperial Bank of Commerce, Toronto Dominion Bank (Canada), Commerz-bank (West Germany) A.G., Bank of Novascotia, Long Term Credit Bank, Bankers' Trust, Chemical Bank (USA).

9. Michael Mortimore, op. cit.

10. Ibid.

11. Ibid.

12. Richard N. Cooper, 'G-7 Co-ordination and Developing Countries', in Jan-Joost Teunissen, *The Pursuit of Reform: Global Finance and the Developing Countries*, FONDAD, The Hague, 1993, pp. 147–9.
13. Richard Dale in Benn Steil, op. cit.
14. H. Askari, *Third World Debt and Financial Innovation – The Experiences of Chile and Mexico*. OECD Development Centre, Paris, 1991, p. 149.
15. E. Rodriguez and S. Griffith-Jones, p. 23.
16. *Financial Times*, 24 June 1988; 'Top 500 Banks by Size', *Banker*, July 1987.
17. *The Economist*, 31 January 1987.
18. E. Rodriguez and S. Stephany Griffith-Jones, op. cit., p. 23.
19. Ibid.
20. During 1981–86, of a total of 94 members in the bank steering committees for eight countries (of which seven were from Latin America) the US controlled 48 positions. Michael Mortimore, op. cit.
21. Askari, op. cit., p. 17.
22. Cooper, op. cit., p. 152.
23. Cooper, op. cit., pp. 152–3.
24. Ibid.
25. Turner *et al.*, *Banks and Bad Debts*, John Wiley, 1995.
26. Mortimer, Ibid., p. 75.
27. Ibid.
28. Ibid.
29. Ibid.
30. *The Economist*, 11 October 1986.
31. *The Economist*, 31 January 1987.
32. *The Economist*, 18 October 1986.
33. Paul W. Feeney, *Securitization: Redefining the Bank*, The Macmillan Press, 1995, p. 20.
34. *Financial Times*, 24 June 1988.
35. *Financial Times*, 24 June 1988.
36. Ibid., pp. 25–7.
37. *Financial Times*, 10 June 1989.
38. J.M. Keynes, 'The German Transfer Problem', and Bertil Ohlin, 'The Reparation Problem: A Discussion', in American Economic Association, *Readings in International Trade*.
39. Robert Devlin, 'Options for Tackling the External Debt Problem', *Cepal Review*, no. 37, April 1989.
40. *Financial Times*, 10 April 1989.
41. *Financial Times*, 4 April 1989.
42. *Financial Times*, 17 March and 3 April 1989.
43. *Financial Times*, 30 January, 22 March 1989.
44. Griffith-Jones and Rodriguez, p. 72.
45. Devlin, op. cit., p. 31.
46. Askari, op. cit., p. 149.
47. *Financial Times*, 11 January 1988.
48. Askari, op. cit., p. 149.
49. OECD, *Banks Under Stress*, 1991.

50. Ibid.
51. Ibid.
52. Ibid.
53. Ibid., p. 75.
54. Asli Demirguc-Kunt, 'Creditor Country Regulations and Commercial Bank Lending to Developing Countries', *Working Paper*, no. 917, June 1992, World Bank.
55. Ibid.
56. OECD, op. cit., 76–8.
57. 'Indecent Exposures', *The Economist*, 31 January 1987.
58. Askari, op. cit., p. 38.
59. *Financial Times*, 22 March 1989.
60. *Financial Times*, 19 December 1989.
61. 'Indecent Exposures', *The Economist*, 31 January 1987.
62. 'Buy backs and External Valuation of Debt', *IMF Working Paper*, September 1987.
63. Askari, op. cit., p. 39.
64. Askari, op. cit., pp. 61–2.
65. *Financial Times*, 21 June 1988.
66. Proposals by Miazawa to ease the recent Asian crisis include a $15 billion medium to long-term loans, funded by Japan's Exim Bank and/or purchase of long-term bonds by the Exim Bank, and another $15 billion short-term credit to finance credits. It also advocated interest subsidies to Asian countries for bonds floated through an Asian Monetary Crisis Aid Fund and a few other devices to help the crisis-ridden as well as other Asian economies trade. http//www.morganstanley.com/GEF data/digests/19981005-mon.html.
67. *Euromoney*, Supplement on Corporate Finance, January 1987.
68. OECD, *Banks Under Stress*, pp. 41–3.
69. Ibid.
70. Terutomo Ozawa, *Recycling Japan's Financial Surpluses for Developing Countries*, Paris, OECD, 1989.
71. *Economist*, 18 October 1986.
72. Terutomo Ozawa, ibid.; OECD, *Banks under Stress*, pp. 38–9, 48, 60–1.
73. Mario Marcel *et al.*, Fabian Society Paper on Third World Debt, 1987 (mimeo).
74. *Banker*, 5 July 1987.
75. OECD, *Banks Under Stress*, 1992, p. 125.
76. Jan A. Kregel, 'Diagnostics before remedies in formulating new strategies for dealing with instability', in Jan Joost Teunissen (ed.), *The Management of Global Financial Markets*, Fondad, The Hague, 2000, p. 32.
77. Robert Merton, op. cit.
78. OECD, *Banks Under Stress*, 1992.
79. Ibid.
80. Ibid., p. 72.

81. Thomas F. Siems, '10 Myths about Financial Derivatives', Cato Policy Analysis, no. 283, 11 September 1987.
82. See for a graphic account of the failure of derivatives to protect a bank from eventual collapse, Stephen Fay, *The Collapse of Barings: Panic, Ignorance and Greed*, Arrow Business Books, London, 1997.
83. 'Today interest rate swaps account for the majority of banks' swap activity, and the fixed-for floating-rate swap is the most common interest rate swap. In such a swap, one party agrees to make fixed interest rate payments in return for floating-rate interest payments from the counterparty, with the interest-rate payment calculations based on a hypothetical amount of principal called the notional amount'. Ibid.
84. Ibid.
85. Ozawa, OECD Development Centre, Paris, 1989.
86. Ibid.
87. Rajna Gibson and Heinz Zimmerman, 'The Benefits and Risks of Derivative Instruments' (mimeo), 1994. Also in *Derivative Use, Trading and Regulations*, vol. 2, no. 1, 1996.
88. Ibid.
89. Ibid.
90. Ibid.
91. Ibid.
92. BIS, *International Financial Statistics*, various issues.
93. Commercial Paper Chase–CFO.com at www/cfo.com.
94. World Bank, *Global Economic Prospect 1998–99*, p. 90.
95. See for arguments relating to endogeneity of money and credit in financial innovations, Hyman Minsky, *Can 'It' Happen Again? Essays on Instability and Finance*, 1982. Paul Davidson, *Money and the Real Economy*. Chapter 7. Stephen Rousseas, op. cit., 1986, pp. 38–50. See Appendix 2A of this chapter for an elucidation of the above argument.
96. World Bank, *Global Economic Prospects*, op. cit., p. 70.
97. See for an explanation of export declines in SE Asia by mid-1990s, UNCTAD, *Trade and Development Report*, 1996. Also Sunanda Sen, 'Growth Centres in SE Asia in the Era of Globalisation'. *UNCTAD Discussion, Paper no. 117*, September 1996.
98. Shares relating to Property and Finance companies indexed at 1993, fell sharply in Thailand, from respective levels at 130 and 149 in February/March 1994 to 80 and 60 in April 1995. Indices collapsed further in the subsequent period and by May 1998, these were respectively at 12 and 10. World Bank, Ibid., p. 93.
99. Ibid., p. 75.
100. Ibid., p. 71.
101. It is interesting to observe that even the international credit rating agencies continued to share the optimism of the market in extending new credit to these economies until their financial markets actually collapsed by the end of 1997.
102. Demirguc-Kunt, Asli and Enrica Detragiache, 'Financial Liberalisation and Financial Fragility', Paper prepared for the Annual World Bank

Conference on Development Economics. Washington, DC, April 1998, cited in World Bank, *Global Economic Prospects*, p. 72.

103. A.K. Bagchi, 'Growth Miracle and its Unravelling', *Economic and Political Weekly*, vol. 33, 2 May 1998, pp. 1025–32.

104. See Jan-Joost Teunissen, *New Challenges of Crisis Prevention*, FONDAD, The Hague, 2001, pp. 25–6.

105. Bank for International Settlements, *71st Annual Report*, April 2000–01 March 2001, Basle, 2001, p. 43.

106. As it has been put by Bill Belchere, the Asian economic analyst for Merril Lynch, the Asian recovery is *dangerously dependent* on growth in the US economy and the volatile technology sector. See Joe Lopez, 'Asian Recovery on "Shaky" Foundations'. Thus '...with continuing stagnation in Japan – the world's second largest economy – and US economic growth dependent on continuing inflows of foreign investment to fuel the unstable Wall Street bubble, the 'Asian Recovery' may be short lived. 'World Socialist Website', 3 July 2000, www.wsws.org.

107. Ibid., p. 37.

3. Pattern of Global Finance and the Real Economy

1. While gross savings was on an average at around 21–22 per cent of GDP in most countries of the OECD during the mid-1980s, Japan as well as Germany experienced even higher rates. Evidently, it was a major problem to ensure a full utilisation of these high order of savings. Consumer credit, advanced against purchases of durables as well as investments in real estates often provided additional demand, thus reducing the pressure on unutilised savings. However, this component of consumption tends to reinforce the cyclical pattern of changes in output and employment, since changes in borrowed consumption are always influenced by the expected changes in disposable income. As for the ability of the corporate sector to borrow from the market, limits were set by the compulsion to maintain safe debt-to-equity ratios. The other major borrowing agent, the government, was pre-committed in its expenditure programme towards pensionary benefits, which in effect supplement household savings. In fact, the current demographic trends in the advanced economies warrant an increasing proportion of government expenditure in the form of these superannuation benefits. It is not difficult to see that such expenses reduce the effective role of governments in these economies to borrow, on a *net* basis, the savings from the household sector. With problems experienced by both the corporate sector and the rest of the advanced economies, which support a large superannuated population in trying not to exceed the safe limits to debt, it is not a surprise that these countries were led to a path of recurrent stagnation and unemployment during the post-Second World War period. See in this context, Joseph Steindl, *Economic Papers*, Macmillan, 1990.

2. Rosa Luxembourg, *The Accumulation of Capital*, Translated in English by Tom Bottmore, London, 1963. V.I. Lenin, *Notebooks on Imperialism* (1915–16) in *Collected Works*, vol. 39, Moscow, 1968, C.K. Hobson, *The Export of Capital*, London, 1904.
3. World Bank, *Global Development Finance*, 2001.
4. In the US, income from a range of bank activities, earned as fees, commissions, brokerages and so on, rose from 24 per cent of annual gross banking income in 1981 to 32.8 per cent in 1990. See Table 2.6.
5. *Fianancial Times*, 16 October 1986.
6. BIS, *Special Papers on International Monetary and Financial Market Developments*, Basle, 1992.
7. Sunanda Sen, 'On Financial Fragility and its Global Implications', in Sunanda Sen (ed.), op. cit., 1996, pp. 35–59.
8. In terms of data released in the Flow of Funds Account of the US Federal Reserve, the index of total debt, based on the year 1965, was at 742.5 in 1985 in the US economy. Of this, maximum expansion was accounted for by financial business, followed by consumer debt, which also was acted as a dynamic force.
9. Gerry Epstein, Dorothy Power and Matthew Abrena, 'Recent Trends in Rentier Income in OECD Countries', (mimeo), December 2002.
10. UN, *World Economic and Social Survey*, 2001, p. 44.
11. J. Stiglitz and A. Weiss, 'Credit Rationing in Markets with Imperfect Information', *American Economic Review*, vol. 71, 1981, pp. 133–52.
12. Joan Robinson, *Essays in the Theory of Economic Growth*, Cambridge University Press, 1962, p. 53.
13. See for an elucidation of the argument, Sunanda Sen. *Finance and Development*, R.C. Dutt, *Lectures in Political Economy*, 1996 (Orient Longmans 1998) pp. 1–4. See, in particular, for the 'skill-mismatch' argument, Adrian Wood, *North–South Trade, Employment and Inequality: Changing Fortunes in a Self-driven World*, Clarendon Press, Oxford, 1999.
14. V.I. Lenin, op. cit., R. Hilferding, op. cit.
15. Rosa Luxembourg, op. cit.
16. See, for an elucidation of the argument, Sunanda Sen, *Colonies and the Empire*, Orient Longmans, 1992, pp. 1–4.
17. World Bank, *The East Asian Miracle: Economic Growth and Public Policy*, Oxford University Press, 1993.
18. See Commission of the European Communities, 'Growth, Competitiveness and Employment: The Challenges and Ways Forward to the 21st Century', *White Paper, Bulletin of the European Communities*, 1993.
19. P. Krugman, op. cit.
20. Ibid., p. 249.
21. Ibid., pp. 254–7.
22. EU White Paper, op. cit.
23. Raymond Vernon, 'International Investment and International Trade in the Product Cycle', *Quarterly Journal of Economics*, vol. 80, 1966, pp. 190–207.
24. UNCTAD, *Trade and Development Report*, 1996, pp. 75–86.

25. See in particular for the 'skill-mismatch' argument, Adrian Wood, op. cit.

26. Paul Krugman and Anthony J. Venables, 'Globalisation and the Inequality of Nations', *Quarterly Journal of Economics*, November 1995.

27. A. Wood, op. cit.

28. See, for the above position, Charles Albert Michalet, 'Transnational Corporations and the Changing International Economic System', *Transnational Corporations*, vol. 3, no. 1, February 1994, p. 19. See, for a similar position on the negative aspects of FDI flows from the national angle, Commission of the European Communities, White Paper, op. cit., 1993. See also A. Wood, op. cit.

29. Charles Albert Michalet, 'Transnational Corporations and the Changing International Economic System', *Transnational Corporations*, vol. 3, no. 1, February 1994, p. 19.

30. Ibid., pp. 19–21.

31. E. Helpman and Paul Krugman, *Market Structure and Foreign Trade*, MIT Press, 1995.

32. To give an example of the conflicting goals, foreign-controlled firms may seek to maximise profits by remitting as much as possible the profits earned, and the host government may seek to retain as much as possible of these earnings while simultaneously trying to attract the foreign firms. It is a standard practice on the part of host governments to offer incentives to foreign-controlled firms which in turn rely on their own firm level organisation to maximise profits. The strategy chosen by one would then depend on what the other is trying on, thus pushing the final outcome towards what is described in game theory literature as 'Nash solution', which is neither easy to achieve nor consistent with the reality.

33. R. Coase, 'The Nature of the Firm', *The Economic Journal*, 1937.

34. A drop in net barter terms of trade (the ratio between price indices for exports and imports) is likely to pull down the marginal value product of labour in the exporting nation relative to its value in the rest of the world where its imports come from. This, of course, would prevail when prices of traded goods dominate the average price level in all countries. Again, with wages roughly in parity to movements in value of labour productivity, a fall in double factoral terms of trade would also signify corresponding declines in relative wages across nations, an aspect which is consistent with the destination of FDI flows towards cheap labour countries. P. Sarkar and H.W. Singer, 'Manufactured Exports of Developing Countries and their Terms of Trade since 1965', *World Development*, vol. 19, no. 4, 1999.

35. Ibid.

36. R. Coase, op. cit.

37. Sunanda Sen, 'International Capital Flows and Global Demand' in Joseph Halevi and Jean-Marc Fontaine (eds), *Global Demand, Growth and Technology*, Edward Elgar, 1995.

38. Tom Kemp, *Theories of Imperialism*, London, 1967.

39. Gunder Frank, *Capitalism and Under-development in Latin America*, 1971.
40. See for the Indian case, C.P. Chandrashekhar and Jayati Ghosh, *A Market That Failed: A Decade of Neo-Liberal Economic Reforms in India*, Left Word Books Delhi, 2002, pp. 138–48.
41. UNCTAD, *World Investment Report*, Geneva, 1999, pp. 165, 410–11.
42. Ibid., pp. 483–530.
43. Ibid., pp. 168, 192.
44. Ibid., pp. 190–2.
45. Suparna Karmakar, *Macro-economic Implications of Foreign Direct Investment: Selected Asian Countries*, PhD thesis at Jawaharlal Nehru University, 2000.
46. Price cutting by exporting firms, implemented with or without government subsidies, entails a process of cross-subsidisation within the domestic economy. While export subsidies may be a direct method of making exports cost-effective, firms in export industries can, even in its absence, try a dual pricing policy; with opposite movements in prices (of exportables) when measured in units of home goods as compared to importables.

    The argument on 'immiserising growth' can be specified in terms of a simple two-sector model consisting of the export and the home sectors. By assumption, investment and capitalist consumption in the export sector consist of imported goods alone, while the home sector invests its own output. Capitalists in this sector, however, consume only exportables, which is exchanged against home goods used up by workers in the export sector. Thus, exchange in this economy is at two levels: the first one is international, between the export sector and the rest of world while the second takes place between the two sectors within the economy. Impact of the changing price relations on the domestic economy, as results from the dual pricing policy of the export sector brings about the immiserisation process in the economy.

    See for details of the argument, 'Strategy of Export-oriented Growth: A Theoretical Note', in Sunanda Sen, *Trade and Dependence*, 2000, pp. 152–68.
47. See for relevant statistics, UNCTAD, *World Investment Report: Foreign Direct Investment and the Challenge of Development*. Geneva, 1999, pp. 410–11.
48. Ibid., p. 165. See for an useful analytical separation between demand and supply constraints on output, Amit Bhaduri and Rune Skarstein, 'Short-period Macro-economic Aspects of Foreign Aid', *Cambridge Journal of Economics*, 1996, vol. 20, pp. 196–206. The 'trade effect' and the 'rentier effect' of capital flows have been discussed in an earlier paper. See Sunanda Sen, op. cit., June 1991. See for relevant statistics, UNCTAD, *World Investment Report*: Foreign Direct Investment and the Challenge of Development. Geneva, 1999, pp. 410–11.
49. Ibid., pp. 190–2.
50. Ibid., pp. 190–2.
51. See for coefficients of variation of real FDI and other capital inflows. UNCTAD, *World Investment Report*, 1999, p. 163.

52. See for an useful analytical separation between demand and supply constraints on output, Amit Bhaduri and Rune Skarstein, op. cit., 1996.
53. The 'trade effect' and the 'rentier effect' of capital flows have been discussed in an earlier paper. See Sunanda Sen, op. cit., June 1991.
54. Ibid.

4. Global Finance and Development

1. Barbara Stallings, 'Euro-Markets, Third World Countries and International Political Economy', in H. Makler, A. Martinelli and N. Smelser (eds), *The New International Economy*, Sage Studies, 1983.
2. Patrick Engellau and Birgitta Nygren, *Lending Without Limits*, Secretariat for Future Studies, Stockholm, 1979, p. 45.
3. Section 4 relies heavily for documentation on Sue Bradford and Bernardo Kucinski, *The Debt Squad: The US, the Banks and Latin America*, Zed Books, 1988.
4. L.A. Sjaastad, 'Where the Latin American Loans Went', *Fortune*, 26 November 1984, pp. 129–30.
5. Bradford and Kucinski, pp. 78–84.
6. Ibid.
7. Ibid., pp. 77–125.
8. See for documentation and analysis of the current economic crisis in Argentina:

   (a) 'Argentina's Crisis, IMF's Fingerprints', by Mark Weisbrot, 25 December 2001, '$17b of Trouble for Top 25 Banks', *American Banker*, 14 February 2002.
   (b) 'Peso float buys time in Argentina', by Mark Mulligan in Buenos Aires, 13 February 2002.
       'Argentina unveils crisis strategy, to ditch dollar', *Reuter*, 4 February 2002.
   (c) 'Middle classes face ruin as Argentina's crisis widens', by Sophie Arie in Buenos Aires, 23 December 2001, *The Observer*.
   (d) 'Argentina seeks billions to survive crisis', by Gilbert Le Gras and Anna Willard, *Reuters*, 14 February 2002.
   (e) 'Crisis in Argentina', by Simon Jeffery, *Guardian*, 4 January 2002.
   (f) 'Peru urges aid for Argentina', *Financial Times*, 5 February 2002.

9. Kuczinski, pp. 89–92.
10. Ibid., p. 118.
11. See for a comprehensive analysis of the current situation at the beginning of 2003, Arturo O'Connell, 'The Recent Crisis of the Argentine Economy: Some Elements and Background' (mimeo), December 2002.
12. Ibid., p. 109.

13. Ibid., pp. 85–8.
14. Ibid., p. 88.
15. Richard Cooper, op. cit.
16. See for the argument, R. Cooper and J. Sachs in Cuddington and Smith, op. cit. Anatole Kaletsky, *The Costs of Default*, Priority Publications, 1995.
17. A. Bhaduri, 'On the Viability of External Debt', in K. Laski (ed.), *External Constraints on Sustainable Growth in Transition Countries*, Research Reports WIIW, no. 281, October 2001.
18. Griffin, K.B. 'Foreign Assistance and Consequences', *Economic Development and Cultural Change*, vol. 18, 1970, no. 3, p. 321. T. Wieskopf, 'Impact of Foreign Capital Flows on Domestic Savings in UDCs', *Journal of International Economics*, 1972.
19. As defined earlier, net transfers are equal to the net capital account balance less investment income payments.
20. Stiglitz, op. cit.
21. See Chapter 1 for more details of the argument.
22. The three types of expectations which are possible when the variable (say x) is not static and is subject to changes cover the following:

   1. Adaptive expectations: $Ex_{+1} = E_{-1}x + \theta(x - E_{-1}x) = \theta x + (1 - \theta)E_{-1}x$
   2. Extrapolative expectations: $Ex_{+1} = x + \theta(x - x_{-1}) = (1 + \theta)x - \theta x_{-1}$
   3. Regressive expectations: $Ex_{+1} = \theta x + (1-\theta)\bar{x}$

   where E stands for the expected values, E_{-1} is the prior expectation before one period, θ is a fraction and $\bar{x}$ is the normal or equilibrium value of x. See for a clear exposition, John Williamson and Chris Milner, *The World Economy*, Harvester Wheatsheaf, 1991, pp. 256–7.
23. Grilli Vitterio and Gian-Maria Fireretti, 'Economic Effects and Structural Determinants of Capital Controls', *IMF Staff Papers*, September 1995, pp. 517–51.
24. Dani Rodrik, 'Who Needs Capital Account Convertibility?', in Peter B. Kenen (ed.), *Should the IMF Pursue Current Account Convertibility?* Essays in International Finance, no. 207, May 1998.
25. Glick R. and M. Huchinson, 'Capital Controls and Exchange Rate Stability in Developing Countries', *Federal Reserve Bank of San Francisco (FRBSF) News Letters*, 20 July 2001.
26. Uri Dabush and Dipak Dasgupta, 'The Benefits and Risks of Capital Account Opening in Developing Countries', *Capital Flows Without Crisis?*, in Dipak Dasgupta, Marc Uzan and Dominic Wilson (eds), Routledge, London and New York, 2002, pp. 15–24.
27. Ibid., p. 15.
28. Stephen S. Roch, 'Learning to Live with Globalisation', Testimony before the Banking and Financial Services to the US House of Representatives, 20 May 1999, cited in Michael Pettis, *The Volatility Machine*, Oxford University Press, 2001, p. 196.
29. Ibid., p. 19.

30. Marcus Miller and Lei Zhang, 'Sequencing of Capital Account Liberalisation', in Dipak Dasgupta *et al.* (eds), op. cit., p. 43.
31. Ariyoshi *et al.*, *Capital Flows to Emerging Economies* (mimeo), 2000.
32. Ramon Moreno, 'Capital Controls and Emerging Markets', *FRBSF News Letter*, no. 2001–25, 31 August 2001.
33. Ibid.

Index